EARLY BRAIN SPROUTS from STATES to TRAITS

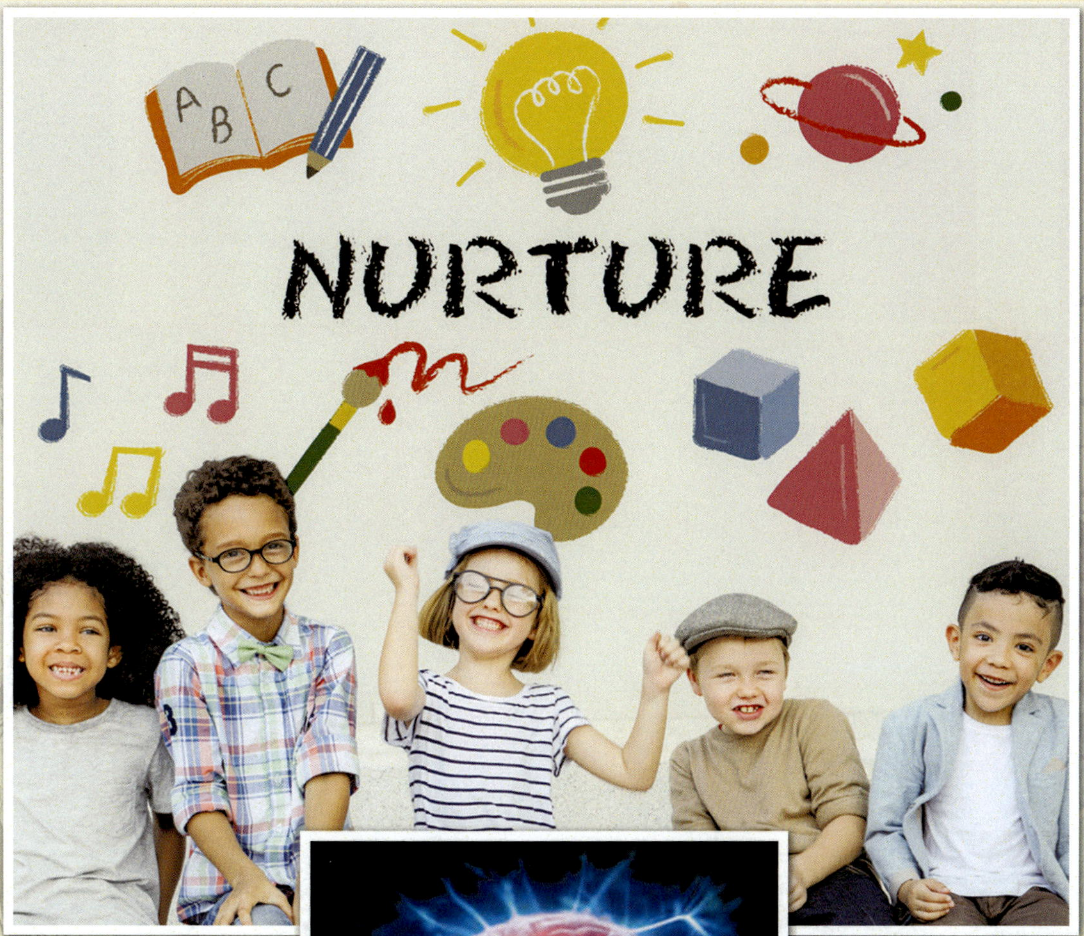

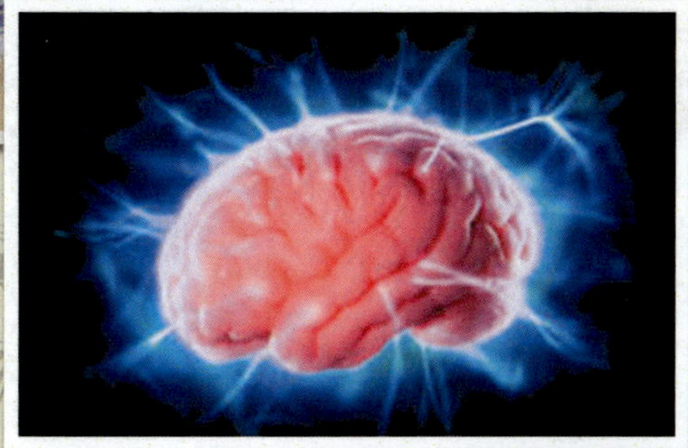

Nurture through multisensory integration 0-3 years and even up to 5 years of life is essential to prevent behavior and learning disorders and health risk behaviors among youth. This book is a humanitarian contribution from S.A.I. and the SAI Institute of Educare.

Meena Chintapalli, M.D. F.A.A.P.

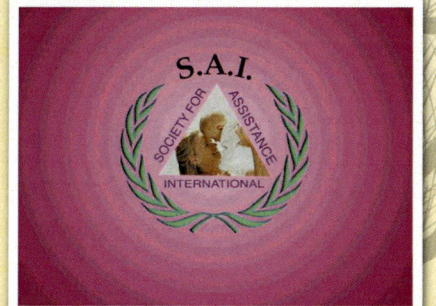
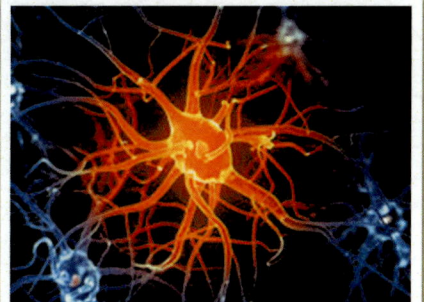

Copyright © 2017 by Meena Chintapalli, M.D. F.A.A.P. 754996
Library of Congress Control Number: 2017906535

ISBN: Softcover 978-1-5434-1916-0
Hardcover 978-1-5434-1915-3
EBook 978-1-5434-1917-7

All rights reserved. No part of this book may be reproduced or transmitted in any form or by any means, electronic or mechanical, including photocopying, recording, or by any information storage and retrieval system, without permission in writing from the copyright owner.

Print information available on the last page

Rev. date: 05/26/2017

To order additional copies of this book, contact:
Xlibris
1-888-795-4274
www.Xlibris.com
Orders@Xlibris.com

DEDICATION

1. First dedication is to my eternal benevolent father and mentor, guide, counselor

   Sri Satya Sai Baba who taught me love and forgiveness as the **highest asset** of human existence and the **highest purpose of human race** is to find the highest divine energy in oneself and in all.

   Therefore a human being is born to "**Love all and Serve all.**"

2. My father Professor **"Bhadriraju Krishanmurti"** who taught me self-confidence, values and virtues with a scrupulous life, even in the challenges of external negative forces. He gave me his genes with enquiry, hope and persistence.

3. **Third but not the least** I dedicate with gratitude this work to my spouse **"Dr.Kedar Chintapalli"** and my daughters "Pallavi Chintapalli Nemani and Sumana Chintapalli Prasad" who are patient with my impatience and are good counselors and helpful in all my endeavors and ambitions.

Meena Chintapalli.

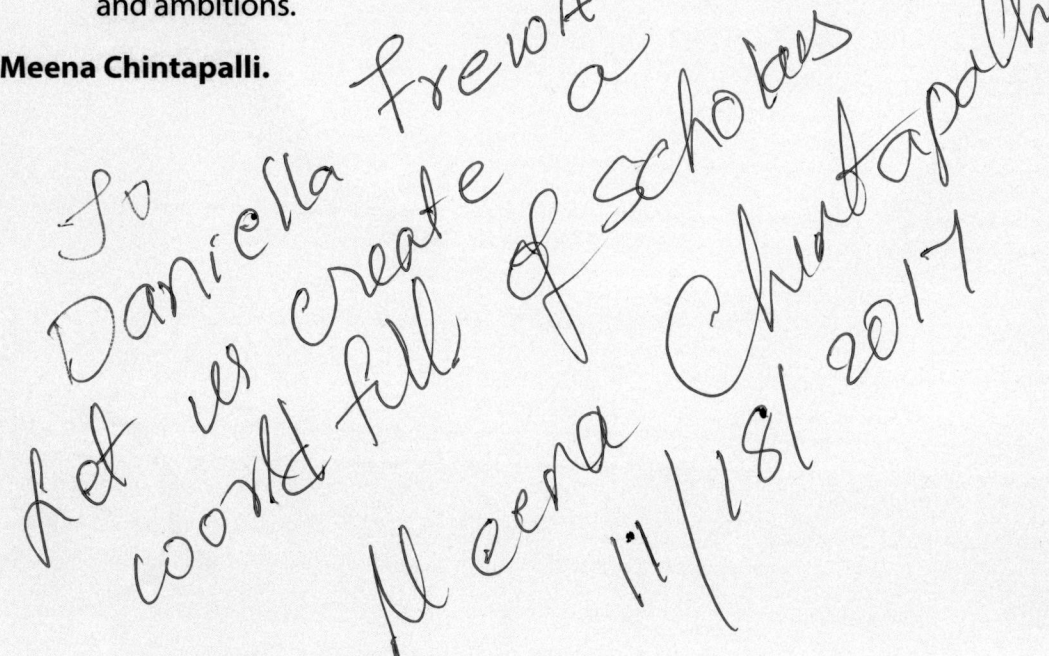

To Daniella Frewa
Let us create a world full of scholars
Meena Chintapalli
11/18/2017

Contents

Preface 2

Chapter 1	Introduction to the Topic and the Current Need for Self-Transformation 6	
Chapter 2	There Is A Need For A Universal Curriculum 0-3 Years 15	
Chapter 3	Need-to-Learn Facts about Neurons and Organization 28	
Chapter 4	Neurobiology of the Brain 35	
Chapter 5	Reasons for Developing a Curriculum for Healthy Dynamic Brain Growth 51	
Chapter 6	Role of the Parent from 0-6 months for Nurture of the Nature 59	
Chapter 7	Development from Two to Four Months 79	
Chapter 8	Six Months' to Nine Months' Development 89	
Chapter 9	Infant Development, Twelve Months to Eighteen Months 101	
Chapter 10	Infant from 18 Months to 36 Months 109	
Chapter 11	4-Year Development and Summarization 116	
Chapter 12	Case Presentations 125	
Chapter 13	What Are My Relaxation Techniques in a Nutshell for the Caregivers and Children Four Years Old and Older? 132	
Chapter 14	What Can Parents Know about Their Own Skills and Where Are Their Parenting Skills Coming From? 136	

Goldie the Goldfish 158

Good Tongue And Bad Tongue 161

Man And Animal Dilemma 164

Poor Man's Wealth 166

Poor Tailor's Luck And Love...168

References..170

Figures and Diagrams 181

Index..183

Figure: 1. Family and Responsible unconditional love

Family Love:

A happy family is one filled with love, that is a string that keeps all working together and happy. Love is a feeling of respect and giving. Selfishness is to get all and forget all. Love binds people and resources together, and selfishness disperses resources and families.

Love for Nature and communities:

Love for nature should make us protect the resources like water, electricity, trees, money, time, energy, minerals, speech, sounds, air systems, food, natural gas, and oil. A great way to do it is to self-audit and develop a ceiling on wants or desires.

Love for the individual self:

Love for oneself should make one take care of the body through proper eating habits and physical exercise, attain a meaningful education to hold a job, and use the money for maintaining family, community, and charitable activities. One cannot be socially and economically equal, but one can attain equanimity through self-confidence, self-reliance and self-sacrifice, and self-effacement.

Preface

This book is the result of my passion to reach out to all and assure that every child is born to give something back to society and every parent loves their progeny and wants to give them the best. I am certain that parents might have read thousands of books filled with suggestions on parenting techniques and regimental reward and reactive limit setting techniques, but there is a core system of positive early experiences that parents can provide help build a holistic, intellectual and effective personality development. A thorough, knowledgeable parent will seek the education that explains how each person is connected to the world and will move away from old theories to develop skills as a good effective parent. There is one universal truth that differentiates a human from the rest of the creation. It is only in human beings that the *five senses* connect the individual to the world with the brain, which sits at the top of the eye sockets (orbits) and helps use discrimination and self regulation with capacity to express emotions and balance the emotions.

A passion that made me become a pediatrician is to give something more than just treatment for an illness. There are a few antibiotics, and microbiology taught us about various illnesses that could be treated whereas biochemistry and pathology taught us what to look for among other biological systems. As a young doctor, what I really wanted to do was to heal the body, mind, and soul and make a difference for everyone who came to me for care. I always was altruistic and explained the findings as they were and gave a reason behind an illness or a symptom. A typical example was when I did not give Orajel along with antibiotics to a nine to-ten-month-old who was brought into my practice by the parent. I got reported to the medical director of the insurance company that I was a quack and did not treat the patient properly as I did not offer antibiotics and consider orajel (A topical anesthetic)for crying from teething. It was a quick fix that the mother was expecting along with antibiotics when the nine-to-ten-month-old infant presented with a fever but no focus was found. I got a call from the medical director, asking me why I would not give Orajel and amoxicillin when there is teething fever. I had to educate him about physiological immunodeficiency from nine to thirty-six months of age,that teething never causes any fever and that overtreatment of viremia without any focus found is suppressing the natural immunological systems, and I would not cause a biological warfare. The crying was from separation and stranger anxiety, and it was natural for the infant to cry from discomfort of low-grade fever and also from the psychological factors that were physiological. Infants go through a phase of stranger and separation anxiety at nine to twenty-four months. Physical, biological, psychological, and emotional developments always go hand in hand rapidly from birth to the first thirty-six months. A clear knowledge on growth and development will clarify the symptoms on systems review for a rational medical approach. In my professional life of forty-one years, I never treated a patient with "Colic" drops in the newborn period and never entertained the diagnosis of teething syndrome. I was fortunate enough to get hold of the textbook **"Growth And Development of Children",** by Dr. G. H. Lowrey (University of California, Davis), which is out of print now but a golden book that every pediatrician should read. Developmental maturity of all systems is reviewed in detail in this book. This helped me a lot not to make misjudgments in diagnosis and approach a problem with developmental pediatrics background.

My approach on this type of counseling about any illness was also from my ambulatory fellowship training under the guidance of the director, Dr. Miyoko Bassett, who always guided me to look at research articles on different cases and the presentation of symptoms. An example was my inquiry on why mycoplasma pneumonia would cause prolonged coughing and how it responded to treatment with beta2-agonists, besides antibiotics, in those days, and I did a small presentation on wheezing management with infections. I got interested in treating wheezing-associated respiratory illnesses and took a different approach in treating cough and chest congestion and avoided cough medicines.

My first inquiry sprouted about how violence and abuse impacted the growing child from the case report presented in this book about *"Psychosocial Dwarfism"* and how the child improved in six months in a stable home environment. Another heart-touching subject was the impact of the improper biosocial behaviors of a sixteen-year-old stepbrother who made a thirteen-year-old child bear an infant and the teen mother had to take care of him with love and nurture at 14 years of age and she lost her childhood and youth. What made that sixteen-year-old stepbrother misuse his freedom and have no ethical values at all? What was causing this irrational behavior? I was inquiring within for causes for this mental illness or psychopathology. The thirteen-year-old child and her family succumbed to circumstances, faith systems, and the adverse effects of youth violence, and the impact and suffering were on an innocent thirteen-year-old girl who lost her childhood and youth. The family was excellent and well supportive of this innocent girl, and the parents adopted the male infant so that the thirteen-year-old could go to school and complete her education.

Touched by these two cases as a young doctor in training and with a background of having a genius father, an eminent researcher, genius in his own field of linguistics, who created his own era in linguistics, "Prof. Bhadriraju Krishnamurti", my inherent research mind began a quest for healing the human soul after looking for underlying causes for many physical and psychological illnesses. I did have an opportunity to do clinical research at the University of Michigan on the unopposed effects of stress hormones on the brain, and, unfortunately, I had to move, as my spouse moved out of town. My destiny led me to be just a clinician with adjunct faculty positions and no opportunity for academic research. I continued to follow my own cases, my own protocols, and my own patients with perseverance on the theories, and, finally, when I saw the research data on ***"Early Child Brain Development"*** from a round table conference by ***"Johnson and Johnson Institute" in 1996–1997,*** environmental influences, trauma, or the injury on brain pathways from abuse and emotional trauma, I became more self-reliant in my approach to teaching parents on how to raise infants while protecting their personality development.

By not offering a quick fix made me lose some customers, but persons who were interested in being a better parent gave me popularity by word of mouth. I received few awards locally and got into Who's Who in America, but the most fulfilling were the AMA Foundation recognition award in 2008 and the World Physician recognition award in 2010 for integrating the brain science in daily child development counseling in my practice and other community initiatives.

I intend to reach out to more people through this book so that the world will realize that Renaissance had helped us in the past, but the current inventions and trends, with metal music, drugs and substance abuse, electronics, seeking instant gratification, looking for quick fix from outside for various curable and incurable problems, and eating poorly for convenience are causing major environmental and human pollution. We are seeing the greatest *"heart bypass"* through the disturbing societal norms and broken family relationships as compared to the early "50's. Hopefully, we all will accept a need for change in the societal norms while accepting the current inventions on neuroscience, make adjustments in life styles, adopt old family and human values that will sustain a crime-free society. Controlling the mind and having a ceiling on desires are good for individual growth. My approach to life is addressed on spirituality scales that one can achieve on the four tenets of truth, peace, love, and right actions and the taxonomy of the five teaching techniques.

(Patent was obtained for the independent work in 2003–2004.)

Truth is an eternal fact that only human beings can transform and maintain the balance in nature and reflect the highest energy standing next to God. Animals cannot communicate, humans can, humans can change from bad to good emotions, and we can certainly change through the process of transformation.

Peace is an inner calmness and balance in life with happiness, contentment, while facing challenges. Peace is within and trying to find peace outside the body is similar to an old lady who lost her needle in the house while sewing, is trying to find the needle on the street under the street lamps. Peace is an internal locus; drinks, alcohol, sex, ice cream, rock and shake, movies, and ball games all give momentary pleasure, but does not confer lasting peace and bliss. When the effect of the chosen object is worn out, person comes back to the same dark, cloudy inner feeling that caused distress, depression, anger and despair. One has to light the lamps of adjustment, control desires, and give up jealousy, comparisons, hatred, and anger that stem from frustrations. ***One has to find peace within and not outside from materialistic sensory pleasures.***

Love: Love is an internal feeling of acceptance, responsibility, self-confidence, self-respect, tolerance, and virtues. The basis is self confidence that is not shattered by external pressures. Self confidence teaches hard work with patience to achieve long term and short term goals.

Right Action: All good things are divine and help all and serve all without hurting anyone. Personal, social, and ethical responsibilities that are accepted with love makes all actions right actions. These good actions reflect a personality in performing personal and family duties and community participation.

I conclude with the statement that I am not intending to hurt anyone's feelings at the individual level, but the knowledge that has been available since early 1996-1997, has not been made public till 2015 - 2016, as the grantees are bound by not releasing any information for public use and make statements. I used the research in my practice because of my own interest as a community pediatrician with the passion that I fostered for four decades, and the quest and commitment with fruitful results. I wanted to share the knowledge for public use, and if it helps families understand what they can do and bring about changes for good in the communities, then my dream of touching all lives on earth is done. Facts are bitter, but bitter medicines cured illnesses. Starting with healthy food initiatives for the body and positive thoughts for the soul, I have given all that I had to offer for a better society. A good society is first and foremost in the hands of the caretakers raising infants from 0-5 years of age.

Food sustains body. Thoughts sustain words and actions. Pure and healthy food helps the body to remain healthy. Pure thoughts help mind with actions that are referenced through the heart.

The ocean gets rid of impurities by pushing it to shore. What can we do as humans to push out the bad in the ocean of life and keep balance in human development and take care of nature to prevent disasters?

Meena Chintapalli

A HAPPY FAMILY IS A HEALTHY BIOLOGICAL UNIT IN THE SOCIETY

Figure 2: A happy extended family

Figure 3: New Born Feet in parents hands

Chapter I

Introduction to the Topic and the Current Need for Self-Transformation

Parents and caretakers love their children, and as we know, every parent and extended family member looks lovingly at the newborn on the day of the arrival with hopes for a successful future. Every parent wants what is best for their child. No one wants the child to struggle in life, education, social relationships, cognitive abilities, sports, and family interactions. Yet we see many children, by the time they reach high school, have shifted away from core human values. Teen pregnancy is high from 36/1000 in some states to 68/1000 in southern states. Teen depression and truancy are on the rise. One out of four schoolchildren seems to have learning and behavioral problems from later elementary to high school education.

The society has to reflect upon why there are health-risk behaviors in youth. Where are those Newton, Einstein, Mozart, Lincoln, Washington, Michelangelo, Florence Nightingale, Martin Luther King, Gandhi, and Tagore?

We need to reflect on questioning what is happening globally in the last four decades, post world war baby boomers' children and grand children, as compared to the Renaissance period a century ago. We need to question and seek answers as a collective group in the society.

1. Why do we not see more people leave a landmark in the history of human evolution?

2. What can parents do to prevent the health-risk behaviors?

3. Are parents and extended caretakers willing to look at the past and see the current global societal heath-risk behaviors and trends?

4. Are caretakers willing to educate themselves to offer transformation measures in raising a whole new generation of children with values and virtues?

5. Shall we hope to see every child attain optimal intellectual and cognitive development with good character?

6. What is an opportune time to create awareness in children and help them make healthy choices, keep these healthy choices for lifetime, and build on that strength?

7. As a global society, are we missing opportunities to create brain pathways that are permanent in the brain that determine future reflective decisions?

8. Why is the prevalence at record high for autism spectrum behaviors at one in sixty-five?

9. Why is ADHD 4% in the upscale neighborhoods and 16% in the inner city?

10. Why are there escalating violence and shootings at schools and in public places that are considered as haven for children?

11. Why are life partner relationships breaking within a short time?

12. Overall, are the caretakers raising children with mental health issues unable to get help, which is affecting the mental health of the children in many ways?

These questions are raised by looking at some of the available statistics at the current time.

National Statistics 2014–2016

Divorce rates

Overall, 48%–50% of marriages are ending up in divorce for first marriage.

Nonvirginity at the time of marriage increases the risk by another 40%–45%.

If one spouse wants a child and the other does not, the divorce risk increases.

In living-together arrangement, the spouse separation is at 80%.

Intimate partner violence

Twelve million women and men are involved in domestic violence.

Intimate partner violence is at 15% for women who are victims and 4% for men who are victims.

The prevalence of rape victims is twenty-four every minute.

Abuse of men and women

One out of every four women, or 24.3%, is a victim of physical abuse.

More than 48% of women who are victims of aggression are between eighteen and thirty-four years of age, the prime childbearing age.

One out of four women and one out of seven men, or 13.5%, are victims of aggression.

Child abuse

There are 1,564 children who died of abuse in 2014. There are 700,000 children who are abused annually in the USA. Out of these, 300,000 children receive help.

Child Protective Services (CPS)s involved with three million cases per year.

There are 24.4/1000 children who are victims under twelve months of age.

Parents are the perpetrators in most of the abuse and neglect cases.

80% of child trauma is secondary to neglect, and the neglect is from the woman who had been a victim of emotional or physical abuse.

18% are physically abused children.

9% of children are victims of rape.

1. Are the parents raising children while they are suffering with psychological issues unresolved in the childbearing age?

2. Is the proportion of parents with mental health needs higher and is getting higher in the last thirty years?

3. Certainly, the National Statistics seems to point towards some form of psychosomatic disorders that stem from different causes that seem to keep the *cycle of violence* among adults going. It is costing the nation up to $83 billion on mental health needs, and yet many poor segments of the society who have mental health needs are unable to get into the system for timely intervention.

   (Kathleen Ries Merikangas's research was on the estimates of the lifetime prevalence of *DSM-IV* mental disorders with and without severe impairment, their comorbidity across broad classes of disorder, and their sociodemographic correlates.)

The National Comorbidity Survey Adolescent Supplement (NCS-A) is a nationally representative face-to-face survey of 10,123 adolescents aged thirteen to eighteen years in the continental United States. *DSM-IV* mental disorders were assessed using a modified version of the fully structured World Health Organization Composite International Diagnostic Interview.

Results

31.9% Anxiety disorder

19.1% Behavior disorder

14.3% Mood disorder

11.4% Substance use disorder

Approximately 40 percent of participants had an overlap with one class of disorder, also meeting criteria for another class of lifetime disorder. The overall prevalence of disorders with severe impairment and/or distress was 22.2% (11.2% with mood disorders, 8.3% with anxiety disorders, and 9.6% with behavior disorders). The median age of onset for disorder classes was earliest for anxiety at 6 years, behavior disorders at 11 years, mood disorder at 13 years, and substance use disorders at 15 years. If we look at this survey, almost 40–45 percent of youth are having one or more than one class of psychological disorders among the general population. This is the community that we are dealing with, and these community members are raising children without knowing where things can go wrong and how to prevent the adverse influences to prevent the *cycle of violence. They need to get help also.*

Factors on aversive experiences determining lifetime mental ill health

These findings provide the first prevalence data on a broad range of mental disorders in a nationally representative sample of U.S. adolescents. Approximately one in every three to five youth in the United States meets criteria for a mental disorder with severe impairment across their lifetime. **The likelihood that common mental disorders in adults first emerge in childhood and adolescence,**

highlights the needs for shifting the focus on treatment of youth in Unites States when changes happen slowly and may not, to that of prevention and early intervention.

A. HOME SITUATION

1. Children have two parents in two homes.

2. The relationships break frequently enough to have a single parent working hard and unable to take care of the family needs of bonding and effective parenting.

3. The home situation is not consistent in both homes. This confuses the children while having two different environmental experiences.

4. The circumstances are so demanding without family support systems that puts strain on single parents economically and physically as well.

5. Two-income families and single parents need more supportive systems to maintain jobs and family and societal relationships, and help to give good nurture to the very young infant whom they brought to this world with a lot of love.

When you read the life stories of these violent men and women who took guns and randomly shot at school and college kids, you will find that they were troubled as children and youth or came from broken homes (e.g., Santa Ana and Columbine shootings). They tried to seek mentoring or love from a neighbor or a relative and could not be accepted. More often among these assailants, there is a history of disturbed social and family relationships that was not taken into serious consideration to get timely help.

We have enough behavioral, EEG scan, SPECT, PET scan, fMRI, sMRI, and DTI studies to show that the early experience creates and determines the architecture of the future brain, laying down pathways of behavioral and intellectual development for life time from 0-3 years. These stay with the person for life. Why can't we then use this early experience to foster pathways of positive adaptation and highest attainable intellectual abilities?(Huttenlocher, P. R., Mills K. L., Lebel C., Pam Schiller, Meena Chintapalli).

Is there a realization by the primary caretaker of his or her critical role of being the first teacher to this dynamically growing infant, layering brain networks based on experience, creating permanent neural pathways at zero to three years of life? These pathways have a direct correlation to succeed in the future intellectually, emotionally, psychologically, socially, physically, and with emotional regulation, which will not hurt themselves and others.

The foundations for reciprocal society and family relationships are rapidly developing in this critical time of the first one thousand days. The knowledge on neurodevelopmental organization is still not a public awareness program till today.

It is nice to prevent problems through massive education about the experience-based neurodevelopment facts into the society and seek help for the current problem by the involvement of each family unit, which is a biological unit of the society.

"Intellectuals solve problems, geniuses prevent them."

—Albert Einstein

No one can incubate a child in a germ-free, crime-free environment. But a child can develop skills to make healthy choices to avoid injury or harm by developing integrity to succeed in all domains of life with health as defined by the World Health Organization.

Health is defined by the World Health Organization in 1997 as "Physical, Intellectual, Psychological, Emotional and Spiritual wellness".

B. GENETICS

1. 50% of the time, genes do not get turned on. Genetic exposure does not mean the genes will manifest illness. Genes do not get turned on when the environment prevents adverse experience in their life.

2. Latest neuroscience and genetics articles with research background have come forth that the epigenetic studies show that mRNA does not get expressed, particularly with anger and explosive personality issues, if the person is in a secure environment that will not cause stress and anxiety. If the messenger RNA fails to take the cortisol on the receptor for DNA marker sites, there is no expression of the gene. Although bipolar depression is genetic, the genes for the increased hormonal imbalance, which raises the cortisol, epinephrine, and nor epinephrine causing the symptoms, do not get expressed if the infant is nurtured and has positive direction in the immediate environment where the infant is being raised (Brian M. Onofrio, Benjamin B. Lahey).

If there is family history of type 2 diabetes and if the eating habits are good from the beginning, the type II diabetes does not manifest.

C. ELECTRONICS

1. **1.** The latest data shows the adverse influence of screen time on the dynamically growing brain.

2. Most of the infants from six-nine months are exposed to 2-4 hours of screen time, even after informing the parent or caregiver about the ill effects of screen time. American Academy of Pediatrics advised no screen policy till 18 months and personally preferably till 2 years.

3. This is creating hyper stimulated sensory input seeking hyperkinetic stimulus constantly, and impulsivity is the result. Brain is getting noisy and disturbed pathways are the result of early screen exposure. The critical time of making connections for life time are from 0-3 years. At birth nerve cells are floating willing to connect with a sensory input.

4. The brain gets over stimulated without any ordered or organized pathways with early life screen exposure. Rapidly moving screen stimulates 250,000 cells per minute; each nerve cell makes ten thousand connections dynamically from sensory signals to the brain through the five senses. These do not get set in an organized pathway but disorganized with disturbed mini and macro columns.

5. If this sensory experience promotes excitement, high-strung messages, and too much of rapid movement and activity, more stress hormones are released.

6. The pathways get arrested at the lower limbic system, and connections to the higher brain are arrested.

7. The synaptic junctions are more disorganized and dispersed. This causes poor communication between the functional units of the brain and changes the structure of the brain.

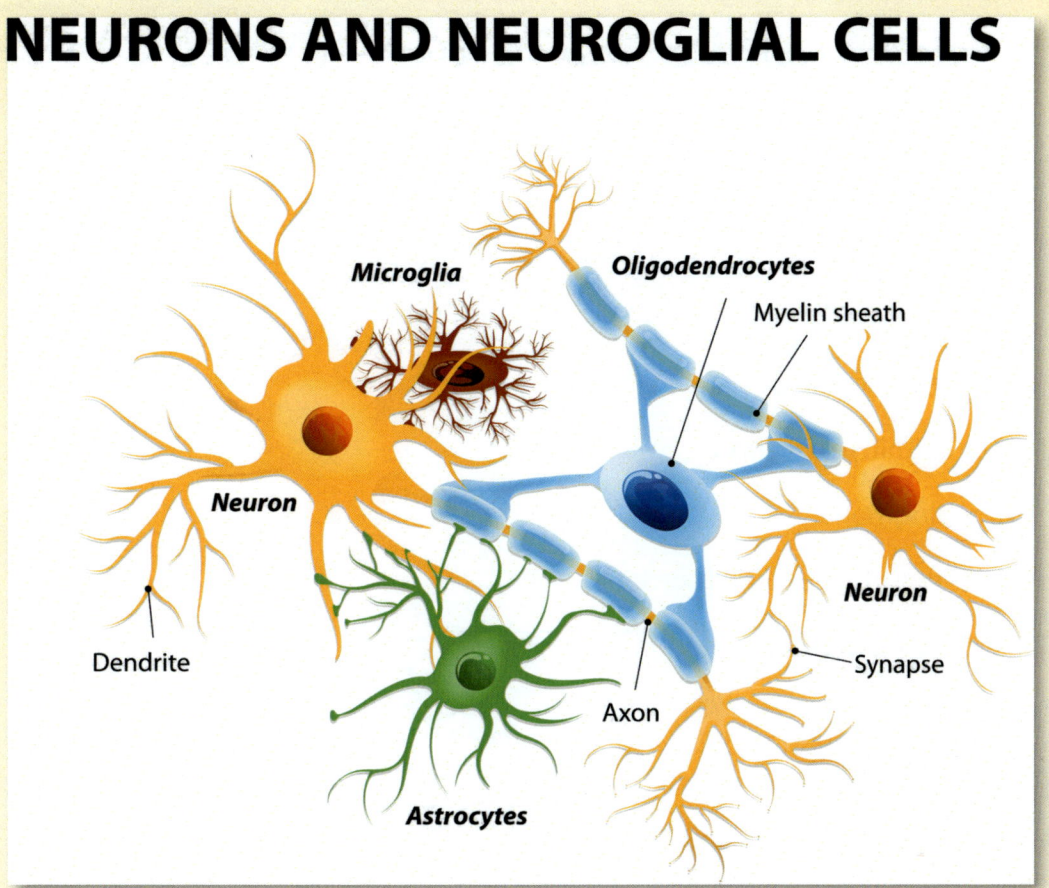

Figure: 4

In autopsies from autistic children's brains below three - five years, the synaptic connections seem to be overproduced. Their brain volume is more than that of autistic adults and youth at autopsy, where there is sparseness of synaptic connections (Eric Courchesne, Karen Pierce, Cynthia Schuman, Joseph A. Buckwalter, Daniel P. Kennedy, John Morgan , 2007)

8. Recent data shows that screen exposure for fun is causing the hyperstimulated brain, poor self-regulation, poor memory, poor cognitive associations, poor motivation, poor social adaptation, and also weight gain problems.

9. Screen and electronics exposure is also causing structural changes that are cutting down dopamine in the right areas of the reward system of the brain and stimulating networks that do not respond to reward systems (more research is ongoing in understanding the role of dopamine).

10. Majority of parents still give apps on iPad or cartoons to a child as young as fifteen months of age as a solution to control and deal with the toddler's demanding and negative attention-seeking behaviors. Many times when there are behavioral disorder and sleep disturbance,

leading questions on screen time exposure reveal that the TV is on all the time, there is involvement with iPad games or EX-Box games, or the infant/child sat in front TV watching cartoons most of the day and after school, at least for two to four hours per day (Yan-Zhou Fu et al.,. Victoria L. Dunckley). The behaviors that are the result of screen time among youth studies show the following:

1. mostly negative psychosocial consequences
2. poor memory
3. poor motivation
4. depression
5. anxiety disorder
6. poor attention span
7. poor cognitive function
8. poor judgment
9. obsessive-compulsive disorder
10. psychosomatization
11. dissociation
12. introversion
13. psychotic behaviors
14. poor anger management and explosive temper

DSM-5 accepted the Internet-associated disorder as an addiction disorder.

D. STRESS AND EXPERIENCES

1. Infants at birth have no previous memory of any experience other than what they experienced through their mother's emotions and vibrations in the womb.

2. Most of the personality development after birth is secondary to sensory input through the five senses.

3. Infants at birth are happy, loving, compassionate, eager to learn, and in a state of safety and security, will absorb all information through the senses, are very curious, and have robust memory for words and actions. They are sponges absorbing everything before they talk or express feelings.

4. They absorb good and tag it with memory, and they tag bad also with some memory or can effectively block the memory, as the bad emotion does not get beyond the right dorsal hippocampus and no further axons develop.

5. In a state of affective mood of safety and security, the perception is that of survival and feeling happy and motivated, to learn everything offered to senses.

6. In a state of perceived danger, insecurity, lack of love, or anxiety, the sensory perception is arrested in a mode of survival to avoid danger, arresting the sensory information to a state of fear and anxiety, preventing strategic planning and learning.

   These earlier states become future traits of a personality (Bruce D. Perry, Child Trauma Academy, Harry T. Chugani, National Scientific Council on the Developing Child, www.developingchild.net, Palmen).

   Every child has the same number of nerve cells no matter where he or she comes from, and every infant has a right to learn and express his or her talents; being poor or rich does not matter. No child should be left alone untouched by the knowledge that we can provide through healthy early experiences for cognitive learning. Even the poor and uneducated can be taught, and this has to be a *massive community involvement and movement.*

7. When there is an experience that fosters the original state of happiness, motivation, and eagerness to learn and interact socially, the child develops good social relationships, family relationships, and emotional and cognitive associations.

8. When the infant feels danger of survival, the brain cannot learn anything with the reaction of fear and anxiety. In this state of toxic fear and anxiety, any information through the five senses is not taken to the frontal lobe, left medial orbital prefrontal gyrus (executive networks), which is the important structure for executive functions like strategic planning, memory and recall, choice making, abstract reasoning, critical thinking, self-control, and self-regulation. The pathways seem to get dispersed and disorganized in the subcortical limbic system.

9. The right side of the brain connects to the world and stores the information permanently in the left prefrontal gyrus. A state of self-trust, self-worth, and self-confidence allows one to enhance on their inherent potential. (see figure 7 for anatomy and functions). Both brains work together through their connections and crossing of fibers between the Corpus Callosum. Each brain has its major role in connecting to the world. When there is more crossover connections of nerve fibers in-between the right and left brain, the intellectual growth also is proportional to this connection.

"Hatred is not an emotion that is natural for a child; it has to be taught by the experience from environment, from community and caretakers. Persons directly or indirectly teaching hatred towards each other, whether it is in-between spouses, or extended family or friends, are making a grave mistake of causing life time changes that are adverse for a child's emotional and psycho-social and intellectual development."

S.A.I. Institute of Educare

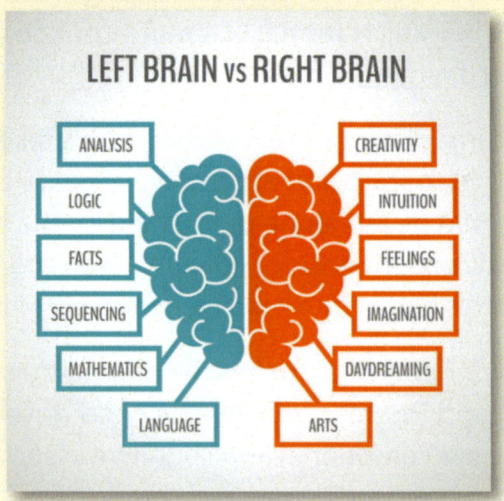

Figure: 5

Chapter II

There Is A Need For A Universal Curriculum 0-3 Years

We cannot see internal pathways development in the brain like we can see the gross motor and fine motor milestones. The development is happening at the molecular level, cellular level, neurotransmitter and chemical balance level, neurohormone level, electrophysiological level, and ionic level.

What if, in the whole world, we make all new arrivals on earth experience the sensory input of the original state of love, family bonding, compassion, self-reliance, and acceptance rather than self-rejection, poor social bonding, with a sense of insecurity, lack of love and sharing, and poor self-esteem?

In a brain that did not have wiring of any sensory input, if the society is trained to offer the above nurture that fosters intellectual and cognitive abilities in a state of happiness, positive values, healthy eating and sleeping habits, that becomes a permanent pathway in the brain before they are three years old.

We have enough behavioral studies on the role of sensory nurture that do not require any expensive gadgets that will stimulate the reward and learning networks, and they are permanent if they are activated and sensitized before the infants can talk and walk.

The experiences and training need to address eating right to prevent cancer through healthy meal plan early on, protecting immune systems, good emotional development, social and family relationships, cognitive development enhanced through nurture to extract that scientist, musician, painter, sculptor, teacher, engineer, physician, and researcher, and so many more (the true meaning of ***educare***) in a developing ***child 0-5 years old.*** They grow up giving something back to society, family, and themselves without causing harm to others to be successful.

The selfish **"I"** can become a selfless **"I"** who in turn is a biological unit in the society to offer something back. The current violence and hatred, jealousy, and retaliating mentality need to be removed from the society by raising children with nurture and human values of love, sympathy, empathy, inner peace, compassion, motivation, happiness, robust memory, persistence, curiosity, and autonomy, which is the natural state of every newborn.

We need parents and caretakers in the society who are willing to see these changes happen. Gun control measures alone will not prevent the current state of violence, but in the next decade, we need to see children who are maintained in their original state at birth in all domains of health by fostering physical, intellectual, psychological, emotional-social, and personal-spiritual wellness. Give them a good foundation to build a strong structure of personality so that there is a safe, strong society.

It has to be a quantum leap, and we are losing time not implementing the knowledge on focusing on the nurture of 0-3 year's age, while still trying to invest money when changes do not occur.

The subsequent chapters will bring out the facts on how the neurobiology from infancy to first three years of life occurs and will bring out the discussion on the need to protect ***the early experiences***

to nurture the infant's overall development in all domains of the definition of health by the World Health Organization.

This brings out a need for a curriculum that fosters ***multisensory integration,*** which can be offered to all newborn infants; teach parenting skills to all parents, grandparents, and all people dealing with children so that they can help hardwire the infant's brain with effective pathways to meet the definition of assuring holistic health. The curriculum has to foster and reinforce the education for all caretakers of 0-3 year old infants, during which time brain pathways form a permanent biosocial, behavioral, hierarchical organization internally in a state of happiness, less threatened with anxiety and fear of survival. Ninety percent of brain pathways are established with a perceived state of mind permanently, memorized and stored by thirty-six months of age. A 333-gram brain has become a 1000-gram brain by the second birthday through this neurodevelopmental organization. No new nerve cells have formed, but one nerve cell to another had connected to form electromagnetic field inside the brain after birth.

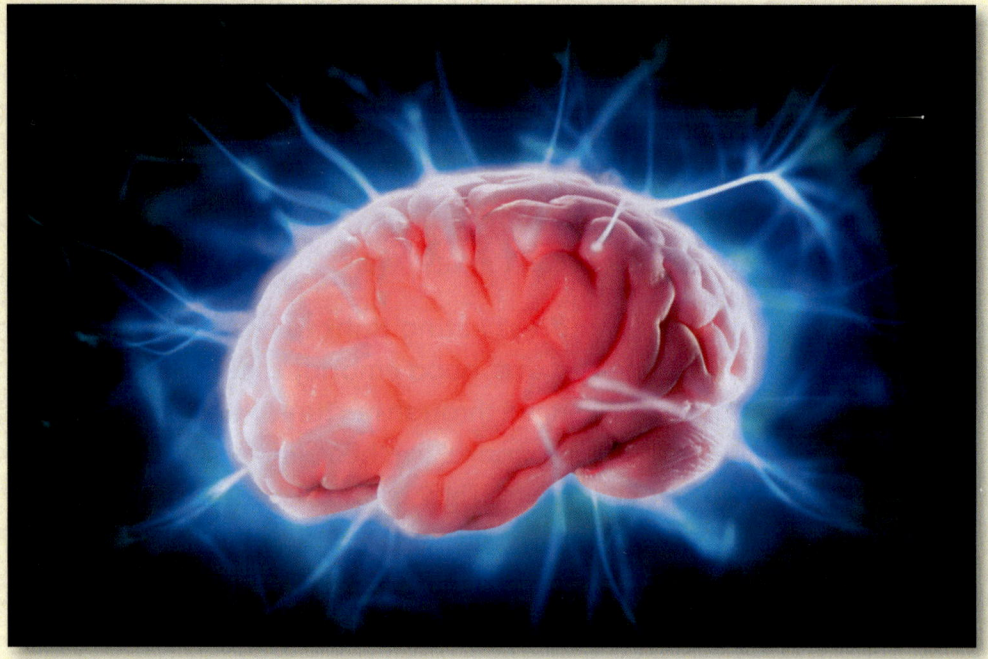

Figure 6: Activity in the brain illustration

This curriculum should not impose any extra expenditure other than what is commonly available at home. Expensive toys and gadgets will not create a human being with sensitive human emotion with self-regulation, empathy, and love.

If the nurture does not support this organizational pattern and is not used for good pathway development, nerve cells die (apoptosis). This means that 600,000 cells per minute are killed or lost per minute if not used. If sensory input is good only 250,000 cells per minute connect to form a pathway. Brain reorganizes all throughout life, but prevention is better during the 0-5 year developmental states that become future traits.

If the brain is a digital analogue, the senses are the software making the broad bands internally in the brain, connecting externally to the world through the sensory input.

The executive networks continue to form through adolescent years, but if the foundation is weak and lay wrong, the plasticity of the brain among youth is also on that weak foundation. All these were discussed with a lot of enthusiasm in my previous writing that was given to society, **Brain, Mind, SAI Educare, in 2004.**

I will offer my experience with real cases (original names were not revealed) with the hope that the readers can understand how the brain, mind, head, and heart connections are impacted with daily life experiences and, if they were positively perceived, could have made a difference in preventing psychopathologies. These early pathologies emerge and stay permanently with the individual.

A real case: 1979–1980

During my fellowship in ambulatory pediatrics, I came across a little three-year-old boy who was at the height and weight of an eighteen-month-old. A very calm and energetic mom brought him for concerns of eating too much and not growing, not talking, not making any eye contact at all, talking in gibberish language, moving all over the place, hoarding of food, and walking at night and opening the refrigerator with a step stool and eating raw bread and meat. I was rotating through child development clinic at that time (1978).

Literature review showed me a similar description of a case report by Dr. Money, 1977, a psychiatrist from Johns Hopkins, titled "Psychosocial Dwarfism." A home evaluation indeed proved that the mother was very moody and punitive and at times locked the infant in the closet and bathroom as a form of punishment. Very punitive measures for disciplining the child were executed by this mother. Paradoxically, the child was very clingy to the mom, and the mom was calm and composed in our interrogations. After the Child Protective Services involvement and home investigation, the child was removed from the home and placed under a very caring foster home. He had music, toys, structure, consistency, and love. He thrived and, in a matter of six months, started talking, grew two inches, and showed growth arrest lines on bone X-ray. His hormone studies were normal. He became calmer and more motivated. It was a fascinating experience for me as a young doctor in training, and it was interesting how a secure, positive home environmental change made a difference in the quality of a child's life! My quest to find the impact of stress on a growing mind was answered when I read the **"Johnson & Johnson Institute"** first roundtable conference on **"Neurobiology of a Developing Child from Birth and Emotional Development,"** published in 1997. I had the pleasure of studying the video clips about the crude but deliberate gestures for learning from the newborn studies by the **Johnson & Johnson Institute**. This convinced me that there is more to behavior disorders from environmental exposure than a genetic predisposition.

Today, it does bother me that people are resorting to blaming the microbiome in the gut and vaccines for causing autism spectrum disorders, trying foods and mineral supplements, and mothers are resorting to fecal transplants to treat children for autism spectrum disorders. **Can we look at all other gadgets and domestic issues that are influencing sensory integration?**

We have come a long way fighting mortality and morbidity from infectious diseases through vaccinations, and parents are taking steps backward in not vaccinating children and helping the resurgence of whooping cough, mumps, and measles. Why cannot we make changes in our thinking and living practices that is healthier emotionally and creates a calm, peaceful, loving, nurturing environment to create a peaceful society globally? Why cannot we address the issues on good eating practices from fresh produce that is healthy and avoid toxic influences on the gut that supplies fuel to all parts of the body including brain and immune system?

We have enough literature reviews and studies that are available to document the need for **healthy eating practices** to prevent cancer, diabetes, hypertension, and behavior problems.

We have enough data on how a calming, relaxing, **meaningful meditation** changes the behavior and immunological systems; increases attention span, memory, and learning; and helps cancer chemotherapy effectiveness. Breathing has to be healthy and put in oxygen to work with the **body fuel "GLUCOSE"** from food to all vital structures.. Nose filters a lot of toxins and nasal breathing is critical element for longevity. Rapidly breathing animals like cats and dogs live only 13 -15 years. Slowly breathing reptiles, like snakes live 300 years.

We have enough research data that shows how effective **soothing music** is on brain networks and in language acquisition, learning, character and cognitive skills development, emotional development, and reading and math processing. Heavy metal music does cause damage to prevent hearing , hearing cortex of the brain, listening skills and damages the balancing systems of the brain, by promoting more **cortisol** type of hormones internally.

We have enough data on how **thoughts influence words and actions**. Thoughts are responsible for producing inner chemicals in the biological systems through autonomic nervous systems, to cause **"fright-and-flight"** reactions or grow with "inner peace and motivation with critical thinking."

This inner quest for truth behind various personality disorders led me to read the works of Dr. Bruce D. Perry from Child Trauma Academy in 1997; Dr. Harry T. Chugani's research on PET scan and brain perfusion studies in exposure to abuse (1997); Andrew Newberg's quest and research on the effects of meditation from Buddhist monks' out-of-body experience studies; Adrian Raine's research on language and social-emotional development on thirteen thousand children prospectively; Jeffrey T. Schwartz's work on unlocking the obsessive-compulsive brain locks; H. Bennet's research on body-mind work and the effect of chants with regulated breathing exercises; Craig Ramey, Peter Fox, and Raichel's work; John J. Ratey's book on the user's guide to brain; and Patricia Kuhl's research on language development. The work of all these eminent scientists documented the need to protect the brain through body-mind-soul connection in a rapidly changing society with devolving human values. The current research data supports now the fundamental principles that I have enumerated through my own clinical work and the plea for changing the thinking pattern in the society so that we can lay foundations for peaceful and secure communities globally. I was very fortunate to have been there for the very first proceedings at the International Center for Integrating Health and Spirituality in 2003 at National Institute of Health to directly listen from the researchers on how stress relief helps the body-mind-soul connections and the immunological systems in general.

Stress causes endocrine disturbances leading to diabetes, hypertension, cancer, and behavior and learning disorders, besides scarring the brain networks. This is because of the over stimulated autonomic nervous system that needs to be brought back to maintain balance of emotions (homeostasis).

During the time that I went to schools with this project, I read the beautiful work done by Dr. Kurt Fischer through his work at Harvard Graduate School of Education on the learning systems that are not working, as they are not using multisensory integration.

Brain, Mind, SAI Educare is a compilation of all the knowledge gained from the data that I collected and read avidly, the spirituality that is an inner quest within me, the results of my own clinical work since 1983, and the many spiritual lessons from my own experiences to control the mind and prevent toxic effects of stress on life, mind, and heart. I also got interested on the application of this knowledge of early childhood brain development on cognitive learning at school and the pedagogy on multisensory integration using multiple intelligence theory in the school systems. The current system of auditory learning alone is not working well in motivating a child for optimal learning. I could find answers as to why ADHD has poor cognitive functioning behaviors, along with poor self-regulation of the behavioral manifestation based on the dysregulated and disorganized neurodevelopment layering, based on the available data from 1997. ADHD and bipolar depression may have genetic predisposition, and genes do not get turned on if the environment and parenting practices change to protect the brain and heart from self-rejection and create good pathways.

The behavioral manifestations of ADHD, autism spectrum disorders, ODD, OCD, and ED/LD all have an overlap, and possibly so because the underlying precipitating cause is getting arrested during the critical phase of brain plasticity in the "fright-and-flight" mode (Chugani).

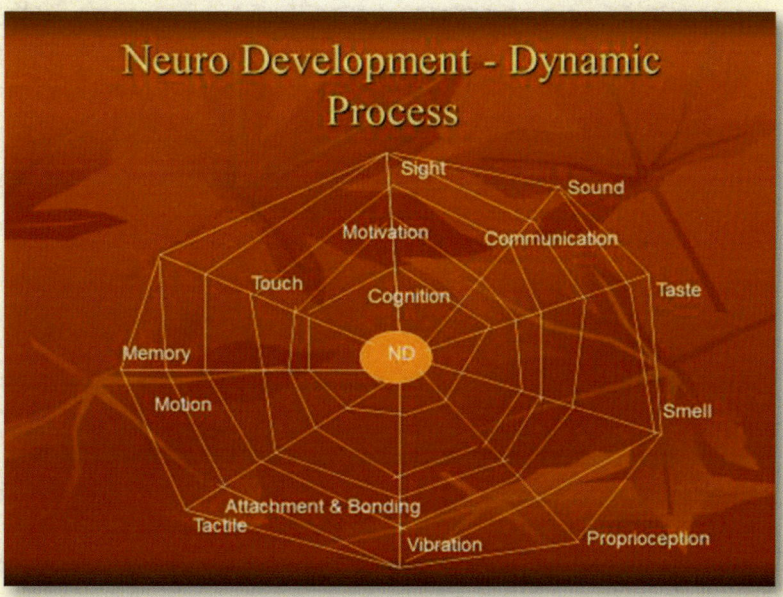

Figure 7: Dynamic pathways that happen that eyes cannot see.

The above is a visual presentation through illustration on how dynamic neurodevelopment simultaneously incorporates the traits into the personality development, and it is like a cobweb where one cannot find the beginning and end. All this happens before the infant learns to talk!

Just like with physical therapy, motor systems reconnect after a stroke, the behavioral and learning systems also reconnect with therapy. It takes longer with more effort, financial drain, and voluntary acceptance of hard work, but they reconnect eventually all throughout life, as the brain is resilient, malleable, and plastic. Thick or broad bands are created in early life, first one thousand days of life, and thin bands are created later on. The broader the band, the faster is the transmission.

We are not talking about hemophilia, juvenile diabetes mellitus, Down syndrome, or other known chromosomal anomalies but more common familial disorders like obesity, heart problems, blood pressure, and type 2 diabetes; these can be prevented if proper eating choices are set in the brain by the third year of life.

Endnotes

1. There is a need for restructuring knowledge and understanding the dynamic brain growth and child development based on that knowledge.

2. Parents are empowered to create excellent children by taking measures 0-3 years of life.

3. Sensory nurture means feeding through all the senses for positive human development.

4. Early child brain development is not a theory anymore but has a value in practical application to ward off negative effects of society on the growing child and the personality development.

5. There are many scholars in different fields in each infant at birth, and they need to be tapped into by the parents and extended family members (educare) and society.

6. One hundred billion cells at birth are ready to connect with the world at a rapid pace, every moment laying down hard wires on twenty-seven trillion connective framing tissues. Unused cells die permanently, and no new cell growth occurs. No new cells form after birth (actually, after 4.5 months of pregnancy), but they connect richly if used.

7. Understand that this phenomenon of neurogenesis is the basis for lazy eye, leading to permanent blindness if not attended to in a timely fashion by the ninth to eighteenth month of life.

8. Infants sense everything from birth and from before birth also, particularly with emotions.

9. Infants are totally dependent on learning from their environment through the adults interacting with them.

10. Toxic stress, anxiety, trauma, witnessing abuse, family dysfunction from spouse bonding issues, poverty, media, electronics, and fast-moving TV cartoons/screen exposure all lead to altering the pathways and brain structure.

ANATOMY OF BRAIN – CROSS SECTION

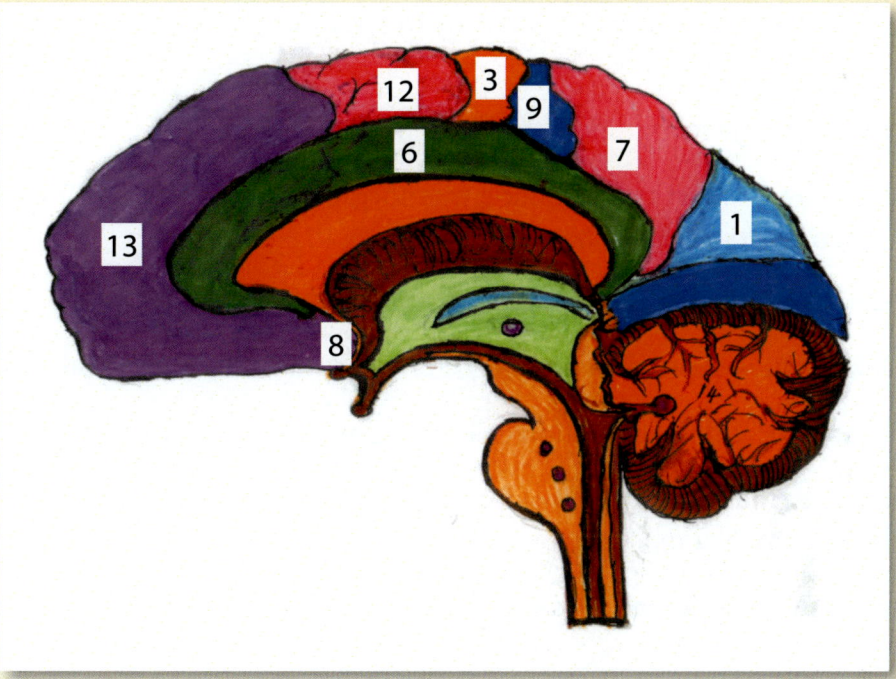

Figure 8: Saggital section of brain anatomy illustration

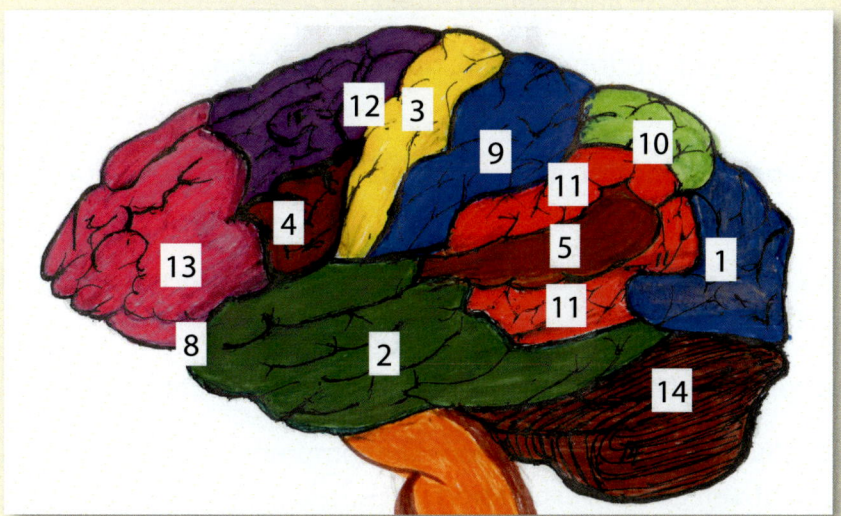

Figure 9: Anatomy of Brain and different functional areas

Anatomy and Functional Areas of the Brain

The areas are numbered and the explanation is by the numbers as to the function and the name of the area

1. **Visual cortex:** Image recognition and perception of seen objects

2. **Association Area:** Short term working memory, balancing, emotion. This area needs to be in focus when instructions are given.

3. **Motor Function** area for gross and fine motor skills

4. **Broca's Area:** Where expression of speech comes from. Has speech related muscle movement

5. **Auditory Area:** Hearing Perception called sensory cortex for hearing

6. **Emotional Area:** Pain, perception of fear, anxiety, anger, hunger. Typical area to cause "Fright and Flight" response or reaction

7. **Sensory Association area:** All sensory input is tagged with safety, security or fear and anxiety

8. **Olfactory Area:** Sense of smell and also memory. Senses danger and alerts other systems or creates pleasure response and calming effect

9. **Sensory Area:** All perceptions of pain, hunger, emotions, touch, heat, cold from muscles and skin

10. **Somato-Sensory Association area:** Recognizes objects by size, color, texture, weight, depth, width, geometrical proportions

11. **"Wernicke's area":** Sensory perception of integrating written and spoken language and comprehending speech.

12. **Motor function area:** All gross and fine motor skills area and also for motor system orientation

13. **Executive Brain:** Higher mental functions like comprehension, concentration, attention span, focus, judgment, self control, expression

    Creativity, abstract reasoning, critical thinking, respond than react, analytical thinking, organization, long term memory and recall.

14. **Cerebellum:** Motor coordination, Equilibrium or balancing, emotional balancing, posture, joint and position sense.

Figure 10: Concept of pathways from outside to inside and behavior out put as Inside to out side

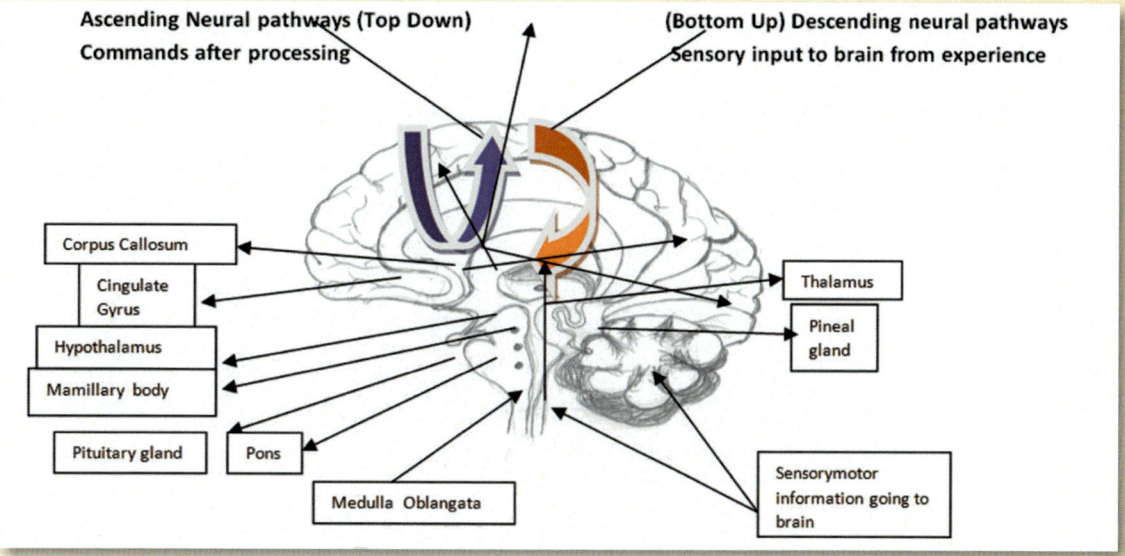

Figure 10: Functional area of the sagittal section of brain

Right insula: Right Insula causes arousal of autonomic system. Gets activated with electronic games

Functions of insula

Insula is involved with consciousness, emotion, and balance or homeostasis. This includes self-awareness, cognitive function, perceptions, motor control, and interpersonal experiences. This is considered as part of the temporal lobe and also part of the orbitofrontal gyrus and limbic system. It controls eye-hand coordination.

It has a role in sympathy, empathy, heart rate control, blood pressure, and pain management, autonomic and visceral.

Clinical importance

Decreased activity is linked to expressive language delay; aphasia (understands phonemes but cannot talk).

Insula is connected with nicotine and drug addictions.

Nucleus accumbens

Increased activity in left nucleus accumbens with electronics on imaging studies was noted. Nucleus accumbens is a part of basal ganglia and ventral striatum.

Nucleus Accumbens is associated with dopamine and serotonin production from rewarding activities like eating food, sex, drugs, sports, etc., or even with negative aversive traumatic stimuli. It is an important structure for memories both good and bad.

Bilateral Premotor Cortex

Premotor cortex is more involved in sensory-guided movement.

Orbitofrontal cortex

This part is connected to visual pathways, visual cortex through thalamus, auditory cortex and pathways, limbic system pathways, nucleus accumbens, hippocampus, insula, amygdala, and uncus.

This is the key structure for most of the executive functions like decision-making, emotion regulation, reward expectation, and punishment systems. Disruption of pathways from thalamus, hypothalamus, and limbic system is involved in ADHD, OCD, and anxiety behaviors. Impulsivity increases.

The inner portion of the region is involved with good associations and positive reward system and learning with memory.

The outer portions are involved with punishment and poor reward sensitivity.

Social judgment and maladjustment occur with damage to this brain.

Temporal lobes

Semantic memory or knowledge of objects, people, words, and facts is the function of Temporal lobes. Other functions include auditory processing, comprehension, verbal memory and visual-spatial associations. Olfactory (nose and smelling) system is also connected, and lesions do cause hallucinations of smell and hearing.

Occipital lobes

Visual learning and processing of color, depth, and spatial reasoning, and connects to motor systems for responding with gazing the external visual stimulus. This portion of brain is responsible for 5–10 percent of seizure disorders (flashing lights and colors). Noise associated with visual signals is associated with better perception by the visual cortex.

Cerebellum

This is right at the junction of the neck and lower portion of the back of the brain structures and is called the small brain. It regulates cognitive activity and emotional regulatory function. It is an important structure for maintaining balance through the vestibule cortical connections. Motor coordination, movement coordination, postural balance, and smooth shifting of visual images are from this little brain.

Dysdiadochokinesia, poor alternating movements of extremities, occurs when damaged. Poor eye adjustment and retinal adjustment happen with damage to vestibular-cerebella connections. Some children have visual distortions that make them scared to see or read, as the letters and words move. Accidentally when they are focusing, it causes fear and they have been misdiagnosed as having Autism as they do not focus and make eye contact. They also get labeled as Dyslexic. Chromagen lenses make a world of difference and the reading improves. But the child need to be assessed fr this disorder.hich are prisms, make them stable emotionally (Dr. John J. Ratey in *A User's Guide to the Brain*).

Cingulate gyrus

An important part of the limbic system, the Cingulate Gyrus helps regulate emotions and pain. The Cingulate Gyrus is thought to directly drive the body's conscious response to unpleasant experiences. In addition, it is involved in fear and the prediction (and avoidance) of negative consequences and can help orient the body away from negative stimuli. Learning to avoid negative consequences is an important feature of memory.

Anterior or front part of the cingulate cortex (ACC) is connected to the amygdala, hippocampus of the limbic system, and hypothalamus. Through these connections, the ACC is thought to be involved with a number of functions related to emotion, including the regulation of overall affect and tagging a quality to emotion, good or bad, from the thoughts of internal stimulus and from the experiences from external stimulus.

This structure helps make verbal expressions of these emotions. The ACC also seems to contribute to the regulation of autonomic and endocrine responses, pain perception, and selection and initiation of motor movements.

Cingulate cortex is involved with social adaptations and decision-making; it is an important structure in the back portion for memory from personal experiences and recall of the memory. This Cingulate Gyrus that sits over the eye sockets seems to have a major role in attention span and cognitive associations, sensory integration, and monitoring conflict and resolution.

Hippocampus

This is a main part of the mesocorticolimbic system associated with reward system, memory for long-term and declarative memory from past experiences, not short-term or active working memory or procedural memory that comes from ACC.

In animal studies, damage to this structure caused hyperactivity and poor control of learned behaviors or poor inhibition as in anxiety disorders to block an internal stimulus.

Spatial cognition and memory and mapping with fright-and-flight reactions and coordination of responses seem to be related to the hippocampus.

Memory: Remembering **new information is episodic memory** of events, places, and experiences (also called autobiographical memory).

Hippocampus is also involved with **declarative memory**, which means an expression verbally of events, places, and experiences.

Procedural memory for making puzzles and playing a musical instrument come from cerebral cortex and temporal lobes and not from the hippocampus.

Long term memory is not stored in the hippocampus, and remote memory is not destroyed when hippocampus gets damaged.

Spatial memory comes from the hippocampus, like knowing the directions in the environment and remembering a place and driving to that place (mapping grid). The size of the hippocampus increases with aerobic exercises, even in elderly. In schizophrenia and Alzheimer's, the size of the hippocampus is small.

Stress response: Stress has a direct impact on the hippocampus as a result of the highest number of glucocorticoid receptors. The first response to stress is excitation in the hippocampus with increased activity secondary to many steroid receptors.

Hippocampus is the only structure that forms *new neurons* after birth throughout life and is use based development. New neuron formation is arrested with long lasting or chronic severe acute stress.

There will be reduction in dendrites to the Neocortex or the Executive brain. In Post Traumatic Stress Disorder (PTSD) and in depression, shrinkage of hippocampus is seen. This structure is most vulnerable with stress.

This structure is very excitable and has a major role in epilepsy, particularly in temporal lobe epilepsy.

Ventral and dorsal striatum

Ventral striatum is nucleus accumbens and olfactory system.

Ventral striatum is involved with cognition secondary to reward system, motivation, and reinforcement. This also responds with a tag for aversive and frightening experiences.

Dorsal striatum is putamen and caudate nucleus.

Dorsal striatum is involved with motor functions, stimulus response and learning, and some executive functions.

This system has high glutamatergic and dopaminergic responses. These responses are regulated in addiction through this structure. Damage to the dorsal striatum is seen in movement disorders.

The striatum coordinates multiple aspects of cognition, including motor and action planning, decision-making, motivation, reinforcement, and reward perception.

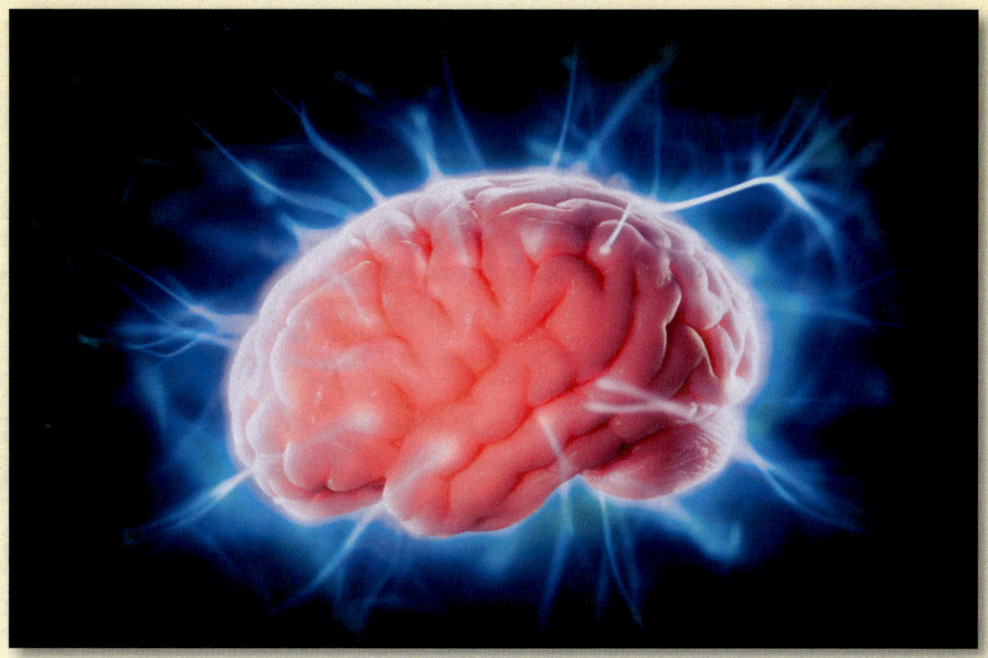

Figure 11: Illustration of fluorescent activity of the brain

Chapter III

Need-to-Learn Facts about Neurons and Organization

By the 4.5 months of pregnancy, two hundred billion neurons form and migrate to the future area of the brain in the head region. Approximately, at birth, one hundred billion neurons remain in the brain; the rest were pruned out (apoptosis). When there was drug, alcohol, or substance abuse during the first trimester of pregnancy, the cells are still at eighty billion in number. There are twenty-seven trillion cells for supporting the nerve cells and the nerve pathways.

The care of the future infant begins in pregnancy, in planning, nourishment, rest, proper nutrition, preventing exposure to illness, and spiritual endeavors to avoid severe emotions. Even a little alcohol can affect the fetus. Minerals are very important; multivitamins are also important. B10 deficiency has been shown to cause neural tube defects. Poverty has caused poor weight gain in infants at birth. If there is a family trend for diabetes, overeating white carbohydrate food can cause maternal gestational diabetes mellitus and an infant of diabetic mother (IDM) with heart anomalies and sugar adjustment disorder at birth. Aspirin can cause birth defects.

We have controlled infections that damage the brain from viral infections like Cytomegalovirus and Rubella or German measles, and parasitic infections like Toxoplasmosis. Group B bacterial meningitis and morbidity are well controlled with increased awareness and prenatal testing. We took precautions to prevent exposure to Herpes Simplex II virus and morbidity and mortality. Even better measures are available for preventing Rh-negative blood group–induced hemolytic damage to the fetus with Rhogam administered to the mother prenatally and after delivery. We are trying to prevent exposure to whooping cough by catching all elderly people from transmitting it to the newborn in the first six to eight weeks of life by cocooning the adults and giving them Tdap. Now we are facing a challenge with Zika viral infections, and CDC has measures under way to develop a vaccine and prevent transmission. We were able to overcome the challenge of preventing morbidity to the unborn fetus and the newborn infants in the section of community-acquired infections.

But we are unable to protect the growing brains in the first three years from the adverse effects of domestic violence, media violence, and electronics and screen exposure that seem to have toxic fear and anxiety effect on the brain to the extent of damaging the gray and white matter with degenerative changes and structural changes in the brain for a life time.

> The role of anxiety and fear, beyond normal separation anxiety, is very toxic to the developing brain. All is tied into early experience and nerve pathway development.

We are still not proactive through legal systems in protecting the neonatal to early three years of optimal brain development and biosocial behavioral outcomes by curbing screen time, intimate partner violence, family dysfunction, and media violence. As a result, adversely perceived sensory input from birth to thirty-six months of life is causing the damage, creating complex brain disorganization structurally, leading to intellectual disabilities, poor social outcome, poor emotional regulation, and poor cognitive organization, which includes math disabilities and language disorders. Stress also adversely affects the immune system that leads to more chronic health problems. Stress causes poor function of D54, natural killer factor that will attack viral infections. Stress also takes a toll on the metabolism, causing a ground for diabetes, high blood pressure, ulcers, poor focus, and poor learning. These states become traits to be carried on into the adult life, which are causing disturbed, insecure communities and society for raising our children. National statistics were already laid out in the previous chapter.

Similarly, addiction to cartoons, using TV as a teacher and babysitter, and iPad and iPhone addiction as young as from nine months onward are causing similar disorganization of brain networks and nerve pathways. There is enough data about hyper stimulation of the brain and hyperkinetic childhood behavior and developmental delays linked to screen time under 2.5 years of age.

The answer to this is that neither the CDC nor the health-care systems nor the legal systems look at ***community violence as an epidemic***. If they do so, they are going to open their eyes to curb the escalating health-risk behaviors by listening to community members who are doing preventive measures in a scattered way and work on bringing about effective legal and judicial reforms, and will bring all community groups together.

In my previous book, "**Brain, Mind, SAI Educare,**" published in 2004, with a lot of enthusiasm, I explained the same facts. I brought the science and spirituality together, explained neurobiology, and gave the curriculum for parent training and a lesson plan development model for three- to five-year-old pre-K children. The book was published by UPA in October 2004 and distributed by Lanham and Oxford Press. It allows readers to comprehend the critical role of early positive experiences to reach out to the community, to make critical changes and create a better world, with understanding the needs at different age groups, and to guide parents through education for proper child development.

A parent is not just a caretaker but the first teacher and then becomes a counselor and friend and guide by adolescence. Schoolteachers and administrators become second parents to understand the needs of the poor learners. Since then, I have additional twenty-three years of experience of implementing the curriculum that I developed, to integrate the five senses to make an infant develop optimal intellectual and biosocial pathways, even among the structurally compromised brains as with the NICU graduates who were one thousand grams or less at birth.

There is more interest on the part of the organized medicine now in getting to implement the knowledge gained from imaging studies on early child brain development (ECBD). I was too ahead of the general application of knowledge in the society and also the organized medicine about ECBD and stood alone in the general medical field implementing the knowledge in daily practice.

This second book venture is to make the general population understand the need to know about neurobiology and the critical role of the parents and the society to prevent the adverse influences on brain pathways and create pathways for optimal biosocial personality development. Fostering the dynamic brain growth toward meeting the holistic definition of health by the World Health Organization is the *duty of the society* through offering education to parents and the community at large on the techniques of nurture.

Judicial reforms by making caretakers take mandatory education on neurodevelopment and the causes behind the disorganization of brain architecture and corrective measures for optimal learning socially, emotionally, intellectually, cognitively, and mathematically, and in linguistic abilities of reading, spelling, and writing are the needs of the day. Parents more often leave all up to the school, and they are not deeply involved in the triangle of teacher, pupil, and parent as a team to work strategically on a student.

The root word for **"education"** is **"*educare,*"** a Latin word. As per Johnson's *New World Dictionary* meaning of EDUCARE is ***"Extracting the inherent strengths or powers of an individual."*** The current educational system is not able to do that, as it has many limitations, as Dr. Kurt Fischer (Harvard Graduate School of Education - HGSE) describes the system as a ***"spoke and wheel"*** pattern. It has to develop pedagogy to foster all the senses for learning and has to be a multisensory integration in a state of happiness in learning and with enthusiasm and calmness of mind. We have to tap into external and internal motivation factors.

For the last thirty-six years of my pediatric practice and in teaching life skills, more so in the last twenty-three years, I worked on sensory nurture; but since 1997, I worked with the evidence-based backup knowledge on the need for sensory nurture after I read the first roundtable discussion materials that I purchased from Johnson & Johnson Institute on early brain development and emotional development. As a provider, I happily, with self-confidence, incorporated the knowledge in caring for all normal children, NICU graduates, and those with behavioral disorders. I had excellent results on many children and parents who were compliant and never failed to follow the five teaching techniques for multisensory integration to nurture the sensory input and through similar adopted techniques for parental education teaching the techniques of nurture to foster healthy brain pathways among zero-to-three-year age group children.

I look at a parent or any caretaker as the first teacher in a child's life and feel that the knowledge and curriculum that I am intending to share can change the behavioral outcomes, creating a peaceful society globally.

Expensive curriculum is beyond the scope of most needy families. The curriculum has to be available without expensive gadgets and universally applicable with daily available tools, parent's knowledge, and preparation for transition. There are many rapid transitions in early brain development, and a fundamental knowledge is very important among the caretakers, teachers, and institutions in general. The role of the parent changes with every transition of infant development.

The following is a representation of society and individual in the society.

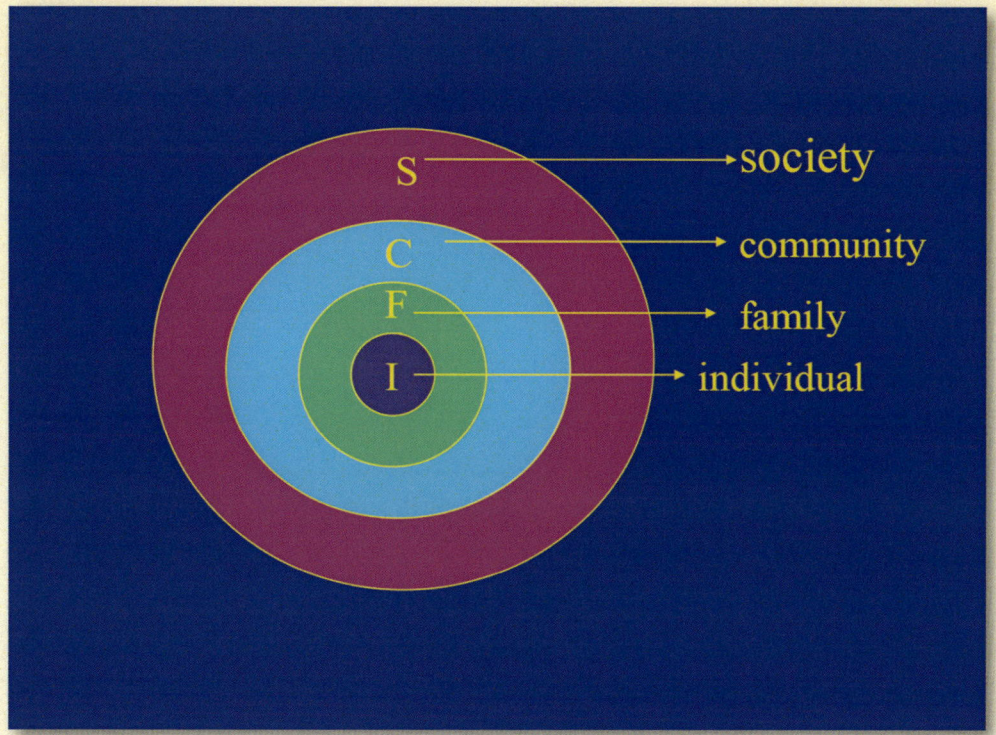

Figure 12: Individual is a biological unit of Society

In the current society, calmness and peace start with the individual character and then family peace and world peace.

"When there is righteousness in heart there is beauty in character

When there is beauty in character, there is harmony in home

When there is harmony in home, there is order in the society

When there is order in the society there is Peace in the Nation and World."

(Satya Sai Baba)

As stated above, world peace starts with individual development that should meet the criteria of definition of health as defined by the WHO in 1997.

"Health is physical, intellectual, psychological, emotional, and spiritual wellness."

Massive education is needed for community awareness of the facts that are being held only in the researcher's domain. We need judicial, school, and community reforms with new approaches in systems of delivery and care. We need to shake the old thinking patterns and replace with new knowledge and reform the rules. Every caretaker of an infant and child needs to be knowledgeable in their role and break away from past with self-respect, self-confidence, and without feeling guilty of making and accepting changes. We need world reforms to make the globe a peaceful entity.

Peace starts first within, and outside is all pieces of broken hearts and lives

Continuing the presentation of brain functions

A diagrammatic representation of how the whole body systems are connected through the limbic system during organogenesis and functionally after birth

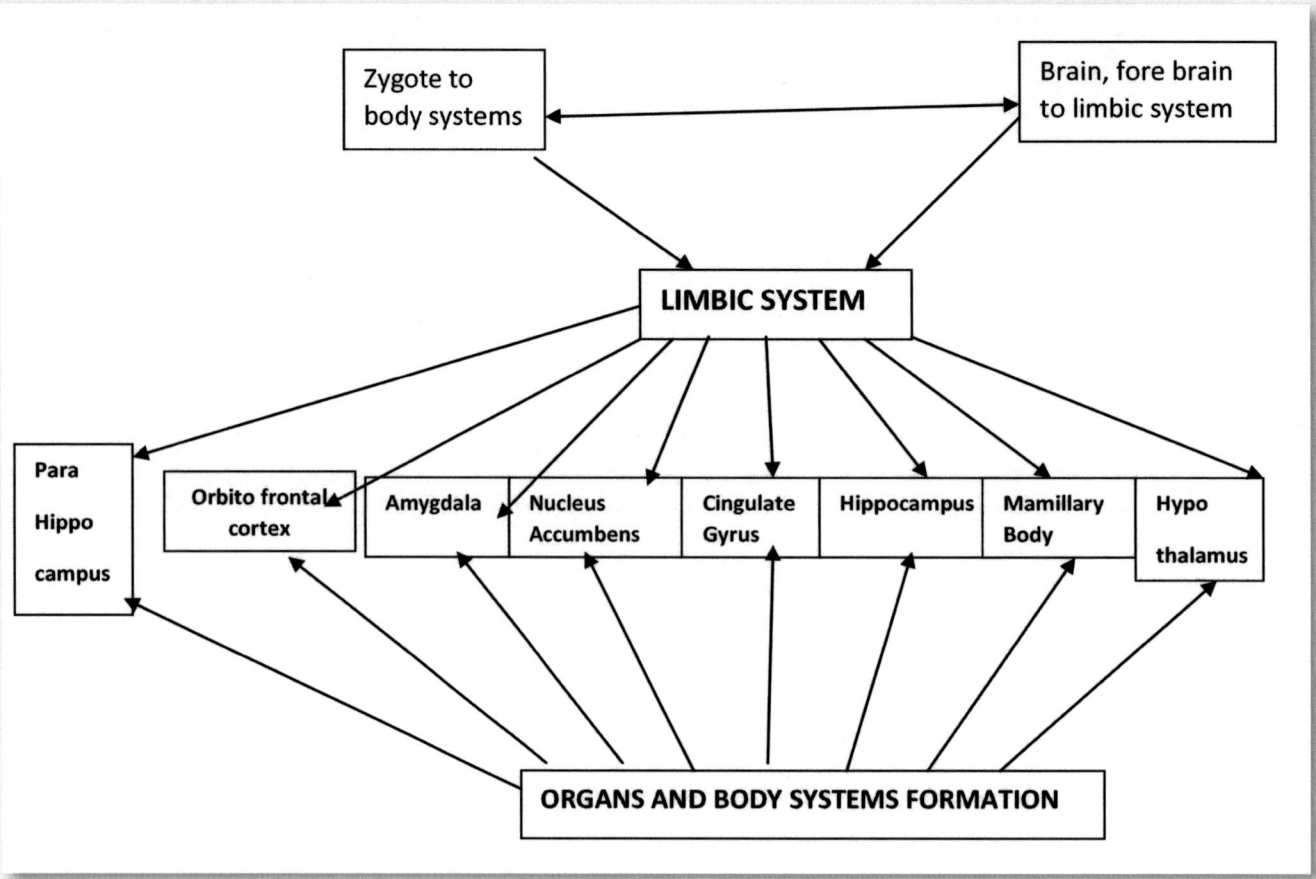

Figure 13: Limbic System functions

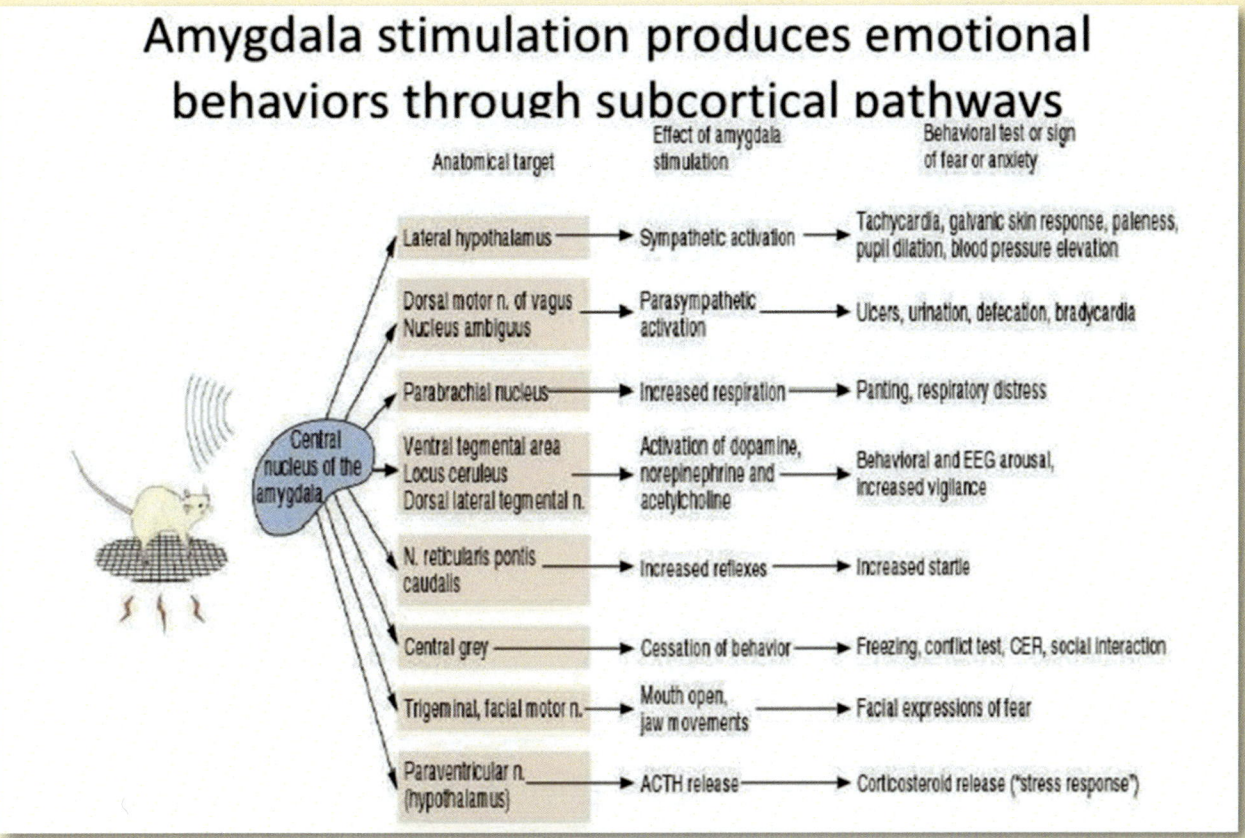

Figure 14: Amygdala Functions

When various substructures of the Amygdala get stimulated, stress hormones are released, muscle tone increases, and the organism freezes and does not move. Because of stress hormone and cortisol release, there will be rapid heart rate and rapid respirations, the face and ears get flushed, tremors may appear, pupils get dilated, sweating starts, gastric acid production increases, cognition gets reduced or down, and the individual will get **into "flight-or-fright"** mode. The reactions are from ventral Amygdala stimulation.

> Dorsal (upper portion) area causes slow heart rate; one may even faint, and urination and gastric acidity increase.

> Imagine the result of prolonged exposure to this response on a daily basis and the effects of cortisol on the brain structures. In a state of vigilance to protect oneself, the brain will not cognize and learn from the immediate environment.

All sensory information has to go through the limbic system and has much more than an emotion regulation, which was a previous thought. In majority of the cognitive associations, memory, visual-spatial reasoning, declarative memory, stimulus that is responsible for autonomic nervous system responses, endocrine regulation, parasympathomimetic responses, inhibition of overgrowing of adult neurons, neuropathways development and organization of the axonal distribution, organization of mini and macro columns of synaptic connections, reward and insensitivity to reward, satiety, and addiction prone centers of the brain seem to be regulated through the vertical and horizontal radiating fibers in the layers within the limbic system.

Misfiring of impulses through the limbic system, which disorganizes the connections, has a lifetime impact on academic, cognitive, intellectual, social, emotional, communication, and organizational disorders, thus making the overlap of symptoms in schizophrenia, autism spectrum, OCD, ADHD, and emotional disorders (Stephanie H. Amies, Jason Lerch, et al., 2016, *Science Daily*). Limbic system is the main system to organize adaptive functions in the human brain.

This is also found to be of similar extent in elephants and some birds. Neocortex in some form is now recognized among certain birds and that explains why parrots talk.

Chapter IV

Neurobiology of the Brain

For the first-time parents, when they hold that healthy newborn in their hands, it is a great and memorable experience. ***The greatest gift in life is the gift of human life.*** It is human life that has the capability of changing behaviors from reaction to response as a result of the presence of the neocortex, frontal lobes, amygdala, and hippocampus. This brain sits above the eye sockets, and animals do not have this brain. All religions taught that human life is the only life that will acknowledge the highest energy within, serve people, and protect the nature by protecting animates and inanimate in nature, and is the only life in the whole creation that can express emotions. In fact, human beings are the only ones who can take care of planet Earth and start a life in space through space stations in the galaxy. Human beings are the only ones who can express and synthesize their emotional prosody to respond than react. This is the eternal truth that will not change till we can find an alien on earth smarter and different than human beings!

It is because of this ability that we are able to socially mingle, have cognitive ability to learn, read and write, adapt to new situations, create relationships, reach out through love as a means of sharing and caring, realize the inner peace, express emotions, and respond than react to situations.

> *"When the people become good, the world will become good."*
>
> *"For millions of students and children who go to school, the mother is the first teacher."*
>
> —Sai Baba (a spiritual leader from India)

What are the facts in neurodevelopment?

By the early second trimester of pregnancy, one hundred billion neurons and twenty-seven trillion glial cells that are the future gray and white matter are in their final destination in the brain portion of the embryo. By the early third trimester, like twenty-eight weeks of pregnancy, the infant can start connecting the nerve cells from maternal hormones and vibrations and music. Most of these connections happen rapidly after birth. De Casper (Duke University) in 1986 proved the above fact that the connections form for emotions and vibrations inside the womb and the infant could recognize the rhyming and language of music and stories read to them while in the womb.

The pictures of brain anatomy and functional description of various parts of the brain were given for people who wanted to learn about the brain in the previous sections. The hindbrain, which is the brain stem that has Cerebellum, Pons, Medulla Oblongata are common to animals, like monkeys, cats, dogs, reptiles, and human beings. This brain connects the spine to mid brain and fore brain through mid brain connections. What differentiates the human brain from that of the animals and monkeys is the presence of neocortex, well-differentiated limbic system, and hippocampus gyrus (amygdala and uncus). The little brain called cerebellum has additonal properties for emotional and cognitive associations in the human brain.

Anatomy and Functional Areas of the Brain

The areas are numbered and the explanation is by the numbers as to the function and the name of the area

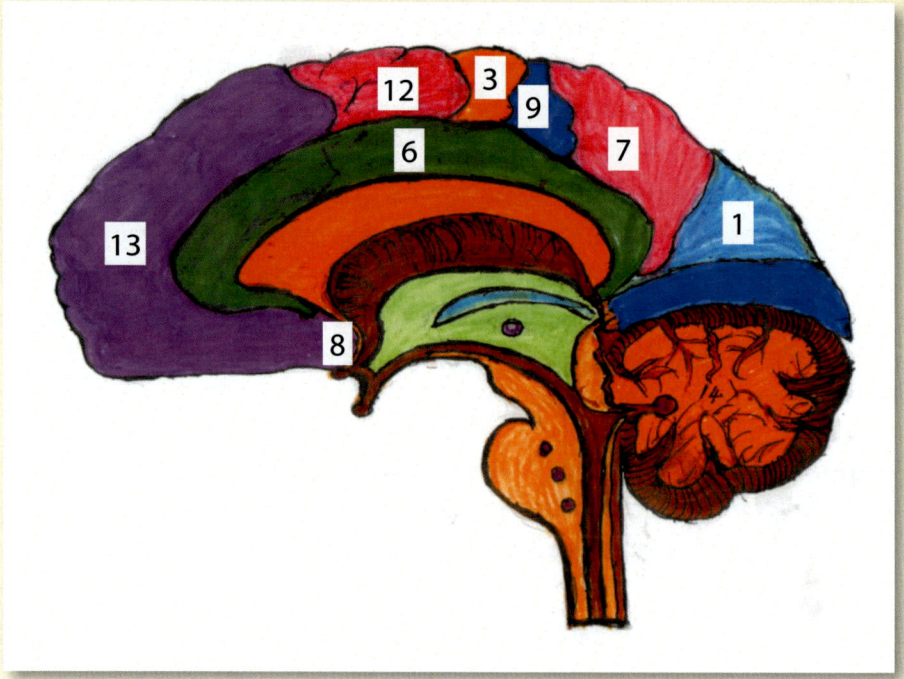

Figure 15: Functional units of brain –Sagittal view

This is repeated from the previous section for quick reference and for convenience of reading

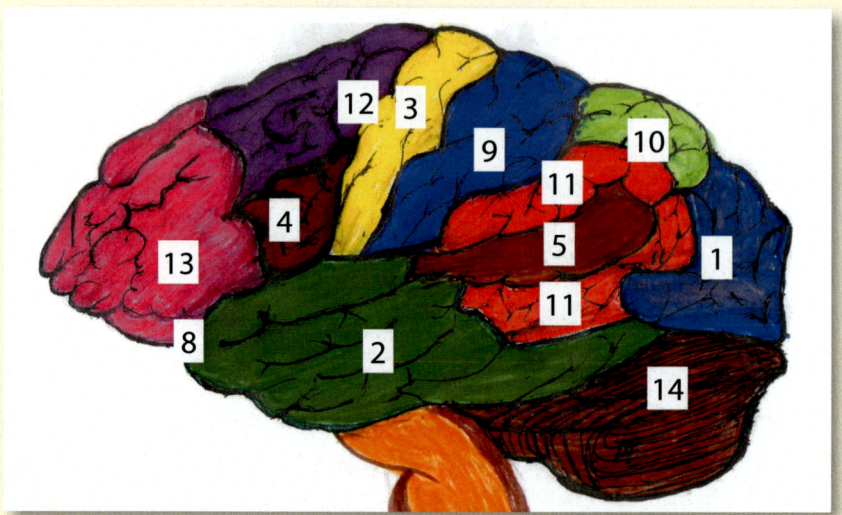

Figure 16: Anatomy of Functional lobes of Brain

Anatomy and Functional Areas of the Brain

The areas are numbered and the explanation is by the numbers as to the function and the name of the area

1. **Visual cortex:** Image recognition and perception of seen objects

2. **Association Area:** Short term working memory, balancing, emotion. This area needs to be in focus when instructions are given.

3. **Motor Function** area for gross and fine motor skills

4. **Broca's Area:** Where expression of speech comes from. Has speech related muscle movement

5. **Auditory Area:** Hearing Perception called sensory cortex for hearing

6. **Emotional Area:** Pain, perception of fear, anxiety, anger, hunger. Typical area to cause "Fright and Flight" response or reaction

7. **Sensory Association area:** All sensory input is tagged with safety, security or fear and anxiety

8. **Olfactory Area:** Sense of smell and also memory. Senses danger and alerts other systems or creates pleasure response and calming effect

9. **Sensory Area:** All perceptions of pain, hunger, emotions, touch, heat, cold from muscles and skin

10. **Somato-Sensory Association area:** Recognizes objects by size, color, texture, weight, depth, width, geometrical proportions

11. **"Wernicke's area":** Sensory perception of integrating written and spoken language and comprehending speech.

12. **Motor function area:** All gross and fine motor skills area and also for motor system orientation

13. **Executive Brain:** Higher mental functions like comprehension, concentration, attention span, focus, judgment, self control, expression, creativity, abstract reasoning, critical thinking, respond than react, analytical thinking, organization, long term memory and recall.

14. **Cerebellum:** Motor coordination, Equilibrium or balancing, emotional balancing, posture, joint and position sense

Meena Chintapalli, M.D. F.A.A.P.

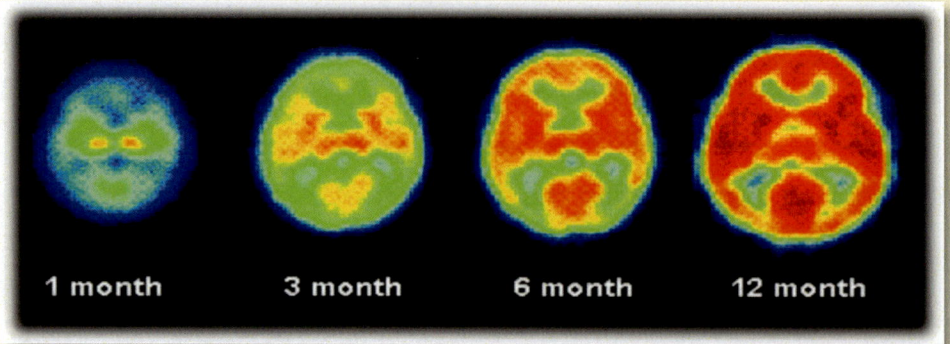

Figure 17: showing brain PET scans of active brain pathways 0-12 months.

Courtesy of Dr. Harry T. Chugani, who used these for community education in 1997 (WSU). Currently Dr. Harry T.Chugani is still actively working on Brain research at Nemours Institute in Delaware.

As noticeable in the above PET scan section from newborn stage to one month, the infant has no red activity; red and yellow means that the brain is forming a mind, wires are forming from outside to inside, and there is activity from recognizing the world around them. There is very little red at one month of age.

That means that the infant is actually forming nerve pathways from the sensory input, called as **"hard wiring."** At one month of age, still at basic needs of eating, sleeping, and crying for a need, and one can see the red activity is a small area in the midbrain. The weight of the brain is 333 grams at one month of age. Every sensory input is new to the brain and is the foundation pathway as it is making connections through the experience from the surroundings.

But by one year, the human connections to the neocortex for future behavioral outcomes have occurred, making the brain weigh 1000 grams. Dynamic brain growth forms connections rapidly at the same time for states of emotional growth, recognizing tempos, rhythms, movement, auditory-spatial recognition, visual-spatial recognition, balancing, communication, motivation, memory, and reasoning, emotionally tagging all experiences either with an emotion of fear, anxiety, sadness, and worry, or happiness with curiosity and eagerness to learn with motivation. Gardner's multiple intelligence factors are rapidly laid down, occurring in a dynamic fashion, before the infant could talk and express feelings!

It is a dynamic combination of layering memories permanently from surroundings and giving it a tag of good or bad emotions, cognitive associations and intellectual learning, social adjustment, and willingness to learn and to communicate; this will be expressed as a behavior after eighteen months if age.

Many ions, molecules, hormones, immunological factors, humoral responses, transporters, receptors, inhibitors, excitatory factors, mood hormones, autonomic nervous system responses, and genetic factors help or block the neurogenesis, layering, and organization. Influencing factors are diets, attitudes, environmental stressors, infections, poverty, substance use, fear, trauma, and illness, which can cause disorganization. An experience is needed to create the pathways by stimulating these chemicals, ions, and molecules.

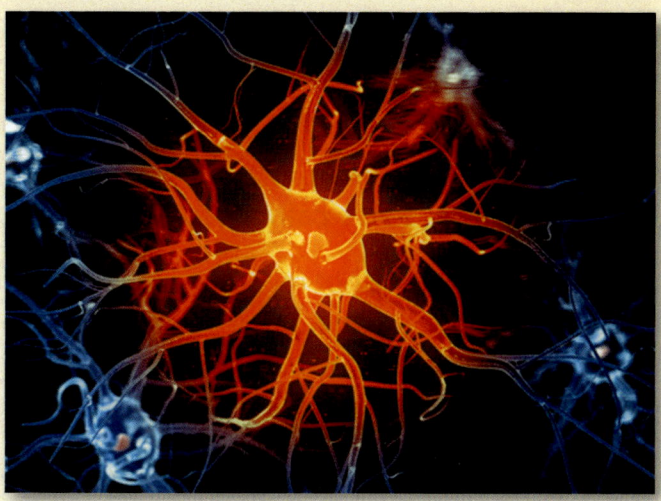

Figure 18: 3D image illustration of Neuron

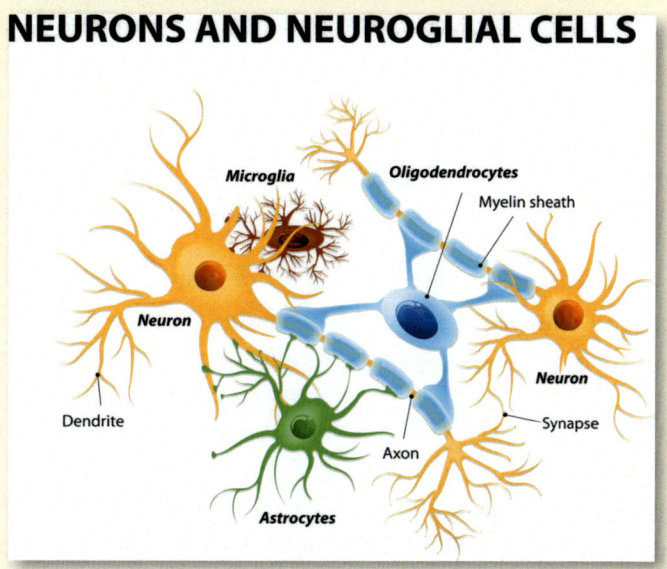

Figure 19: Illustration of various connections forming synapses, axons and supporting glial cell frame work. These are mini columns and aggregates of these mini columns form macro columns based upon the functional use of a pathway. If pathways are not consistently laid down through experience, the aggregates are scattered in functional capacity and chaotic.

Every experience is a new experience and is formed as a permanent part of the brain, and this is a foundation for personality development.

Therefore, care has to be taken early on in pregnancy through stabilizing all of the above factors for equanimity of mind and body, certainly avoiding aversive factors, and stabilizing the community limb as shown in the triangles below to prevent inadequate outcome in infant-raising practices.

All newborn infants develop social smiles by two to three weeks, wherein they love and trust caretakers and are very happy to see a face that has been taking care of their needs. When a designated brain area is stimulated, there is a rapid transmission of message from nerve cell to nerve cell, which forms a connection called a **synaptic junction**, where each nerve cell makes ten thousand dendritic connections (small hair like structures) to the other cell multiplied by 250,000 cells per minute, among one hundred billion cells. Unused, or not stimulated from birth, ten thousand cells die per second, called apoptosis, which translates to six hundred thousand cells per minute, to the power of ten thousand connections for each cell.

Myelination protects the cells and the axons from getting short-circuited in conductance of electromagnetic transmission along these nerve pathways.

We do newborn hearing screen so that we do not miss the opportunity to identify sensory neural hearing loss. We pay attention to the lazy eye so that there is no suppression amblyopia or permanent cortical blindness in a child from blocking vision through one of the eyes. We do massages to make them walk or move early. All are done to optimize the brain connections before we lose opportunities.

Infants getting too many ear infections and impaired hearing will develop speech and cognitive deficiencies. As the conductive hearing loss prevents proper hearing, listening pathways thin out (atrophy) or they die called apoptosis. Unused memory tasks cause poor memory and retention. ERO scans and tymapanometry shall be done more often for frequent ear infections in a small child under three years of age to prevent hearing loss and language processing delays.

0-3 years is an opportune time, to create pathways of memory, attention, redirection, choice making, focusing, self confidence, critical thinking, abstract reasoning and self-regulation. When these pathways are not used, an opportunity for a good foundation is lost.

The formations that we cannot see inside can only be measured through indirect methods. Direct interventions in stabilizing home, with good experiences in the home environment and teaching nurture to parents, have definitely shown better results in preventing suboptimal development.

Organization and overgrowth with no inhibitory control of neurogenesis happens early on, and then, pruning to a certain extent happens prenatally. After birth, most of the impulses are tagged with a memory, synapses are formed, mini columns to macro columns of synaptic junctions takes place, layers of these columns are formed for a functional purpose, axons develop, and microglia and astrocytes take away unnecessary pathways and organize working pathways. There ***are GABAergic controllers*** that have critical role in firing systems, controlling signals to the brain, controlling the axonal pathway stimulation, controlling inhibition or stopping certain pathways, helping white matter and inter neurons, dopamine receptor functions, and so on. ***We know very little of any chemicals, hormones, molecules, ions, and electrolyte pumps within the brain. We certainly know that the fear, toxic anxiety, and emotional trauma seem to have deep impact at this level, and that is enough for a common man to know***. This knowledge is enough for us to create relaxation responses all the way in life and definitely at the critical phase of zero to five years (Palmen, Mark N. Ziats, et al., Filipek, Herbert, 2002). At birth, there is more neuro genesis in the hippocampus, and then inhibitory control and organization take place, which is a very intricate balance, and studies are evolving in this field.

Causes for psychopathologies

Psychopathologies were higher for males and related to violent acts with substance abuse. Similar patterns were discussed in a study of acutely disturbed psychiatric patients (Binder 1990). The more a child's developing brain was exposed to hyper arousal or dissociation states from a violent environment or adverse sensory information, the more likely the child would develop neuropsychiatric symptoms (Perry 1995). The reason for this is that nor epinephrine, epinephrine-1, and cortisol are secreted by the RAS (reticular activating system), which consists of the locus coeruleus and ventral tegmental nucleus. As a result, there is increase in blood pressure, heart rate, body temperature, increased acid secretion in stomach, urge to void with nervousness, and rapid respiratory rate or panting. This arousal/alertness state increases muscle tone, impulsivity, and movement, freezing the body, which remains in a state for survival. This state does not allow focus and attention for critical thinking and learning. The brain stops taking notice of information coming through the senses in this state of fear. The brain will not recognize and store information and does not pay attention in this state of mind. There will be failure of long-term memory and active working memory while listening and seeing. As a result of this lack of attention, poor learning, poor critical thinking, poor processing, poor problem solving, poor motivation, anxiety, and frustration, leading to poor self-control, will result. As the pressure on learning increases, anger that is held back will escalate, and there will be lashing out with aggressive behavior or withdrawn behavior with poor self-esteem. The brain gets arrested *in "fright-and-flight" mode.* This anxiety and fear are very toxic to brain cells, as the cortisol causes burning of the cell and the cells die (Bruce D. Perry, E. Ron de Kloet, Marian Joels, Sonia J. Lupien, et al., K. Pham, J. Nacher, V. Lemair, M. Koehl, Christian Merescue, Jennifer D. Peters).

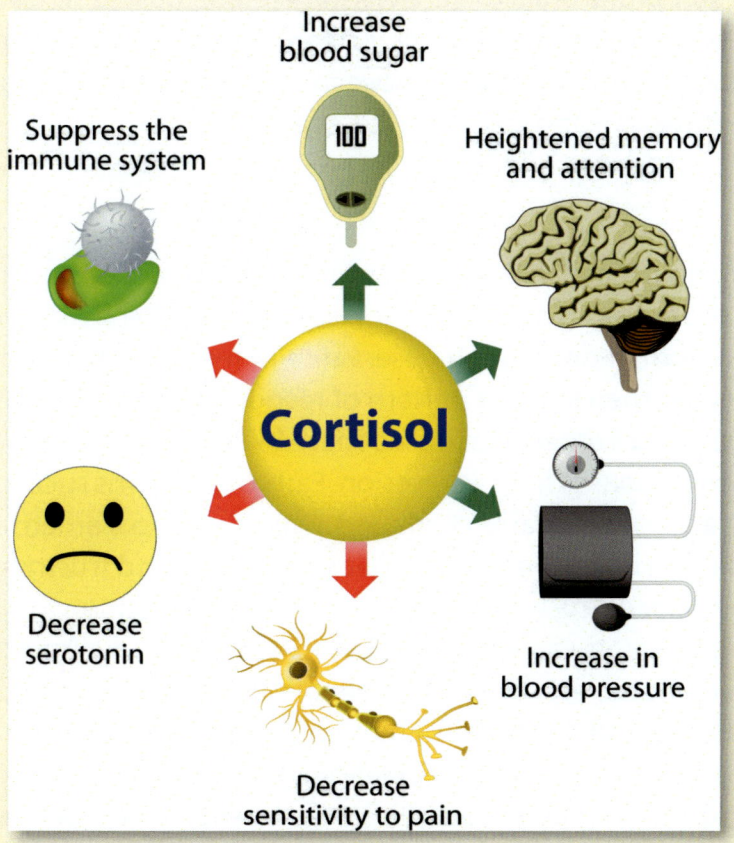

Figure 20: Illustration of stress and effects of Cortisol

In the figure, the heightened attention and memory are for fear, avoiding danger and trauma and not for critical learning and thinking.

This arousal, if it happens repetitiously, as an experience to the growing mind, gets to a point of hyper arousal freezing and dissociation. In boys, this is exhibited as explosive aggression and oppositional defiant disorder. In girls, this is expressed as fainting and lack of memory, orientation, and social withdrawal. The X chromosome seems to be related to increase in oxytocin levels in girls and vasopressin for aggression in boys. As a result girls' day dream and faint with stress and Boys escalate with aggression and fight. Underlying cause is a feeling o flack of power and poor self confidence and self esteem.

There is built-in balance in biological nature, and that is called homeostasis. That is lost in repetitive trauma, anxiety and toxic stress, or severe trauma of onetime toxic stress. Instead, the neuro genesis through a cascade of molecular, biochemical, neuro endocrine and neuro humoral states becomes a trait with permanent life time structural changes in the brain, particularly from the limbic system to the neocortex. These changes get expressed as various adverse behavioral outcomes.

The amount of trauma to the growing brain can be one that is of intense trauma at one time, as in accosting and witnessing a crime like a murder, and it can be over a period of time as daily exposure to abuse and witnessing abuse or violence that can be physical or verbal. Therefore, duration and intensity of trauma both are important factors in disruption on smooth nerve pathways formation.

The latest studies do show that screen time has a similar impact on the developing brain, arousing and making the addiction-prone brain to get over stimulated, causing similar effects on the state of mind and poor cognitive and linguistic abilities. Screen time seems to arouse poor impulse control and stimulates aggression and random motor movement, poor memory, focus, and motivation (Daria J. Kuss and Mark D. Griffiths, Yan Zhou, Fu-Chin Lie, et al.).

Social learning

Social learning theory points out that a person notices which actions succeed and which fail or produce no results. It also indicates how the person adjusts his or her behavior accordingly (Bandura 1977). A person gains information through observance of response and its consequences from his or her home or society. He then learns a pattern of responses in set circumstances. The literature findings on violent acts toward others that did not have biological basis were interpreted to suggest the existence of learned responses from aggression. Early on, patterns such as crying, shouting, and bullying are a result of a chaotic unstable childhood, which leads to learned violent behaviors. Later as teenagers, when playing computer games that excite them and frustrate them when they fail, they will act with more anxiety, frustration, and anger than the situation merits. Therefore, multiple socio-cultural stimuli and events can induce the neuro-endocrine and humoral responses, causing sensitization and hyper-arousal responses. These steroid-mediated responses exhaust the brain and lead to rebound withdrawal and depression. Emotion and motivation are results of complex neural pathways. Gram per gram, cortisol burns the brain cells (Lou Zhang's article reference). Unless there is constant redirection guiding for proper adaptive adjustment through discussion, social adaptation is one of imitation from environment, and what succeeds gets picked up.

The hypothalamus, amygdala, uncus, limbic system, and neocortex are involved in learning from threatening experiences early on from domestic and community violence, video games, cartoons, and other toys that encourage shooting, guns, and archery. Violent acts were correlated with unstable childhood family life and living in a violent community (Costa 1991; Estroff 1994; Farver 1999; Monahan 1994; Casanova, Mark N. Ziats 2015). Violent stimuli incorporated into memory can become triggers for impulsive aggression in later stages and can become a problem-solving skill. The violent act of aggression becomes a lived experience through family and community and thus becomes a constant interactive aggression of the cycle of violence (Mayer 1995; Rutherford 1995). **Therefore, violence is a learned behavior from environmental exposure and not genetic.**

Sensitized brains are when they had no prior memories and the only learning is what they are exposed to for the first time. This has deep impact on creating permanent pathways of maladaptation in a society, interfering with adaptive personality development, cognitive and intellectual development, and social and emotional development. Even when there is no current external stimulus, the acts of aggression will be chosen from fear, anxiety, and reassuring attention from negative behavior (like bungee jumping, self-inflicting injury, making a cat suffer, or pyromania). A person who witnessed a gunshot and death gets scared by any loud sound, like a falling tree branch, thunder, or a rock hitting the dashboard while driving and causing a noise. The pain and stress in life secretes internal hormones of pleasure or "Opiates", that seek pain and stress to find relief. This explains some of the dangerous behaviors and self inflicting wounds in depression and trauma.

Children witnessing fighting with guns, even if it is on screen time, get aroused with anger or anxiety with loud noises. A loud airplane can cause fear and anxiety and random motor movement. Loud male husky voice can also cause fear (Dr. Bruce D. Perry did excellent studies with the Branch Davidian complex children who were victims of aversive environmental experiences).

Emotional learning

Emotional learning occurs with the parents and caretakers as the first teachers. The natural state of a newborn is with love, sympathy, empathy, and motivation to learn and absorb all experiences.

The role of the parent changes with every transition from being a care taker to be a teacher. By adolescence, a parent's role is that of a counselor and a friend. By youth, the role of the parent includes friendship with the young adult and creative guidance. Parents need to have an open mind to understand their changing role with each transition, and that is very rapid, every day, from 0-3 years.

Every infant can make a fluid shift or smooth change of emotions if the parent becomes a critical player in balancing an infant's emotions. An insecure parent fearful of a crying infant can cause ineffective wiring and personality development. Every parent needs to know the transition that they have to be prepared for, as the infant is rapidly developing in all domains of health. Health-care providers have to address these issues of rapidly evolving physical and emotional growth and make the parents get ready for transitions every two to three months till the first two years of life.

Any disturbance in these roles during critical transition periods can lead to disturbed family relationships. Maternal disturbance in attitudes can include depression, family dysfunction, child abuse, maltreatment, poverty, or poor parent-child-peer communication. Poor parenting skills can lead to inappropriate regulation of emotions and poor balance of emotions. Inner peace is lost, and learning with frontal lobe processing and cognitive association gets disrupted. Post partum depression is often missed if the provider and family support systems fail to recognize the signs and address the need about helping measures.

Maternal depression left unrecognized, lays the basic foundation for poor social outcomes and intellectual development ultimately.

Literature suggests the important role of touch in human cerebral processing. Maternal touch stimulates both cerebral hemispheres. Both right and left hemispheres demonstrate brain activity in PET scans if left and right extremities are touched or massaged. In very preterm infants, touch therapy enhanced survival and early dismissal from the prenatal intensive care unit. Touch causes the release of oxytocin, which relaxes the muscles and eases emotions. Oxytocin has negative feedback suppression on the stress hormones epinephrine, cortisol, and nor epinephrine. The Touch Research Institute in Tampa, Florida, did controlled studies to document the drop in urinary catecholamine as a result of touch therapy (Mooncey 1997; Hernandez 1999).

Emotions also are learned from music. Music tunes can create positive and negative emotions, and the tunes have much influence on the mood for sad, joy, excitement, fear, horror, and anxiety. It depends on what music a child is exposed to, to create emotions.

Language development and hearing are very early in infants. Phonemic schemes are presented to the brain if infants are spoken to, with external stimuli as reinforcement. Language is an expression of the highest evolution of the nervous system. We are the only beings in creation that are capable of expression and communication as a result of hearing, seeing, and spoken to as a sensory input. Sensory input involves complex cerebral processing. The left hemisphere of the brain is known for written expression, organization of different words into complex sentences, reading, processing words from sounds, and speech, even in left-handed persons. Audiovisual sensory input is located in the Wernicke's area, the left side of the brain. This area connects to the Broca's area, and this area allows speech sounds to big sentences later on (syntax to pragmatics). Injury to Wernicke's area is known as **receptive aphasia.** Injury to Broca's area is termed **expressive aphasia.** The right hemisphere of the brain is known for visual-spatial reasoning, storage of mathematical algorithms, and memory of objects, facts, faces, and geographical locations. Both sides of the brain do similar work to a certain extent. Music therapy stimulates all brain centers and is critical in the optimal phase of permanent wiring from zero to three years. Music does more than just helping to hear.

Language seems to be universal until four to five months of age, and a definite speech pattern becomes obvious between nine and twelve months of age. Hearing or auditory communication and temporal cortex stimulation are also enhanced through classical music. Extensive literature reviews are available on the Mozart effect, which stimulates the sensory cortex of the child and promotes inner peace, creativity, visual-spatial relationships, depth perception, motivation to turn and listen, communication, social development, and effective math processing skills. PET scans of people engaged in prayer or listening to music show frontal lobe activity as well as temporal-parietal lobe activity. Shamanic or devotional music listening demonstrated good results of behavioral outcome on elementary schoolchildren (Wiand 2003). Music does a lot more than develop listening comprehension in creating speech, cognition, and expression.

Music plays a major role in the dynamic brain neurogenesis and organization internally and behaviorally; on the outer side, music does more than develop listening and comprehension. It is very important for cognitive development, comprehension, expression, depth perception, spatial reasoning, math development, focus and enhanced attention span, development of emotions, enhances memory, and critical thinking.

1. Music enhances social participation. Kirschner and Tomasello (2010) documented that the social participation in play was better, and music-trained children were cooperating better with each other in challenging games than children not exposed to music in solving problems.

2. Cognitive and physiological effects of music go along with emotional development. Music associated with happy and sad memories cause happy and sad mood, respectively.

3. Mostly soothing music is therapeutic in cancer, anxiety disorders, and mood disorders.

4. Music listening increases activity of the reward and pleasure systems in the brain, nucleus accumbens, ventral tegmental nucleus, hypothalamus, insula (Menon and Levtin 2005), orbitofrontal cortex (Salimpoor 2013), and auditory cortex, which interacts with nucleus accumbens, amygdala, ventromedial prefrontal cortex. This is why listening to music causes pleasure. (Snowdon, Elke Zimmerman)

Discrimination of speech starts by the fifth month. If exposed to different languages at a young age, infants are capable of picking up all languages (Ramirez 1991; Kuhl 1999). However, one parent would need to speak English or vernacular and the other parent in some other language to encourage early language acquisitions (Cummins 1985).

If, with the same pitch and frequency of voice tone, a single parent speaks two languages, each language storage, called thematic, phonemic presentation, to the brain gets scattered all the time. But if one caretaker speaks only one language and the other caretaker speaks the other language, infants can learn multiple languages by three years.

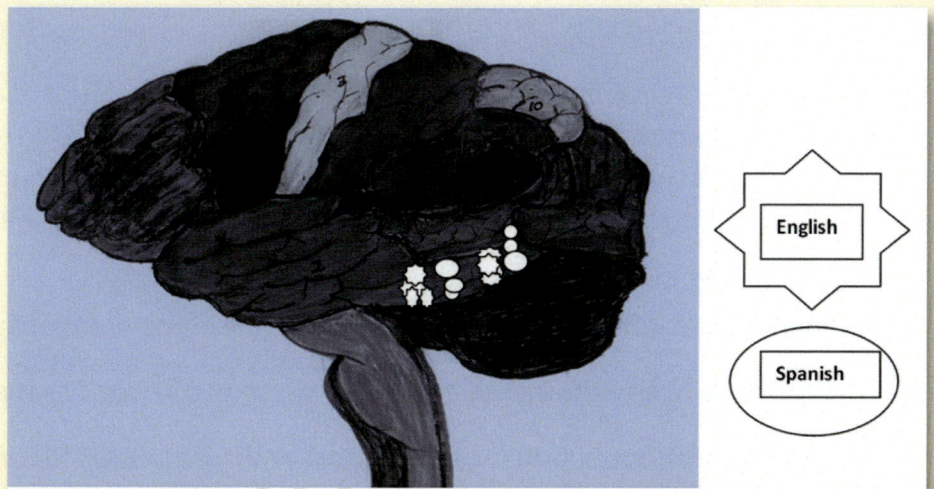

Figure 21: Exposure to language switch by same person for 2 languages and scattered phonemes

If one tone and pitch of voice switches between 2 languages the sounds get stored in different areas and no language gets picked up. Phonemic presentation is scattered.

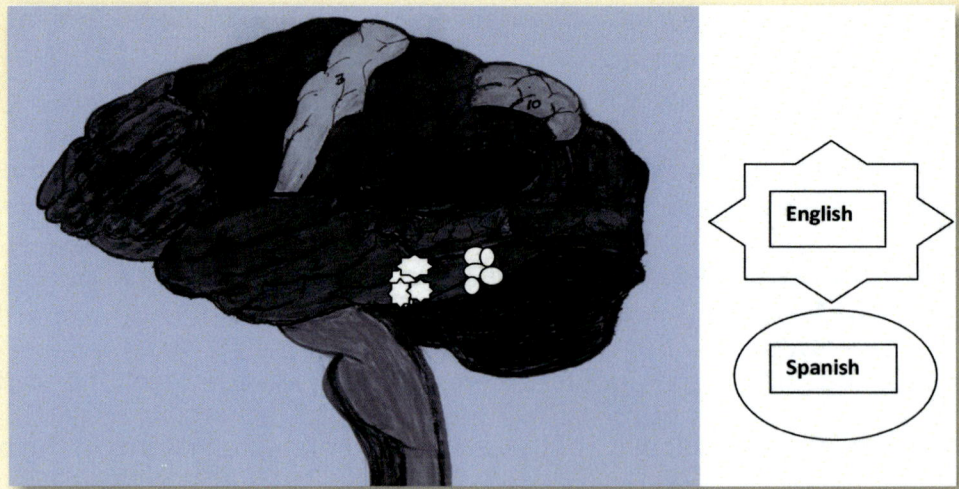

Figure 22: If one care taker speaks one language and the other another language both will be stored in their own site and multipel languages can be picked up. Phonemes stored structurally.

In the subsequent chapters, a sincere attempt is made to take the reader through an understanding of the role of the five senses, neurodevelopment organization and hard wiring of brain, environmental influences, parenting skills at each level of development, and the role of educare (extracting the inherent strengths) in all professions, fields, and all walks of life. Furthermore, the following chapters will address concepts of brain development and the role of caretaker skills in creating an optimum child who will be immune to adverse environmental influences and consequent maladaptive biosocial behaviors. The areas that will be addressed are the organic factors influencing neurodevelopment organization, the influence of behaviors from the position of synaptogenesis, and the symbiotic relationship of learning and neuronal structures. Discussions will bring about how developmental synaptic connections are greatly influenced by the age of parents, prenatal nutrition, teratogens, and genotypes, as well as how personality reflects biosocial processing of lived sensory experiences.

The information from these chapters is used as a foundation for the development of a multisensory intervention in all walks of life from womb to tomb. The intervention has been labeled the SAI Educare Character Development Program (www.saicdp). "*Educare*" is the root word in Latin for "*education.*" Educare means extracting the inherent powers from an individual per dictionary meaning.

This program extracts an individual's assets by way of life application of human values using a planned curriculum that stimulates frontal lobe processing. The program has three areas of application.

A. **A. Internal locus needs to be stimulated for motivation and reward systems.**

B. **External factors that influence neurogenesis and environmental factors have to be addressed for proper neurogenesis and to prevent aversive factors.**

C. **The response cause and the need for daily transformational habits and tools with daily life application have to be addressed.**

D. **Taxonomy of transformation practice and the spiritual scales that need to be weighted are elaborately developed by the SAI Institute of Educare, which worked well in my personal practice.**

1. **SAI Educare in parenting with nurture and bring out the nature**: this is the current book and the previous book.

   These classes are twelve-hour training sessions, divided into two six-hour sessions. They teach parents how to understand, respond, and discipline a child with love and nurture. The sessions teach facts about brain biology, the emotions and their origin. Focus is given on methods of anger management and how to build self-reliance. These parenting skills help in developing an authoritative parent.

2. **SAI Educare in child care** is for teachers from all walks of life, particularly those in the preschool to elementary education levels. Lesson plan preparation training is given to integrate asset building and management into the existing core curriculum. Curriculum will be given to rewire ADHD brain pathways till head, heart, and hands get connected with self-esteem and self-regulation and industriousness to succeed, as well as five teaching techniques to help rewire the lost pathways.

3. **SAI Educare for therapists** includes training of brain biology, neuropsychology, brain nurturing activities, and parent training programs.

4. **SAI Educare for staff development for teachers** is to explain neurogenesis, behaviors, lesson plan development that incorporates the relaxation techniques, and transformational character development integrated into the core knowledge subjects.

The parenting intervention program was done as a pilot study with the families at the Salvation Army Hope Center in San Antonio, Texas, June–July 2002, called Scattered Sites. It included six sessions for training the adults and the children in brain activity understanding and multisensory processing. The sessions were constructed from the latest information on brain biology and child development.

- The first session was constructed to provide information about brain activities, the impact of sensory information on brain activities, and the impact of sensory input in shaping human development and interactions.

- The second session was used for the processing of how brain storage of certain childhood memories impact present-day choices and behaviors, how memories include multisensory information, and understanding where certain memories may be stored.

- The third session processes how choice of partners comes from own family experiences, how multisensory information from own family is related to partner choices, and understanding partner interactions' impact on raising children.

- The fourth session's focus is on the identification of current parenting style attitudes that can be attributed to different developmental memory experiences from childhood to adulthood and to explore strengths and weaknesses of the present parenting style.

- The fifth session describes maximum conditions for multisensory learning at different developmental ages and introduces how values can be integrated with the multisensory interventions.

- The sixth session was constructed to be an overview of the previous session through the explanation of the use of their knowledge of brain activity, multisensory information, and value information from own family of origin for raising children.

In each of the sessions, human values teaching is conducted through five teaching techniques of silent sitting with regulated nasal breathing combined with music therapy, meaningful meditation with guided imagery, theme of the week, positive thinking, quotations or prayer, storytelling and discussions, group singing, and group activity. These human values teachings are done with the children as well as with the adults. The families who attended the sessions provided valuable guidance in the construction of the model for SAI Educare program development as a strategic intervention. What was modified in the sessions was presenting the information in an understandable format without patronizing the participants. The feedback from the participants suggested a perception that their integrity and value as a person were respected while being provided complex information valuable for themselves and their children.

Endnotes

What do sensory input and learning do in the critical phase of zero-to-three-year development?

It makes an individual

- Learn to survive in an environment;
- Learn to adapt to survive;
- Recognize the near and dear, to establish group identity;
- Protect the self and family;
- Fight for self, in the family, or self and family in the community through emotional bonding or dissociations;
- Create more progeny as a form of basic human need or instinct or as a planned order of creation;
- Develop eating habits, good or bad, which have impact on future health;
- Develop a better immune system.

All these happen before the infant learns to talk. Unused pathways are lost for life. Used pathways are sustained for life.

Modern literature supports that the environment is a critical stimulus. Intervention programs should include the whole family unit to learn and participate in fun-filled activities to stimulate the frontal lobe processing, and that should be supported by the communities, judicial reforms, and social media.

Cases from pilot study at Scattered Sites presentation (genuine cases and names not revealed)

1. A seven-year-old young boy who is living at the shelter with biological mother seeking shelter and father visiting regularly while taking parenting education. The family participated in all six sessions. The little boy was not responding to any meds at all for his ADHD for the last two years. After our sessions and revelation of neurobiology of developmental disorders, father started meaningful meditation; music therapy, guided imagery, and he controlled the tone of his voice and started effective parenting skills. The boy since then did not need Ritalin, and he has done well since. Family made big changes with anger management, self-regulation through meaningful meditation techniques, and authoritative parenting skills, and life was peaceful for them through the SAI Educare program.

2. A middle-aged lady had been a victim of trauma and abuse and is now dealing with cancer. Her treatment results improved as she practiced the five teaching techniques taught through this SAI Educare parenting course, and her white cell count increased with no other additional medical interventions. Of course, guidance was given on eating healthy.

3. A mother who was spending her time at the shelter had a son who had severe constipation problems with fecal soiling and a daughter who was not doing well at school and felt lost between parents' fight over the custody. After our sessions with the SAI Educare five teaching techniques, mom felt that she needed to forgive and let the father (a police official with poor anger management) of the children "off the hook" to provide and support and had forgiven him. She went to Oklahoma and completed her education as a teacher, and the kids overcame their somatic complaints and completed college and are still in Oklahoma. Mom practiced the life application of the five teaching techniques and felt internally relaxed, and that helped her children. What was needed was an insight and attitude change. Many prior parenting education classes did not help her overcome the problems of adaptation, till love and forgiveness and detaching from the "hook" of ill feelings were taught.

Likewise, we have many cases that are around us who are suffering at various levels of poor adaptation and poor coping with stress from anger, anxiety, and fright-and-flight nature; when the education on the pathology of stress opens their eyes, they are willing to love themselves, forgive their current status, and help themselves. Building self confidence, accepting weaknesses to work on and building on strengths at any age is the key to life skills.

No one is an idiot as a human being, but spirituality in a scientist could foresee that human connections will be lost five decades ago.

Nice quotes from Albert Einstein:

"We cannot solve our problems with the same thinking we used when we created them."

"Intellectual growth should commence at birth and cease at death."

"Human beings can attain worthy and harmonious life, only if they are able to rid themselves, within the limits of human nature, of the striving for the wish fulfillment of material kinds. The goal is to raise the spiritual values of society"

"One should cultivate the human values for healthy living. This calls for harmony in thought, word and deed. When you cultivate this harmony you will be free from desires and fears"

Sri Satya Sai Baba

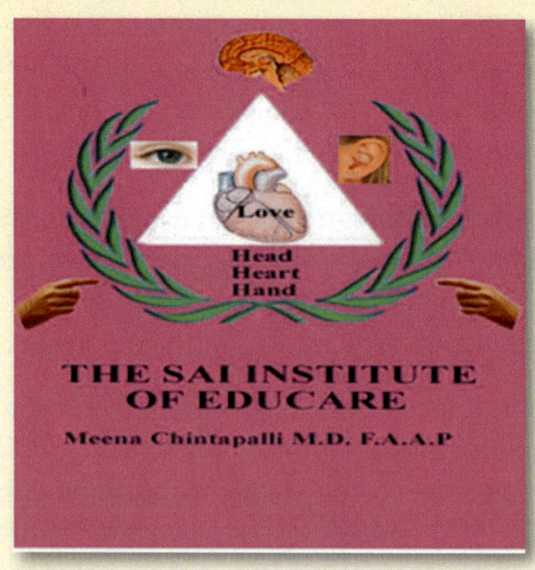

Figure 23: Head-Heart-Hand with The 3 Human Values

The Highest purpose of Human life is to give back to universe the love that created this creation and seek nothing back. The highest purpose of Human existence is to find that highest energy within them so that their strength will is used for the benefit of Individual, Family and the Society. Once that energy is realized that cannot go anywhere but the persistence pays off in securing and realizing the dreams of the gift of human life. Reflect all thoughts originating in brain through heart and take hands into the society professionally and through benevolence. That is the union of Head- Heart and Hand.

Chapter V

Reasons for Developing a Curriculum for Healthy Dynamic Brain Growth

The following imaging studies are from my literature search on how the brain has connected to the world, and they were very informative for me and for my concepts on perception of trauma arresting the brain in a state of fear and anxiety, a concept that I personally fostered in my heart and mind since 1979. This concept made me look deep into family issues that could have caused adverse biosocial behaviors. It was not easy to counsel parents on that concept, although I knew in my heart that was the reason for most of the behavioral disorders. It took me from 1979 till 1996–1997 to find evidence back up, and it is still an uphill battle to make parents understand their role in changing the society with their involvement and being proactive for judicial reforms.

Facts about Sensory Integration from Signal to Attention Perception: Sound and Acoustic Sensitivity

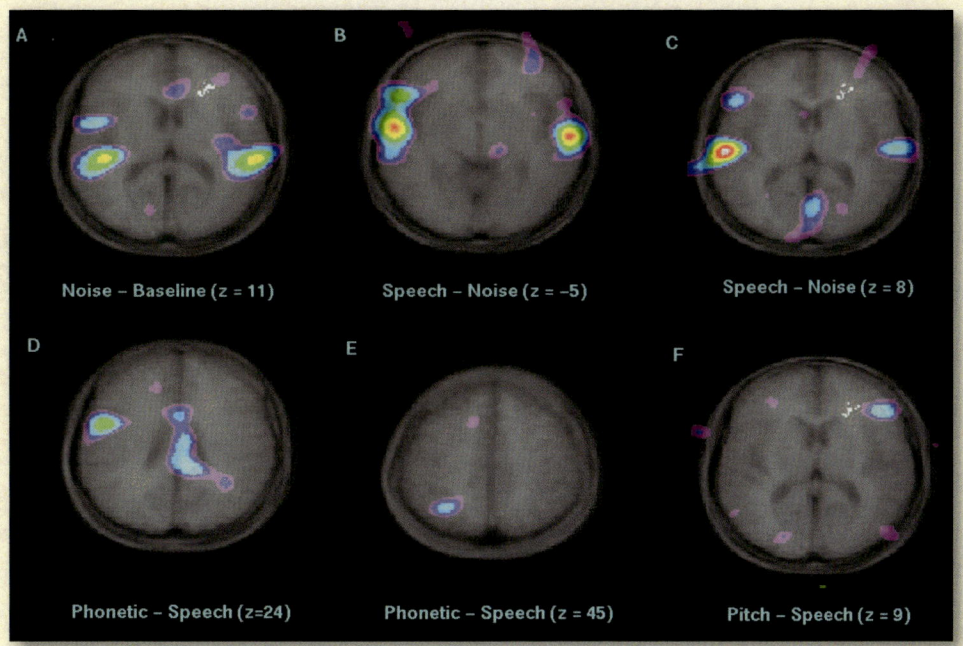

Figure 24: Noise control and sensory blocking of high pitch and loud noise

Courtesy Pet monitoring from the site bic.mni.mcgill.ca/users/robin/bic/bic6.gif(1997)

There is an internal noise in our brain and a hum that we are not sensitive to while being busy with our daily chores. When there is a brassy, low-pitched horrible sound, our brain systems are sensitive to that noise, and both sides of the brain pay attention and perceive the stimulus. When it goes to speech frequency of eight to twenty-four hertz, only the left brain notices the speech, in the Wernicke's area for lefty brains and righty brains; it is the same area in the temporal lobe of the left brain. When the phonetic speech becomes high at forty-five hertz, as the pitch of the sound increases, even low nine hertz, the brain stops registering and perceiving the sound signal and not taken noises to the auditory cortex.

How many times have we tuned out nagging, disparaging sounds? Infants can do this, as that is all they can do other than move away from the unpleasant sounds. Imagine what metallic sounds and rock music can do the ears of infants zero to three years? They cannot close their ears and run away, and they tune out, killing many significant brain centers the perception of sound, listening and learning. That means unused cells, 600,000/minute X 10,000, are dying.

We do newborn screening for hearing capabilities and invest energies to prevent hearing problems. The idea behind newborn hearing screening is to prevent communication problems. Ongoing vigilance should be given to prevent **sensory tuning out** for hearing as well as **acquired conductive hearing loss secondary** to reoccurring ear infections. We have ERO scans for checking hearing even in a nine-month-old with chronic ear infections to guide parents on auditory perception and the need for ear tubes. Poor hearing and listening, poor language development, sensory disintegration from severe emotional trauma of witnessing violence, loud noises, and angry communication at home result in tuning out the senses and scarred brain.

The following is the visual illustration of research Article 2 decades ago by Dr. Peter Fox and Dr. Raichel on the activity picked up by PET scans after presenting visual words and lexicon to the sensory input of volunteers. The red is the activity. Modern literature review discussed the positive effects of music on brain and the neuronal activity even among cognitive association brain and the sensory motor brain. When brain gets stimulated through mutli- sensory integration of sight, sound, touch, there are simultaneous rich and thick connections to the prefrontal Gyrus which is the executive brain for critical thinking, associations, abstract reasoning and much more. Visual presentation alone to the brain, without the emotional bonding of caretaker's touch, emotion, visual contact and auditory presentation, like sitting in front of a screen watching, theoretically, frontal lobe connections are not made, as presented in this illustration only the occipital lobe or vision brain gets stimulated and activated. When meaningful words(Lexicon) is offered without visual stimulus there is activity in Temporal lobe for hearing, sensory and motor cortex and most important is the frontal lobe or executive brain connection that happens.

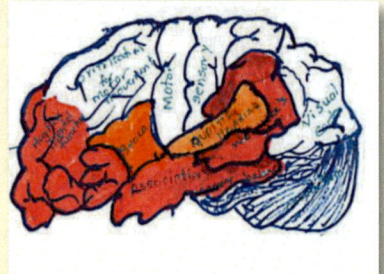
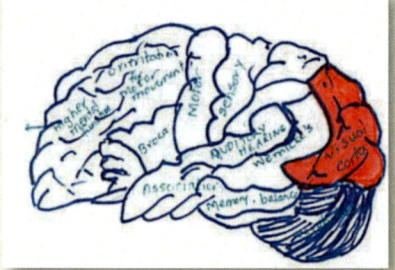

Figure 25: Hearing Brain activity   **Figure 26: Visual Brain activity**

This is a very important fact when optimal multi sensory integration with proper nutrition and nurture is not done 0-3 years when all pathways are new and are life time foundation. These are permanent wiring internally for future personality and intellectual development. As the infant is exposed only to visual stimulus, the infant makes robust connections to the occipital cortex in the hindbrain. Frontal lobe connections are important for speech and language development and executive functions. While listening to soft music, soft sounds, or pleasant words, lexicon and phonetic skills happen automatically as a part of development as the brain recognizes the signals and takes it to the frontal lobe. Phonemic presentation seems to connect through the limbic system not only to hearing cortex but also to the prefrontal gyrus, which is responsible for permanent memory and other executive functions. Can we understand the impact of quickly moving objects on screen time with cartoons—that figures that are jumping around and moving fast over stimulate the occipital or visual cortex and is a permanent memory? While that is a major tool to distract a crying and whining child, the rest of the brain does not perceive any educational input between newborn periods till twenty-four months with electronic or screen exposure alone. The loud bangs and sudden movements are distracting the sensory input to the limbic system. The distorted brain pathways are preventing the organized pathway development for speech and spatial recognition through sight, kinesthetic and sound (a concept of mini columns, macro columns, and layering in a radiant fashion is lost to dispersed synaptic junctions).

Sensory Perception for Touch

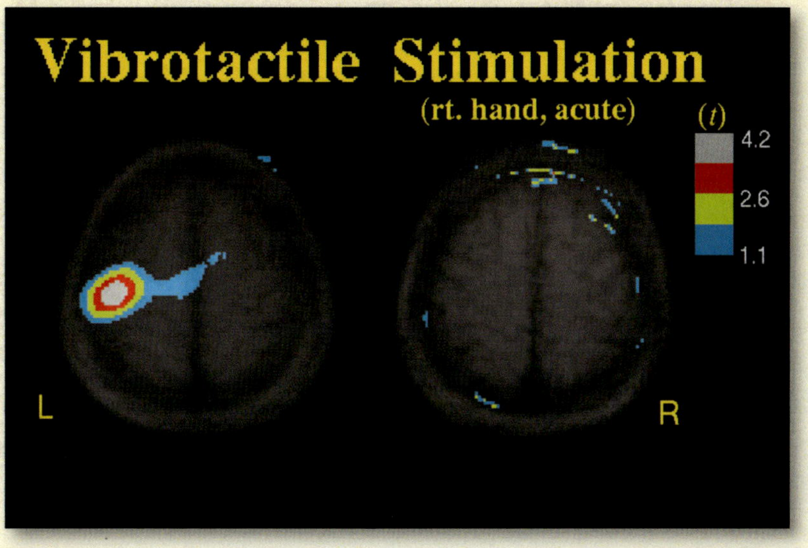

Figure27: Courtesy Pet monitoring, bic.mni.mcgill.ca/users/robin/bic/bic9.gif (1997)

This figure explains how the sensory integration is poor in an untouched infant and if touched while asleep. The left side is normal response to touch. The right one is under sedation and no response to touch.

Touch is very important for internal relaxation and reassurance and bonding. When a caretaker is not touching the infant and interacting while awake and then comes to touch the infant while asleep, there is no sensory integration. Will depression, alcohol, or substance use cause toxic stress to the developing brain while witnessing the care takers under altered sensorium?

When massage therapy with music, touch, eye contact, and visual tracking is offered as a nurture, the infant gets all assigned systems of the brain stimulated along with motivation, memory, spatial reasoning, discrimination, cognitive associations, emotional stability of happiness and peace, internal relaxation, language abilities, and motor coordination toward symmetrical reflex release of the tone of the muscles (infant starts rolling over both sides), and eye-hand coordination (infant reaches for things). Nine- to ten-minute slots, six times a day, the tummy times with music therapy and touch therapy enhance great sensory pathways for future cognitive and intellectual development. Unused, no nurture offered to the infant, the infant is losing opportunity every

minute to connect robustly using all senses. Too much screen time has adverse effects in the infant's dynamic brain growth and organization. Love is a Meta energy transmitted through eye contact, touch and soothing music and personal communication by the care taker.

Infants Are Linguists

When one parent speaks one language and the other parent speaks the other language, a phonemic organization happens in the brain to speak both languages, and information and thematic presentation to the brain do not get scattered. If one pitch and tone of voice switches from one language to the other during communication, the brain perceives differently at each time, and the information is stored in a scattered fashion. The infant does not acquire language in both languages. **(Illustrations were given on pages 45 and 46).**

When parents and caretakers do not invest their time to let the multisensory integration happen with hands-on activity, touch therapy, music therapy, and eye contact with hands on exploration, the infant has potential for developmental delays in rolling over, reaching for things, and exploring to self-stimulate and self-soothe with happiness. Active hand grasp gets delayed. Emotions mature before the progress in the gross and fine motor skills. This lag in motor skills can result in future frustration. Language delay also leads to future behavior problem and frustration and results in screaming spells.

Parents and caretakers are the first teachers. Making the infant watch TV/iPad nursery tunes leads to hypersensitivity of sensory stimulation, and there is no scope for sensory integration, and a seed for childhood hyperkinetic syndrome has formed. Let us all focus on preventing future behavioral and learning problems. The rapidly developing synaptic connections are over stimulated from frequently changing screen, almost every five to ten seconds. This leads to hyper responsive motor and emotional pathways of wanting to move and being less reflective.

Adverse effects of screen time in any age group are enumerated from literature review, and most of the studies are on teen and adult nonprofessional addiction to Internet and Internet gaming.

DSM-5 accepted the Internet-associated disorders as addiction disorders:

1. mostly negative psychosocial consequences
2. poor memory
3. poor motivation
4. depression
5. anxiety disorder
6. poor attention span
7. poor cognitive function
8. poor judgment
9. obsessive-compulsive disorder

10. psychosomatization

11. dissociation

12. introversion

13. psychotic behaviors

14. poor anger management and explosive temper

Internet exposure does cause molecular and structural changes, causing poor psychosocial behaviors and poor learning adaptations.

Altered activity in the brain that is responsible for reward, motivation, memory, self-regulation, cognitive control is also associated with addiction with Internet exposure.

In the initial stages of substance use or Internet addiction, use is voluntary and can be controlled; this control comes from the ***prefrontal cortex and striatum, ventral portion***.

As prolonged use creates a dependency leading to addiction, child gets hooked on to TV/iPad/phone. The brain activity changes, ***sensitizes the dorsal portion of the striatum,*** which blocks the reward system or causes poor sensitivity reward systems.

As the addiction gets further prolonged, ***there is increased dopaminergic release and reward and motivation to use more electronics or substance, which comes from the nucleus accumbens (affiliated with reward), cingulate gyrus, and orbit frontal cortex, with increased dopamine, and later on poor response to a reward system and poor control or self-regulation. Dopamine receptor availability goes down***.(Kuss, Daria J. and Mark D. Griffiths.)

The following references were given from a review article noted above:

(Yuan2011) proved atrophy of many brain areas in Internet addiction daily, two to four hours per day, or thirty hours per week.

(Dong 2012) proved that Internet addiction increased activity in the reward gaining system and poor sensitivity to reward loss systems.

(Han) showed that Internet addicts had poor impulse control, persistent errors, and brain atrophy.

There was increased activity on fMRI left occipital cortex, left dorsolateral aspect of prefrontal cortex, and left parahippocampus, which decreased after using Bupropion for six weeks. This shows that the same drug used for alcohol abuse is potentially working for Internet addiction.

Lin: There is overall abnormal white matter activity in areas associated or linked with emotional processing, executive attentional networks, decision and abstract reasoning, and cognitive self-regulation.

Zhou: Measured the gray matter density (sMRI).

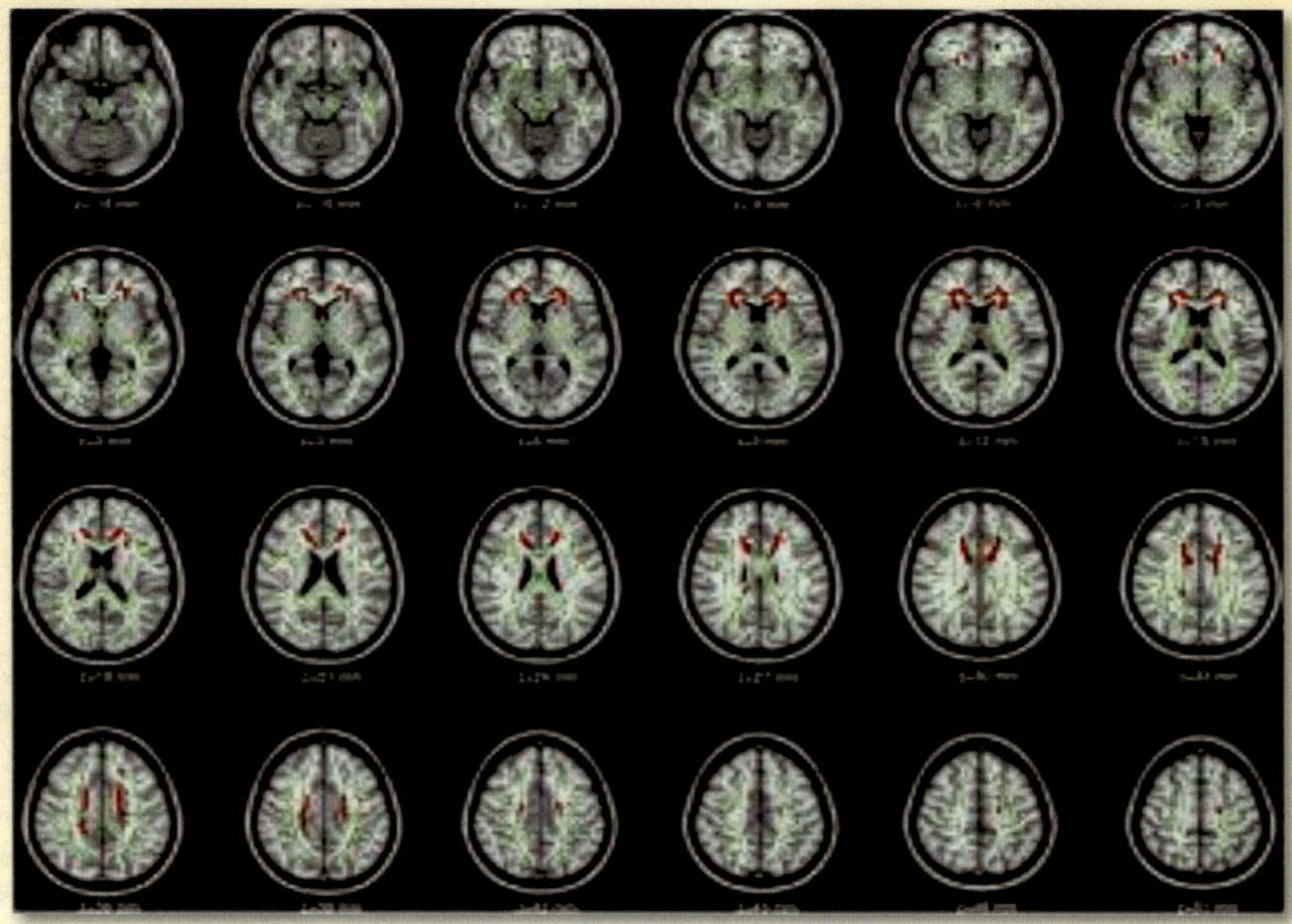

Figure 28: (Courtesy of Lin, Zhou)

"Gray Matter Abnormalities in Internet Addiction." European Journal of Radiology 79, no.1 (July 2011): 92–95. doi:10.1016/j.ejrad.2009.10.025.

There is significant structural anatomical change and frontal lobe attrition, the anatomy is disturbed, and the initial hippocampus increased activity is ultimately replaced with loss of axonal degeneration. The increased red is from the limbic system overstimulation and final loss of anatomy from gray and white matter attrition. The impact is from the same pathogenesis of toxic fear and anxiety and stress on brain that causes burning of neurons and the pathways from cortisol and noradrenaline.

I have worked with autistic children who came to me at thirty months to five years of age. The causes were multiple cases of domestic issues that could have caused multisensory disintegration and sensory withdrawal, particularly from social and family dysfunction, poor spouse bonding and communication, custodial fights and angry exchanges between family members, loving the children so much with no TV and cartoon controls, or leaving the TV on thinking that the child was not watching, or using the iPad to calm a screaming infant at nine months in a bouncer, and similar conditions. Many of these are toxic to brain and the stress hormones do cause inflammatory response internally. The effect of toxic stress is studied only indirectly through sMRI, fMRI and DTI techniques, by measuring the brain activity. These precipitating factors would not have been tracked down as significant aversive sensory stimuli if there is no knowledge and understanding on how the brain gets affected with toxic stress 0-3 years.

The SAI Educare curriculum was developed to educate the parents on neurobiology, development of biosocial behaviors, from perceived threats, toxic effect on brain from fears and anxiety on the evolving nerve connections, and the adverse biosocial behavioral effects. The curriculum was offered to many families at an individual level, and multisensory integration to nurture the sprouting nerve connections was taught diligently, as it is a very sensitive and new subject. This education and hands-on floor activities that were taught brought about positive changes within the family members and the home environment improved with effective communication between the spouses; exposure to music and making associations with phonics and objects with kinesiology and floor-time activities also was integrated into the teaching. Many NICU graduates, ADHD children, autism spectrum behavioral children go to regular schools now and have a mild ADHD, which is being handled with music therapy, "tuning in" or yoga with meditation and nasal breathing, and guided imagery. Because of the HIPPA rules, I cannot give out names, and I had kids from Dallas, Victoria, and Laredo, and mostly from San Antonio, who have no trace of autism today as we worked hard to rewire brain pathways. I educated parents mostly on multisensory integration. There are many patients in my practice who were told by specialists that they would be functioning at retarded level who are now going to regular school. Few are now going to college.

A case presentation labeled autistic and ADHD not amenable to conventional therapies like speech, occupational, recreational, and play therapies

During one of the professional development lectures at San Antonio Independent School District, during parent training, one of the parents was convinced that her 5.5-year-old son labeled as irresolvable autistic and ADHD, could be helped. She is not very educated and comes from a poor family, but the medical information that was offered at that time convinced her to work with him. She made appointments, and we worked together after reviewing the history with SAI Educare curriculum of five teaching techniques, family changes, and mom and dad problems to be resolved. At the time of his entry to the practice, he was 5.5 years old, never looked at any face, had no speech at all, had significant random motor activity with impulsivity—meltdowns were for forty-five minutes at a time, and he would lie down on the floor and would not get up for thirty to forty-five minutes—and was very oppositional and obsessive to do his way. He passed ERO scan for hearing test, and he could comprehend what was said, as he used to become oppositional when he was negated or corrected; he went under the sinks and examination tables. It was a challenging case after the experience-expectant brain development had completed by thirty-six months of age. We had the opportunity to use the experience-dependent brain organization pathways.

Mom became equally strong-willed and educated herself (I needed a Spanish translator at each visit, till she took adult education classes for English). The family had to make many adjustments in interpersonal communication, home environment, structure, consistency, music and touch therapy, changing the meal plan and making him gluten- and casein-free with organic meats, legumes, greens, and fresh fruits as choice snacks, besides the multisensory integration of the SAI Educare developmental program. The TV was disconnected, and there were no computers at home. The father controlled his anger and improved his communication skills and tone of the voice. The family started going back to church. Yoga and meaningful meditation with music therapy, guided imagery, and nasal breathing were done three to four times a day, fifteen to twenty minutes each session. He started going to the library and getting rewards for learning and reading. He developed vocabulary in five to six months and communicated well, and he started reading and writing well by seven years. He has now graduated from high school with A and B honors and is going to college. He is very functional. ADHD is being treated with psycho pharmacotherapy. He never received any ABA therapy. His insurance would not cover ABA therapy and they had limited resources financially. The school gave him speech and physical therapy for writing skills. He did not need occupational therapy. This is an excellent case of how toxic effects in the home environment and poor parenting can affect the neurodevelopment organization causing detrimental effects and how acceptance by parents of their own misgivings, correcting themselves, has helped prevent morbidity. The family is a happy family now with good long-lasting human values.

Chapter VI

Role of the Parent from 0-6 months for Nurture of the Nature

Newborn care

Through the teachings of a health-care provider or through self-education, parents need to be prepared for transition. An expectation at birth by parents of a certain new born behavior prevents a good transition to become calm first-time parents.

At birth, every infant is at a basic need of love and needs comforting during the changes in physical and chemical adaptation from the womb to the external world for survival. **The first realization for a parent is not to expect a behavior from the infant and not to have comparisons**. No two brains are alike, and there is no perfect brain. Crying means communication, and parents need not get agitated with crying. Actually, a strong, lusty, robust cry, demanding attention for care and need, is very reassuring. Parents need to adapt, understand, and accept the basic needs of the infant and learn about the infant in a state of calmness and peace. Parent needs to know and understand the normal newborn behaviors.

Becoming a parent for the first time is the first transition from a care-free life to parenting life with responsibilities. It is learning in process through experience, and experience is the best teacher.

1. It is too much to ask a parent to adjust, but if the parent is prepared for sleepless nights while the infant is adapting, there will be no stress. If the parent is not prepared for this, there will be stress from expecting a good night's sleep and not being able to get it! Five percent of infants never sleep through the night even after the first ten weeks.

2. Likewise, breastfeeding stresses out a parent as she pumps and does not see milk flowing in. It takes a first-time mom usually three to four weeks to produce a higher volume when pumping, and it is not advisable to pump milk and get stressed out. Mother Nature takes care of a lot of things to get good breast milk flow establishment. Breastfeeding is the best for its nutritional value and unknown immunological properties, and also for myelination of the rapidly forming axons every second. Formulas are trying to match breast milk by adding DHA, ARA, and probiotics. They are comparable and may not surpass the breastfeeding from the nutritional point of view to the emotional bonding. If it does not work out for any reason, in spite of best effort, no guilt feelings should bother the parents.

Because of allergies to foods, we had to stop breastfeeding and give hypoallergenic formulas like Elacare and Neocate for nutritional requirements. So a parent should never feel guilty if breastfeeding does not work out in rare cases, but this works the best even when there is poverty, as the infant thrives on breastfeeding.

Case reports: The names are not real names for privacy purposes, but the cases are genuine and reported from my involvement with care. The cases may look like your own, but they are not. The similarity can be appreciated by the readers, as many parents have similar complaints. A few cases are presented before the theory is presented to let the readers know that what goes by the book is not true medicine, and practice of medicine is an art.

1. Patty had an infant, and Patty was determined to breastfeed, as this is their first infant after five years of marriage. Patty and her husband were well prepared with all literature on the importance of breastfeeding and the role of sensory nurture, and they visited the pediatrician prior to the infant's arrival. With all love and tender care, Patty followed the directions on breastfeeding. Milk flow was good, initial weight loss and then gaining back weight were good, but, as usual, the colic started and rash started at three to four weeks of age. Patty's diet was controlled for egg whites, gluten, casein, corn, tomatoes, red and yellow dyes, soy, chocolate, peanuts, and caffeine. Rash or eczema and colic temporarily improved, and then the infant had crying spells again, and there was blood in stools, which progressively increased within two days. The infant was hospitalized and then given Neocate. Bleeding got under control, and the infant was sent home on breastfeeding, with Neocate as supplement. The infant developed severe diarrhea and dehydration and was almost in a state of shock, with rectal bleeding, and was readmitted. With the PICU care and post recovery, biopsies were taken from all the areas of the gastrointestinal tract, which showed allergic eosinophilic infiltration throughout. Breastfeeding needed to be stopped, and the infant grew up on Neocate, and solids were carefully introduced. That infant is a healthy, bright 3-year-old toddler at this time with no delays in all domains of health and is a bright child.

2. Johnny was a product of full-term pregnancy, born to a mom who will not supplement other than breastfeeding. Johnny was not gaining weight as he should but was well developmentally where he should be at nine months, but has gained only five pounds in nine months since birth, which is suboptimal. Mom nurses him every two hours, even at nine to ten months of age. Mom is not willing to wean or give supplement formula. Home assessment and psychological assessment of mother are normal. Infant's nutrition is compromised, and no one can force the mom, who is a good caretaker. One can make a person see the light if they are willing to be educated. There may be higher chances of morbidity in learning faculties at a later date secondary to poor nourishment, and it is hard to pinpoint now. An eye-opener for this type of parent will be to look at the education offered on nutrition and calorie intake and understand the consequences of poor nutrition. Caretakers have to be flexible in their notions and adapt for better outcomes.

3. Nicole and her husband have been married for six years, and they had their first son after many failed trials. Luis is very precious for both of them. They would not put him down, as they could not stand to see him cry. If he cried for a few seconds, both of them ran, dropping all that they are engaged in doing, and comforted him. Their expectation was that the infant would feel neglected and would feel the withdrawal. He was always held by one or the other parent. He slept in the parents' bed since birth, and no sleep training was done at six to nine months' transition time. By twelve months, this crying for attention got worse; no simple phonemes like "mama" or "dada," no willingness to sleep in crib, and needed to co-sleep with parent. By eighteen months, the marriage broke up. The infant developed more screaming; no communication. Mom needed to take him to the bathroom in a stroller so

that he would not cry when she was bathing. A lot of counseling for the sensory need of demand followed by gratification of the needed demand was explained at length early on in neonatal counseling. During the transitioning into six months of development, behaviors from separation and stranger anxiety were explained to the parents, and the need for sleep training was explained. An infant exposed to adult strangers in a social circle like play and music learning places, library, and infant/toddler reading programs were discussed. Nicole was giving in and was very permissive. Crying could not be tolerated. She came from South American cultural background where co-sleeping was a trend and felt it was OK. She was even upset that I talked at length about the importance of sleep training by nine months. It took four to five years of training and teaching for Nicole to overcome her fears. Her fear originated from her own upbringing of neglectful parenting issues that left trauma at a subconscious level, interfering with the current need to change her understanding of parenting. This insecure parenting skill led to autism spectrum disorder, as the infant had deficiency in getting emotional state of demand, gratification, trust, self-security, self-soothing, vocalization of a need, and attachment with insecurity to primary caretaker. After the education, the family is a happy family, and the child is now communicating well and is successful at school. But to get there was pricy with many therapies. Could we have prevented that by being an effective parent and not a weak parent?

4. Paula was born to parents after eighteen years of marriage. Parents never wanted her to cry and feel lonely and gave her all the toys that they could get and made her watch **four hours of television** to make her learn alphabets, rhymes, numbers, and language. Paula developed colic, crying, and avoidance of looking into eyes, and was declared autistic by three years. Mom and dad gave very loud applause for every motor milestone that she accomplished, like rolling over or having a few steps toward walking. Paula was getting plenty of reciprocity and good bonding but was exhibiting the hyperkinetic child syndrome with social, emotional withdrawal, and communication was zero. With the sensory nurture of sight, sound, touch, nutrition, and reading and music therapy, voice and tone control of parental reward system, social participation, meal plan with no prepackaged but organic foods, mostly gluten-free, Paula learned to look at people and learned all alphabets not through screen time but with floor time and face time. She started making associations with the world around her. Screen time was totally eliminated. Paula still has hyperactivity but now falls into Asperger syndrome. She has special needs at school. If she was detected early on instead of 3.5 years of age, the morbidity could have been better. Again, the learning skills are different for different people. She is a middle school student with few special needs now but is successful. Her ADHD is being treated with psycho-pharmacotherapy.

5. Allen came at two months of age, born to a drug addict teen mom with heroine withdrawal symptoms and also premature at birth by six weeks. PGM was taught about sensory nurture, music and touch therapy, and the role of optimal sensory input that has calming effect while she was the sole caretaker. At four months of age, he was taken away by the biological mother to West Coast and was brought back by CPS to PGM at ten months of age. The infant was not rolling over, has no eye contact, was seen with apathy rather than interaction, and cried a lot. PGM invested her time on floor time and face time with the curriculum that encompasses touch therapy, music therapy, hands-on activities for spatial reasoning, and eye movement

therapy. He started integrating senses, started talking well by eighteen months, memorized Dr. Seuss books and rhymes, but still was temperamental and had hyper behavior. The five teaching techniques were taught through the PGM, and he is now a fourth grader with self-control, verbal expression that is good, but needs some psycho-pharmacotherapy for ADHD. He is filled with love, compassion, sympathy, and empathy. He was diagnosed as autistic by the behavioral checklist, ADOS, and neurologist. Multisensory integration and SAI Educare program made him show no features of autism by the third year of his life, and he is doing well. He is a straight **"A"** student and is very compassionate. He was prevented and incubated by paternal grandparents from screen time toxicity and environmental fear and anxiety from parent custodial battles.

Truth and the facts of the matter

Raising an infant to early childhood-toddler stage means parents have different roles at each visit that should prepare them for the rapid transitions of development internally and as expressed behaviorally from the external view.

Normal Newborn Adaptive Behaviors That Stresses Parents

Normal newborn behaviors

Infants take ten weeks to adapt chemically, physically, and physiologically for feeding, elimination, sleep, and basic needs. Majority of the time, parents get anxious over the normal newborn behaviors that are mistaken to be pathology or a sick problem.

1. ***Crying is basic survival and not pain***: Parent needs to understand that the newborn behaviors are basic survival behaviors initially from the brain stem and midbrain, as a result of sudden physical and chemical changes from inside to outside the uterus or mother's womb.

    a. Crying is a means of communication. This adaptation takes about eight to ten weeks.

    b. Crying draws the parent's attention for different needs of the infant. Examples include feeding, soothing vocal interactions, changing of diaper, and the caretaker's touch, scent, and body warmth.

    c. **No Colic medicines**: Medicines at this age are in certain ways dangerous and unnecessary. For example, sedatives like various colic medicines might mask an underlying serious condition by promoting drowsiness. Some drops have atropine products, and can cause dry mouth to heart problems. In general, colic drops do not help. Crying is not a pain from gas or any kind of pain but a *reactive reflexive behavior* seeking a communication—*"Hold me!"* Maternal stress for whatever reason makes the infant more vulnerable to reactive crying. A new mom needs a lot of family support and spousal understanding. An infant cannot be spoiled at this age for holding them on demand and needs to be held.

2. ***Acid reflux runs in the family and can cause colicky pain***. 85% of infants have acid reflux at birth, as the food pipe and stomach junction is a weak spot and there is no valve mechanism there. Acid can reflux into the lower end of the food pipe and can cause a burning sensation

and discomfort. The PH of this acid is 4 and is very acidic. Just by elevating the head end of the bed by twenty degrees will help, and lying down toward the right side will help relieve the burning sensation. If not better, it is worth trying H2 pump blockers, with doctor's advice (for example, Lansoprazole or Prevacid, Pepcid, and Nexium).

3. **Food Intolerance can cause spitting up and Colic: Milk protein intolerance, gluten in maternal diet, peanuts, corn, soy, egg whites, chocolate, and nicotine can cause agitation and discomfort in the infant.** Anything in moderation is good, and if there is colicky pain, pay attention in avoiding the above basic foods that can potentially cause allergy, particularly when the infant is being nursed.

4. **Sneezing is common.** The infant, who floated in a sterile saline solution and was in a dark space, being directly fed by the mom's nutrition directly into the blood, after birth, has to transition to learn and live by using its own systems. As the infant is getting colonized with thousands of bugs with every breath, the beautiful immune responses make the infant get colonized with WBC, macrophages, and histiocytes that cause release of chemicals that cause sneezing, and it is not an infection. If there is dried-up mucus, use normal saline nose spray or drops and suction the mucus out. Infants need their nasal passage spot to be patent. FRIDA nasal suction tube works better than a bulb syringe.

5. The feeding transition takes a while, and stomach capacity increases with every feeding. The infant has to adjust to food intake, maintaining body temperature and sugar levels, use the elimination process, and still develop that bonding of feeling the need, gratification, and contentment. All this adjustment takes a while, more like eight to ten weeks.

6. **Hiccups** are common and do not need to be stopped. Infants fall asleep through the hiccups.

7. Infants at birth **do not have circadian rhythm** to make them sleep at night and be up during daylight. That gets established in 95% of infants by ten weeks; 5% will never sleep through the night.

8. Infants have a **gastro colic reflex** that makes them pass a bowel movement after every feeding in the first three weeks of life, and that becomes like once in three to five days in exclusively breastfed infants. Infants do try to grunt and turn red in the face to make a bowel movement, as their muscles are very weak and they are working against gravity. This process looks painful to parents and calls it as constipation, but it is not and does not need any intervention.

9. I have seen formula-fed infants have hard stools, and if so, go to a casein hydrolysate formula available in the market, like Nestle's Good Start, Nutramigen, Alimentum, which are good choices. There are more hypoallergenic formula products in the market that do not need a prescription. In general, it is better to avoid soy for constipation (hard stools), as soy makes the stools more stiff. Casein hydrolysates are a better choice. It is better to avoid stool softeners, and never even think of Karo syrup. The Karo syrup has too much salt content and can cause brain swelling and electrolyte imbalance. Give no water to the infants, as the formula and breast milk have 85% water content. Giving plain water causes electrolyte imbalance.

There was a case presentation while I was reviewing a case for quality assurance a while ago. An infant was given 5 ml of Karo syrup twice a day in the formula for "constipation" from two weeks of age. At six weeks, the infant presented with symptoms of somnolence and meningitis. The spinal fluid was indicative of group B bacterial meningitis, and the sodium level in the serum was 150 MEq/L, which did not go with the Inappropriate Secretion of Anti Diuretic Hormone (ISADH) or natural Desmopressin that is seen in meningitis. The reason for this was the Karo syrup in the bottle daily for the previous four weeks made the serum Hyperosmolar or concentrated with salt. If too much water is given to dilute the salt level, there will be too much water load on the brain and tissues. The infant could not be saved in spite of appropriate, timely antibiotics. **Since that review, the hospital nurses from the nursery were told not to advice on Karo syrup for presumed constipation. It is a good practice to avoid unnecessary medicines in neonates.**

10. Infants' skin is very sensitive, and it takes three weeks to start a dry, eczema type of rash from perfumes in the body lotions and the soaps. Better to use body washes that are perfume-free and unscented body ointment-based emollients. Powders can cause talc sensitivity and rash and also can be inhaled and can cause talc sensitivity and hyper reactive airways. Vaseline petrolatum jelly is the best, the least expensive emollient. Cradle cap causes much of red rashes and that will disappear after 2 months

11. Circumcision is still a personal choice and is not one to stop horrible STD infections or UTI. These infections will occur whether there is foreskin from the choices in adulthood and from personal practices.

The things that parents can do in lieu of medicines and before becoming anxious

What are the right decisions and things that parents can understand and do?

1. **Encourage breastfeeding.** This enhances bonding from the beginning and helps the mother relax also. Breastfeeding is the best, and the nourishment is excellent from immune system development to brain nutrients that are just right. Moms can take Fenugreek capsules two to three times per day, Yogi Tea for enhancing breast milk production two bags three times per day instead of plain water, dill and fennel seeds, raw papaya Thai salads, gluten-free oatmeal, quinoa, collard greens, kale, spinach, green beans, and whatever the galactogogues moms can find online. Drink plenty of liquids and continue multi vitamins.

2. Indians use suran root, raw papaya curry, and drumstick leaves, and they are available at Indian grocery stores. They are good herbs and help with lactation. The best breast pump is feeding the infant every two hours; twenty minutes on one side, and the other side for at least five to seven minutes. Start where you left off the next time, and reverse the time cycles. Gradually, the infant will increase the intervals, and the time taken for nursing usually drops to seven minutes on one side and two minutes on the other side by the third week.

3. Satisfy emotional needs by picking the infant up within thirty to forty-five seconds of crying. This is a demand of a need and gratification and satisfies the infant when done this way. If the infant is never kept down from the caretaker's hands, as the caretaker does not want the infant to cry as it is painful to hear the cry that infant has no scope for meeting the emotional

needs of contentment after demanding and seeking attention and being gratified when answered for that demand. The pathway of belonging and attachment is lost emotionally. If infant is not picked after a prolonged cry like 1-2 minutes, that infant also feels deprived and withdraws the senses to seek attachment and bonding. An infant cannot be spoiled at this age as there is no recognition of social awareness of personal identity associated with anxiety, but a basic need for sustenance.

4. Try to establish eye contact as much as possible with soothing vocal responses in a soft, low-volume voice, called **"parentese"** with some rhyming.

5. Take the infant to a dark, quiet room and gently massage his or her back while putting a lukewarm heating pad under the tummy. Breastfeeding and touch therapy will release oxytocin, a stress-relieving hormone. Soothing classical music also helps the relaxation response. Both release stress in the infant. Rocking and shaking the head and bouncing the infant up and down can cause harm, as we do not know the impact of adult force on the developing richly vascular brain called a "hot zone."

6. **Touch therapy.** Start as soon as you are settled in postpartum, ideally from birth. Massage from gluteus (child's hips) areas upward in a fanning, circular motion, starting in the middle using outward strokes, taking hands upward toward the neck in a series of stroking circular movements. Stroking movement from the head to neck and shoulders should go downward. Another touch intervention is touching palms/soles. This is conducted with thumbs applying firm pressure starting at the heel from the midline and going outward toward the little toe (going upward). Gentle touch is conducted with the palms against the palms. Circular movements include touch of upper and lower extremities (going from ankles to the thighs and hip joints and then from wrist to shoulders) (Hernandez-Reif 1999). Bicycling exercises in prone and supine positions relieve stress and colic, and gases pass out easily. Play classical music, as it increases spatial awareness and induces relaxation (Hoffman 1982; Bilhartz 1999) while doing the exercises on a gym mat. Never do these against the chest of an individual or on the bed mattress.

    Classical music does a lot more than just for listening and hearing pathways. Avoid rock or heavy metal and electrifying music, as they can injure the hearing cells in the cochlea. The Mozart effect comes from soothing music of any kind. Music has more benefits than just listening and relaxing, as it connects to all higher cognitive functions from day one.

7. While in supine or face-up position, start the massage down from shoulders, chest, and abdomen with one hand, while one hand moves toward the other hand from the pelvic bone and pubic area. Perform bicycling-type movement while playing music, and also making eye contact while gently talking to the infant. Infants at birth to three weeks cannot sustain attention on face, but upon repetitious stimulation, they will focus earlier than expected at a familiar face. (Johnson & Johnson Institute has a YouTube video clip on infant massage.)

8. **Music therapy is very important while doing massage and tummy times.** The music stimulates not only the temporal lobe, Wernicke's receiving center for the brain for speech, but also the neocortex or the prefrontal gyrus. There is sense of rhythm recognition, tone and

pitch recognition, discrimination from what space the music is coming from, and motivation to turn toward the music. This enhances the parietal motor cortex development and helps myelination of the nerves; motor system matures well as a result of this motivation and curiosity promoting intention to move toward the stimulus. Listening pathways develop. Remember now that all these are happening dynamically every minute 250,000 cells x 10,000 connections each nerve unit. Unused, 600,000 cells per minute die down x 10,000 connections each cell. The latest research articles and fMRI studies show that the music listening enhances memory, language skills, critical thinking, and ability to learn multiple languages at zero to three years (Ewa A. Miendlarzewska, Wiebke J. Trosl).

9. Music with tummy time. Tummy times need to be done on the floor on a gym mat by various makers, Einstein, Fischer Price, or Bright Futures. These mats are meant for multisensory integration with various visual, sensory for kinesthetic and auditory stimulations. Every infant will cry when they are placed on tummy times. Distraction is needed with music and a toy. Lay the mat on the floor and not on the bed.

When music is played from the 2 o'clock position, the infant develops motivation to turn, listen and make pathways to hearing centers in the brain, storing it in the prefrontal cortex; infants discriminate musical tone quality, phonemes, rhythms, and spatial recognition of direction of origin of sound. Using motor coordination, the infant turns to the side of the sensory signal from where the music is coming (motivation pathway) and turns toward the sound. Neck and back muscles are building their strength at a physical level, and every moment, the infant is trying to get relaxation of the inner brain at the emotional and social level. Ultimately, the infant gets to develop relaxation of the increased tone of flexor muscles. This is called the symmetro-tonic release of the muscle tone, when the infant becomes strong enough to roll over from front to back.

If the same music is played from the same direction, the infant had hard wired for the sound and stored it well that the infant tunes out the stimulus to the brain if offered more than twice or thrice. The note should be played only for the second time from another direction. This teaches spatial reasoning. This is very important for developing mathematical skills. If the caretaker plays loud music, infants tune out, as they do not know how to close their ears and run away from the noise. The more that the infant is exposed to touch therapy with music, better listening, cognitive, and reasoning skills and phonetic and language skills develop in the infant. Encourage to offer music therapy from different directions diagonally opposite, like the 2 o'clock position and the 8 o'clock position. The next time around, change the music and have one tune from the 3 o'clock and the 9 o'clock position, and another tune from the 4 o'clock and the 10 o'clock position. Each time do three to four minutes on tummy and three to four minutes in supine position and establish eye contact.

Hanging toys stimulate and motivate the infant for motor development and spatial reasoning as well with hands and feet.

The curriculum that I use to achieve these goals has been very successful in creating very bright children coming from very impoverished families. Recent fMRI studies show that the brain structure is different in gray and white matter in children exposed to listening to music from birth and learning an instrument at a later date. Better IQ and better problem-solving skills develop (Charles T. Snowdon, Elke Zimmerman, Eckhart Altenmuller).

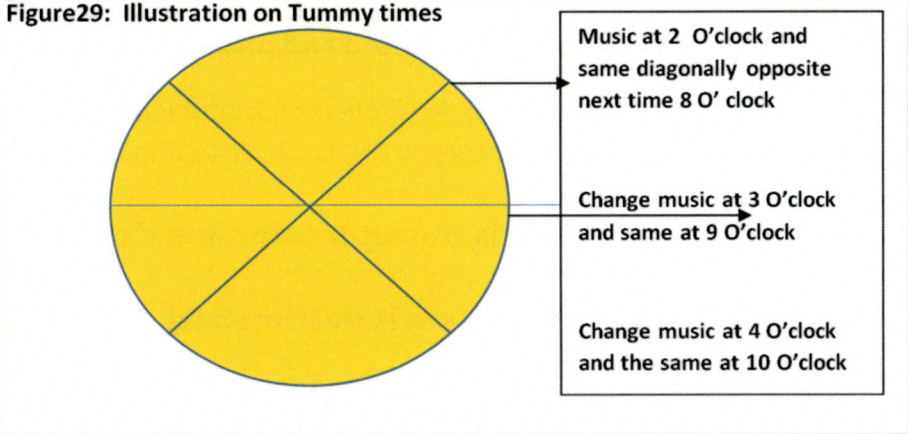

10. Parents should relax by understanding that the crying is not necessarily a pain in majority of the instances but just a reactive response for communication and an expression of the infant's need to be held, reassured, and attend to for basic needs. An infant who is not sick will calm down when held, and when the infant cries as if not recognizing the caretaker's attention and sleepy with bouts of high-pitched crying, check the temperature and call the doctor. Infants may not have high fever, but they show low temperature and can have infections. It is the alertness and calmness when held that is the key to a healthy infant.

11. In summary, a combination of music therapy, touch therapy, eye contact, therapy with tummy times, and limb and upper extremity exercises, in a relaxed state, creates pathways of motivation, listening, memory, spatial reasoning, happiness, bonding, music note, pitch and tone recognition, spatial discrimination, memory, and strengthening of the back muscle

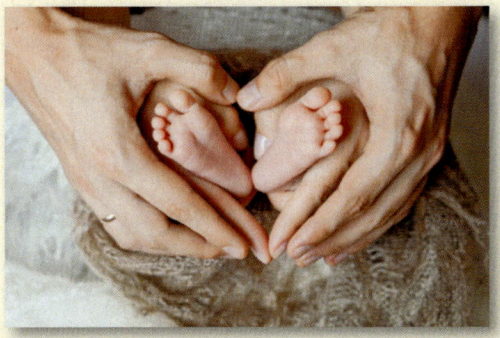

Figure 30: Infant's feet entrusted in the parents' hands

How does the music help better learning in the brain?

Music enhances social participation

Kirschner and Tomasello (2010) documented that the social participation in play was better, and cooperating with each other in challenging games among music-trained children was better than children not exposed to music in solving problems.

Cognitive, emotional, and physiological effects of music

Music associated with happy and sad memories with happy and sad songs, respectively.

Mostly soothing music is therapeutic for cancer, anxiety disorders, and mood disorders.

Music listening increases activity of the reward and pleasure systems in the brain.

(Menon and Levtin 2005, Salimpoor 2013). Auditory cortex interacts with nucleus accumbens, amygdala, and ventromedial prefrontal cortex. This is why listening to music causes pleasure.

Peace: Inner peace of the infant is through caretakers' responsiveness

Reactive caretaking is detrimental

1. Realize that peace is a natural property of every infant. Understand that a child sleeps comfortably when fed and the diaper is dry. Peace will result upon holding and comforting an infant if he/she had demanded attention and cried. Denying this comfort will result in further crying and swallowing of air. This will build up as gas, and the infant will be uncomfortable secondary to air swallowing and cramping. After thirty seconds of crying, the infant needs to be picked up to gratify the need. Infants crying for a long time and not attended to will withdraw senses.

2. If the infant is never given a chance to demand attention through crying briefly, that infant never developed a sense of belongingness and comforting. This can happen with weak parenting skills of not being able to see an infant cry, as they think it is a sign of neglect. Mind you, this is done out of love, but love should not prevent nurture.

3. If the child has not been attended to within a reasonable time of sixty seconds, the infant will fly off the handle, as they have no prefrontal lobe connections for self-regulation. The ideal time is forty-five seconds of crying before responding. This infant, after repetitious crying, will stop demanding and withdraw from social contact and will feel rejection if the demand is not gratified by just picking up the infant and giving body warmth and scent from the primary caretaker. Infants are very sensitive to different scents. An infant will not be spoiled till the infant develops separation and stranger anxiety, demands to be picked up not knowing how to fight a frustration, and gets picked up for crying. Till then, the infant needs to express its needs and then get gratification of the demand by an adult or caretaker to reassure with a response in a state of calmness.

When fed, cuddled, and cared for, an infant is in a natural state of peace, happiness, and contentment. Infants do not have a biological inclination to hate themselves or others. Their natural state is one of love and attachment without distinction to various persons who handle them. An infant's peaceful state is a reflection of the caretaker's state of happiness, knowledge, emotional needs, support systems, and physical needs. It is after four to six months that the stranger anxiety and separation anxiety develop.

Love

1. Infants are born with love, sympathy, empathy, trust, and happiness. They are born to learn and absorb everything through their experience. Everything is a first experience.

2. Infants still need a caretaker who is willing to selflessly care for them and to establish proper attachments and bonding for social and family interactions. The caregiver fosters this love. Poor bonding and attachment secondary to unhealthy emotional state of the caretaker leads to poor attachment disorders in the future (Stifter 2001).

3. Limitation of appropriately lived experiences by the infant resulting from maternal depression can cause global developmental delays in speech, social and emotional maladjustment, motor function, and cognitive associations. The caretaker should envelope infants with love at this age (Halpern 2001).

4. Love cannot be expressed to an infant but can be felt through eye contact, demand and gratification of a brief period of crying, touch therapy, music therapy, and **"parentese."**

"Love as Thought is Truth.
Love as Action is Right Conduct.
Love as Understanding is Peace.
Love as Feeling is Non-violence."

—Satya Sai Baba

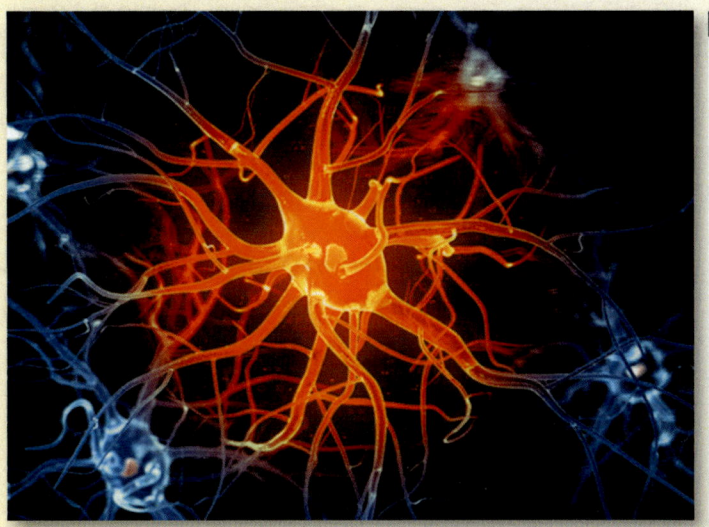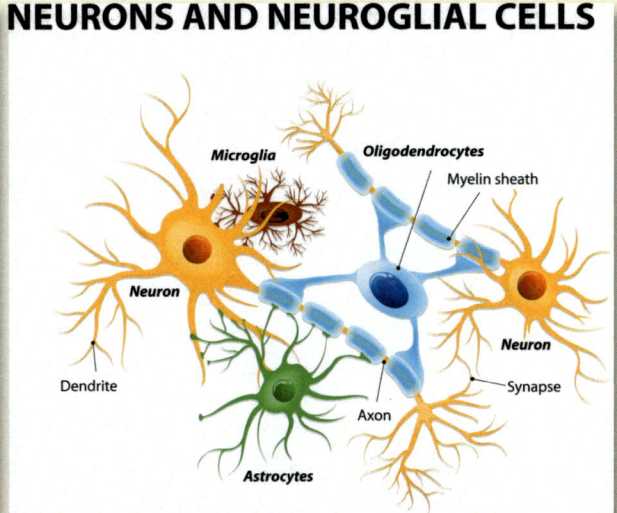

Figure 31: Neuron and synaptic junction

Fundamental unit of neuron-developmental organization is the synaptic junction. Many single units form mini columns, and many mini columns form macro columns. Macro columns are formed based on the use of the function that it is meant to be used for. This function is determined only if the clusters of macro columns receive short and long axon fibers through sensory stimulation. Layers of these nerve segregates are formed from lower brain stem areas to higher functioning brain areas like Limbic system to Neo cortex. These get disintegrated in autism, ADHD, and OCD, and changes are similar on imaging studies. These do get affected with stress and electronic gaming and TV/iPad use two to four hours per day. These aggregates make themes in brain organization. Discussing layering is beyond the scope of current discussion. These aggregates are formed in a chaotic form in Autism Spectrum, ADHD, OCD and Learning disorders. With excessive electronics exposure, or cartoons, there is a potential for sensory over load and over stimulation which results in large volumes mini and macro column aggregates. They are not put in a pathway without any set pattern of multi sensory integration with optimal productive learning. The potential for losing effective cognitive learning pathways will ultimately cause disuse atrophy of the unused pathways at the rate of 600,000 cells/minute x10,000 dendrite connections per each cell. When they connect it is only 250,000cells/minute x 10,000 dendrites per cell to make a pathway based on use. In the recent studies autopsies on Autistic children less than 4 years shows increased brain volume and in autistic adults the volume of brain shrinks with gray matter attrition.

(Eric Courchesne,1,2,* Karen Pierce,1,2 Cynthia M. Schumann, et al., Palmen, Mark N. Ziats, Flipek, Herbert, Timothy J. Schonfield, Stephanie H. Amies, et al., Christian Mirescu, Jennifer D. Peters, CTA, Bruce D. Perry, Henriette Van Praag, Brian R. Christie, V. Lamaire, M. Koehl).

What disturbs nerve organization and disperses it or prevents it from forming?

1. Postpartum depression and poor family and community support.

2. Parental expectations were different from the facts after the birth of the infant to what they expected prior to birth.

3. Fear of inability to feed the infant and natural anxiety of any parent.

4. Poor communication with the infant with or without drug or alcohol or any substance abuse.

5. No tummy times allowed by elders in the family with music therapy and touch therapy for fear of breaking the neck. This is the usual concept by some old-fashioned grandparents. Not having enough rest after delivery prevents actively nurturing the brain.

6. Resorting to medicines to control the colic with colic drops than exploring the relaxation techniques and milk protein intolerance. Acid reflux also causes severe colic in some infants.

7. Spouse bonding disturbances and family dysfunction and poor anger management.

8. Explosive temper and physical and verbal abuse witnessed. The infant cries, and the parent (mostly a mother) is not responding within a reasonable time of forty-five to sixty seconds. After repetitious attempts to cry and seek attention, which is not answered, the infant withdraws, and there is noticeable anaclitic depression as young as two to three months of age; a very quiet infant who fails to make eye contact. Many consider this infant easy to take care of but during examination shows lack of eye contact and no social smile; that is an infant at risk, and we need to pay attention to the parents' needs.

9. Any loud noises in the house can cause sensory withdrawal. Infants cannot run away or close their ears for loud noises but certainly can tune out and block sensory signals. This means listening to voices is also blocked to auditory cortex via the limbic system.

10. General expectations by parents are to feed the infant through mouth and the infant should sleep for several hours, and these therapies and nurture activities are presumed to prevent rest for the infant. A well-informed parent will want to nurture the proper way and willingly participate in feeding the brain through all senses and not confined through mouth only.

11. Screen time exposure had been shown to over stimulate the infant's brain, and this is while parents are watching their shows or the infant's exposure to cartoons. Screen has repetitious movement that over stimulates the senses and the brain, creating the beginning states or roots for hyperkinetic child syndrome. Any fearful scene can be a permanent print in the brain and can make an infant withdraw senses (Eric Courchesne, Karen Pierce, Cynthia M. Schumann).

Endnotes

1. A child with motivation, listening skills, processing, spatial organization, and phonetic acquisition, can learn multiple languages, will have good cognitive development, reasoning, physical strengths, relaxation, happiness, sense of belonging and attachment, good social bonding, social and family relationships, and eagerness to learn more.

2. If the infant is exposed to multiple languages, one caretaker, using his or her pitch and frequency of tone, uses one language to communicate, and the other parent speaks another language. No switching between two languages by the same person. Then the infant can have a phonemic presentation that becomes very well organized in certain areas for each language. If one person speaks two languages and switches around, the infant cannot develop any language, as the phonemic presentation gets scattered. We have enough studies from Japanese and Chinese infants and the exposure to language at different age groups. It is difficult for a Japanese infant to pronounce *r* and *l* if English is taught after ten months of age.

3. Multisensory integration from newborn period is very important.

What do parents need to know about normal newborn care?

1. Crying is for basic need and is a communication.

2. Crying does not mean pain.

3. Sneezing is common as the nose is getting colonized with histiocytic and mast cells and white cells that filter and protect against infections. We breathe eighty-four thousand bugs per breath. Infants are protected from maternal passive antibodies against common viral infections.

4. Straining with stool and passing soft seedy stool is not constipation. Infants are trying to push out and do not have strong muscles. In the beginning, infants make a bowel movement after every feeding. This is normal gastrocolic reflex, and after two to three weeks, breastfed infants will go once in three to five days, and that is normal. Karo syrup will harm the infant and can cause salt imbalance and should not be used. Glycerin rectal suppositories will break down the nerve endings if done routinely.

5. Infants in the first three weeks need to nurse every two hours and as needed. Some infants do sleep three hours between feeds. Infants' contentment and six to seven wet diapers a day is the best guide for parents. Some infants cluster more than others. They take four to five minutes and wake up to do some more. The most important aspect is to learn to have a good latch; otherwise, there will be cracking of areola and nipples.

6. Oils, powders, and lotions that have perfumes do cause sensitization of skin and dermatitis. It is better to use body wash that is hypoallergenic like over the counter perfume free body washes.

7. When the cord gets separated, there may be mild ooze of blood, and it needs to be cleaned with alcohol, as it may seed bacteria if left alone.

8. Water should never be given to infants, as it results in water toxicity and brain swelling with electrolyte imbalance.

9. Infants do not have circadian rhythm from melatonin in the brain till ten weeks of age, and they get up very often for their basic needs. They do not sleep through the night.

10. Parents are the first teachers to prevent brain disorganization and structural damage.

11. The combination of tummy times, exercises, music therapy, and touch therapy all need to be done several times a day to stimulate effective neurodevelopmental organization.

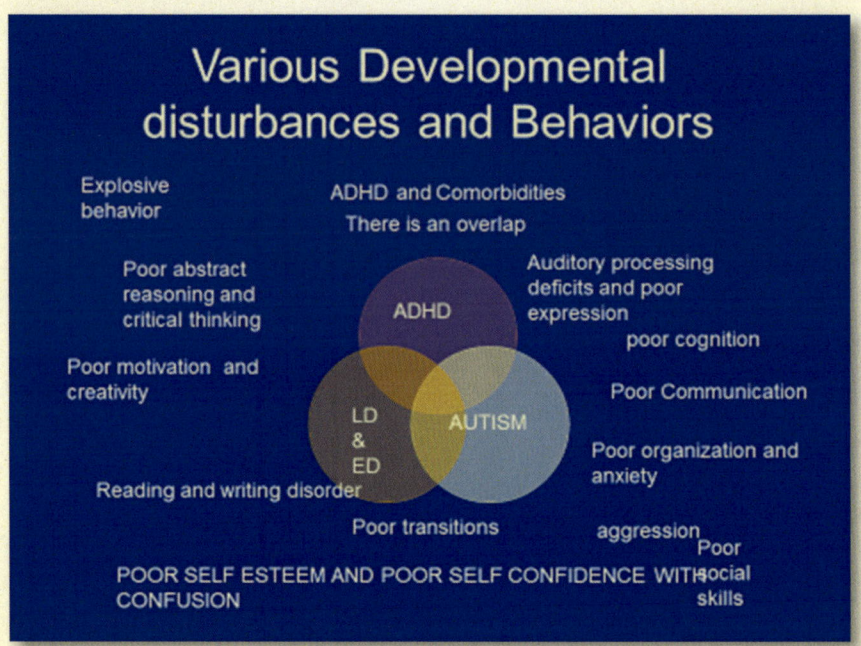

Figure 32: Illustration of overlap of learning and behavior disorders

There is an overlap of disorders like autism spectrum disorder, ADHD, learning disorders, emotional disorders, and OCD, and the imaging studies are also showing the overlap.

Bottom up is the connections going from outside to inside, and top down is the messages coming from inside to outside as behavioral outcome.

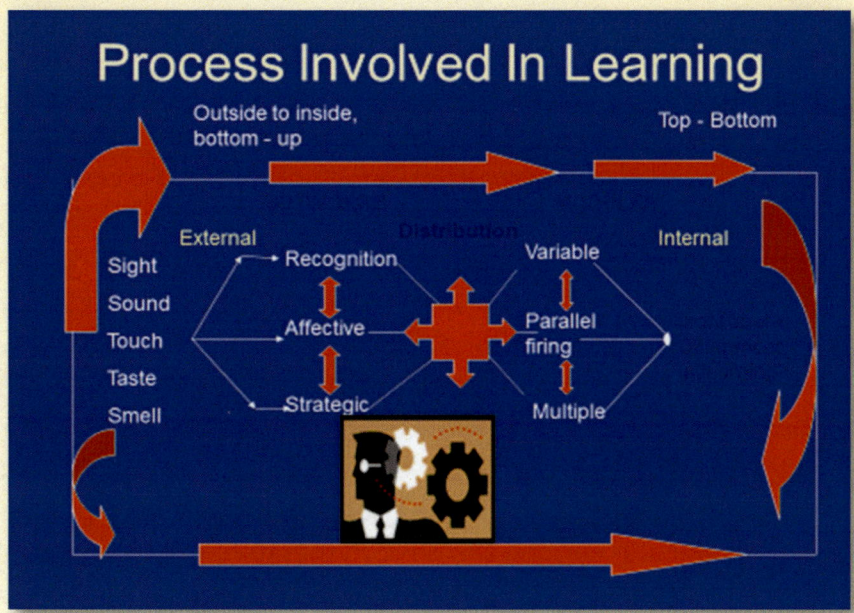

Figure 33: Sensory Input – Factors in perception and learning

The above slides represent the symbiotic relationship between the external influences, sensory input, and affective state of mind to create a strategic planning for development. Critical age is 0-3 years as every information and learning is a first experience and is a permanent part of the brain structure. The brain structure seems to be altered by adverse influences, and the hierarchical development from brain stem (basic lower brain) to neocortex (higher cognitive brain) seems to be structurally influenced adversely with toxic experiences and perceived trauma.

1. There is such an overlap of the psychopathologies of learning, development, and behavior based on experiences and internal nerve pathways development.

2. The global communities are spending millions of dollars after the hard wiring for sensory input and pathway development had occurred based on the environmental and society culture, family values, and electronics exposure. Some of the adverse outcomes are the result of actual and perceived toxic influence of situations, electronics, and poor nurture 0-3 years. If all caretakers in the world can adopt a unified sensory nurture with a curriculum that offers multi sensory integration in a state of internal mental relaxation, we will create golden children who are impervious to negative influences in the society. Genes do not get expressed if the sensory nurture can overcome with a safe, secure environment fostering skills to be extracted. I had fetal alcohol syndrome infants who went into a good home through pathways, an agency through CPS, and adoption, and they are doing well with learning and behaviors. I am not saying chromosomal disorders with significant micro array disturbances can be taught like normal children, but their morbidity can be better with the concepts of 0-3 brain sprouts if nurture fosters learning.

I have many cases of Williams Syndrome, Turner Syndrome and some short arm deletion syndrome children doing very well.

Case presentation

Children of 2 Bipolar Parents with History of Emotional and Physical neglect

1. Two children were brought by their maternal aunt for breathing problems. The infant boy was wheezing away at ten months of age and requiring oxygen for respiratory distress, and the seven-year-old girl was very hyperkinetic and aggressive. The boy needed to be admitted, and a Child Protective Service case was filed. Maternal aunt gave the history of child neglect secondary to her sister's and her husband's drug problems. The infant boy was coughing and wheezing for over ten days with no medical help. The older sibling was a six-seven-year-old girl who was on medicines for ADHD. When the infant boy was discharged, SAI Educare program was taught to both the foster parents. The seven-year-old sister never needed medicines for her hyperactivity; at sixteen years of age, the expression of bipolar depression of both parental inheritance started affecting her, and she needed therapy, breathing exercise, and redirection to set her back on SAI Educare path of multisensory integration and is doing very well and now a college graduate. The infant boy, now an eighteen-year-old high school graduate, never developed any behavior disorders with a stable maternal aunt and her husband, who fully supported the SAI Educare training and the multisensory integration. Brain architecture can be altered for life time, with stress and aversive environmental influences, but it is better to prevent toxic injury to the brain from adverse societal factors through knowledgeable, effective parenting in the wake of modern knowledge on neuroplasticity and experiential early child brain development.

2. I work with a lot of foster placement children who were adopted for giving a better life and the history is usually that of abuse, assault, witnessing violence and self rejection with built up anger internally. This has a toxic stress effect on brain, till the child is taught through healing arts of programs similar to SAI EDUCARE with multi sensory integration and positive Dynamic thoughts for life. All of them got off medicines by 16 years of age, found the real inner self with confidence and hard work and acceptance of past life with love and forgiveness for themselves first and the care takers also. Most of them went to college after High school graduation and some chose to take jobs to figure out life.

Neocortex connections fail to happen if there is perception of emotional trauma and freeze the networks, thalamus down in *"Firght and Flight"* mode. With Visual stimulus, the infant only connects to the occipital cortex in the hindbrain. Frontal lobe connections are important for speech and language development along with relaxation and that happens with listening to soft music and not loud tunes or death metal. As described in the previous chapter, massage therapy music, touch and eye contact, and visual tracking are offered as a nurture, the infant gets all assigned systems of the brain stimulated along with motivation, memory, spatial reasoning, discrimination, cognitive associations, emotional stability of happiness and peace, internal relaxation, language abilities, and motor coordination.

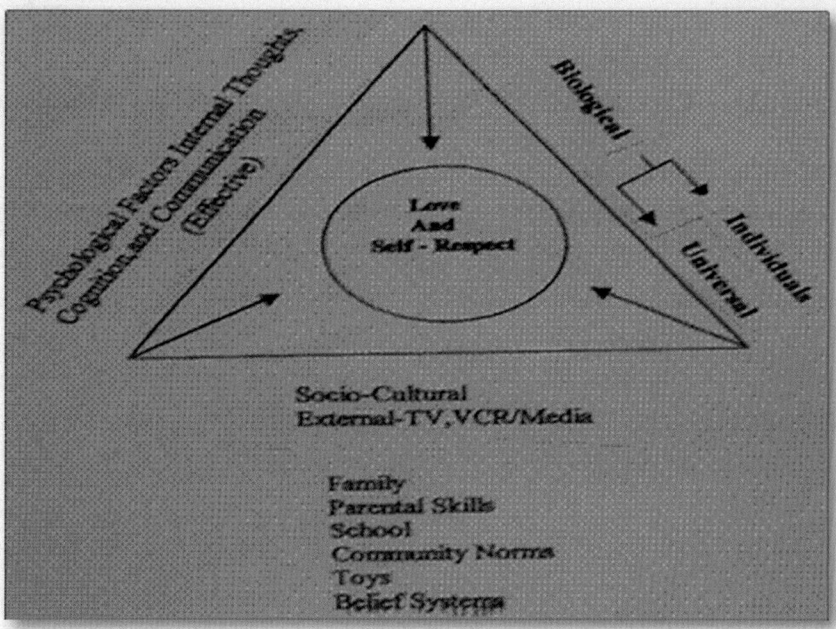

Figure 34: Positive Personality development influences

This is a visual concept developed explain in a diagram that most important determining factor for creating an excellent child as written as the base of the triangle. Left limb is individual genetic traits at birth and right limb has 2 factors. One is Universal like puberty that is not in ones' hands. The other is Individual factor and choices made in eating, drinking, and relationships. The base of the triangle and the right limb are very important to foster self respect and confidence in an individual during rapid growth. An excellent child represents an ascending pyramid.

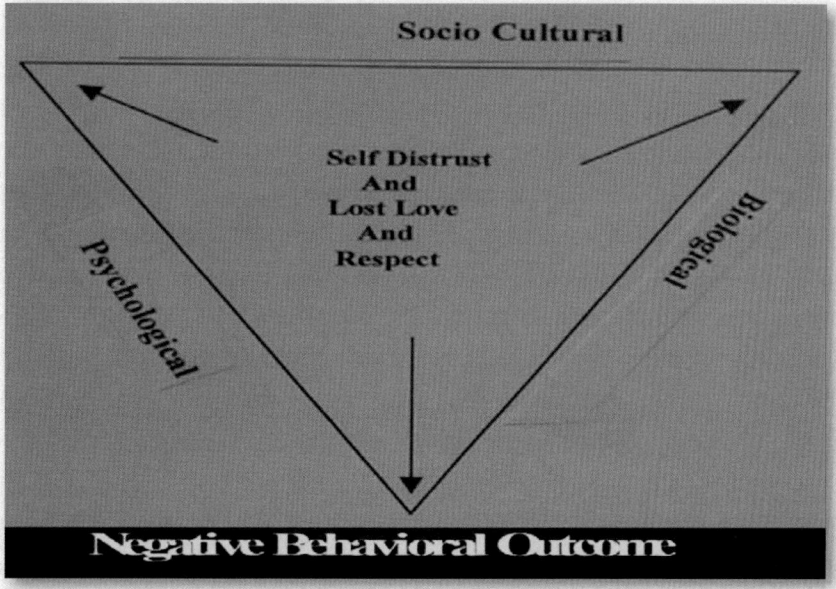

Figure 35: Negative Influences from environment

The upside down triangle represents an individual torn with experiences that caused and promoted chaos, poor self reliance and trust and felt rejection. Nurture was disturbed by experiences that did not center on the infant getting positive experiences by care takers but placed their personal needs above the infant's needs.

All this happens dynamically by investing one hour of quality time, broken down into ten-minute slots, six times a day. Unused, no nurture offered to infant, the infant loses opportunity every minute to connect robustly using all senses.

I have worked with autistic children who came to me at thirty months to five years of age or even at a later age. The pathogenesis was noted to be from multiple factors when reviewed with the background knowledge on hierarchical neurodevelopment organization of early child brain development (ECBD) perspective and looking for factors that could have caused multisensory organization disturbances. With a good history taking, the multiple factors were about domestic issues that could have caused multisensory integration problems; this results in sensory withdrawal, particularly from social and family relationships' perspective; poor spouse bonding and communication, custodial fights and angry exchanges between family members seem to be the most common causes. Some parents are in good relationships, they love their children so much with no TV and cartoon controls from permissive parenting; in some cases TV was always on thinking that the child was not watching; allowing watching for good reasons of learning something, or using an iPad to calm a screaming infant at nine months in a bouncer.

If Autism Spectrum is at 1 in 65 cases, certainly all of these are not from genes that are bad as the prevalence of genetic disorders falls under 14% of the population. There has to be other causes that we should really tackle and reeducate ourselves and prevent the toxic effects 0-3 years. These precipitating factors would not have been tracked down as significant aversive sensory stimuli if there is no knowledge and understanding on how brain connects to the immediate environmental experiences and what kind of impact it would have on zero- to thirty-six-month's early child brain development and the resulting biosocial behaviors.

The SAI Educare curriculum was developed to educate the parents on neurobiology, development of biosocial behaviors, role of perceived threats, fears and anxiety on the rapidly developing nerve connections, and the adverse biosocial behavioral effects that the innocent parenting practices can cause. The curriculum was offered to many families at an individual level about the multisensory integration to nurture the sprouting nerve connections and was taught diligently, as it is a very sensitive and new subject. This education and hands-on floor and face activities that were taught rigorously 0-24 months, brought about positive transformational changes among the family members and the home environment, effective communication between the spouses, exposure to music and making associations with phonics, kinesiology, and floor-time activities. Many NICU graduates, ADHD children, autism spectrum behavioral children who attended and practiced this teaching go to regular schools now and have a mild ADHD that is being handled with music therapy, "tuning in" or yoga with meditation and nasal breathing, and guided imagery, which are part of the SAI Educare curriculum of five teaching techniques. Because of the HIPPA rules, names cannot be given, but patients who came from Dallas, Victoria, and Laredo and mostly from San Antonio have no trace of autism spectrum but need treatment for ADHD, inattention, and some auditory processing disorder.

Case presentation on above facts

1. In Head Start conferences, I went to the Southern Texas areas and gave a lecture on the above information of early childhood brain development, the role of sensory nurture, the way SAI Educare program works, and the curriculum that is curing infants. Someone who heard me referred a case from the valley. The infant was thirty-two months old when the mom drove just to see me, as he was diagnosed with autism and he would have an "animal-like behavior and would not communicate," per their local neurologist. I spent an hour just trying to take the history and immediately realized that there were spouse relationship problems between both highly educated mom and dad. Their four-year-old son was also acting up and had a temper, and I was wondering if he was a hyperactive child (ADHD). This boy who was brought was staring into space, avoiding eye contact, and had no speech at all; he was hyper with random motor activity. History had the following salient points for toxic effect on Early Child Brain Development (ECBD).

He did have two hours of screen time per day. Dad had a drinking problem and came home late, and there were heated exchanges between spouses in their own room. The parents thought the kids would not have had chance to listen to the arguments, as they were sleeping. The dad was described to have a male husky voice. The mom was trying to save the marriage and was very depressed. She did have a flat affect during our entire communication and history taking. Both the parents felt that the vaccines caused the autism. They tried diets, and the effort was in vain, and they stopped diet regulations.

The next two hours were spent on showing literature that was available at that time, (2005) PET scans of neurodevelopment organization of the brain, and the causes for sensory withdrawal. I requested her to stop screen time, to get therapy, and continue speech therapy and occupational therapy that he was already receiving, teach the five teaching components of SAI Educare, do touch therapy with music as given above, and do hands-on activities and phonics and associations of alphabets with daily objects that are around so that sight, sound, and touch will help procedural learning. Numbers were to be taught on blocks and abacus. Not to give up as he was under thirty-six months of age, and till that time, the brain connects dynamically. The father was to be educated by the mother on the knowledge and let him seek therapy on his weaknesses and anger management. The mom was advised on low volume of speech tones at home. I taught the mom the basic meaningful meditation with nasal regulated breathing for twenty minutes, three times a day, to calm her and for focus and direction. When the mom went home with a lot of hope and enthusiasm, she shared this information with the local PCP and the neurologist and the father. I was labeled as a **"quack"** by their local neurologist in October 2005.

Mother called me back and expressed concern. I gave her the reference articles to read once again, and I insisted that she learn from cross references herself and, if she did not, at least to follow and implement what I taught her.

By November, the child called his mom "mama," and the mom was excited and called back and reported to me. By July 2006, the father and paternal grandfather came to see me and took some notes on the patient, as he was talking and ready to be enrolled into pre-K, very cooperative, and self-controlled. Further therapies continued, and he went to regular school, and no therapies were needed afterward. **The neurologist said that it was nothing short of a miracle.** *The miracle was connecting neurons in a state of calmness and sensory nurture in a state of trust, security, and selfless love, giving in to each other by both the spouses, getting some help for their mood disorder, no screen time, increased family time, and no toxic information to the brain from domestic issues*. This is a real case (one out of many), and for privacy reasons, the names and cities will not be discussed.

2. Having an anomaly of chromosome 15, the child presented with global developmental delay and no speech at all at six years of age and diagnosed as a severe autism spectrum disorder. After the multisensory integration was taught and discussing the adverse effects of electronics and screen time on language development, the mother immediately stopped iPad exposure for teaching and learning and did more hands-on therapies on the floor and with chin lift, music therapy, and eye contact. With music and touch therapy and hands-on activities, making associations with daily life application objects and phonemes and numbers, the patient started communicating within six months. It will take longer to make her develop pragmatics.

3. A young boy came at 3.5 years of age with no speech at all and poor eye contact and was impulsive and hyperactive. Only child for both parents in a two-income family. Grandparent has been the main caretaker. He has an excellent family with no domestic issues of violence. He was in front of TV cartoons and iPad for action figures and knew how to manipulate the mouse and play games for at least three to four hours per day or more. He was given everything that he demanded for, and it was easy to make him stop crying by sitting him in front of the TV or giving a game. After exposure to teachings from SAI Educare curriculum and being educated on neurobiology and where things could go wrong, the parents stopped screen time absolutely, and the patient started talking. Being an only child, naturally, the parents felt limit setting and authoritative parenting skills were difficult for some time, till the parents started seeing good results with self-regulation, speech, and eye contact from two months to twelve months with SAI Educare, multisensory integration, and parent education on consistent limit setting and behavior modification. Of course, he was enrolled into speech therapy prior to the introduction of SAI Educare curriculum. Currently, he is in high school, needs meds for ADHD but has excellent behavior, makes straight A's, and may come off meds soon after he builds his self-confidence in his own effort and self-regulation. He practices daily as much as possible the five teaching techniques of SAI Educare program for overcoming ADHD. His family is wonderful and very cooperative. He is enrolled into many activities, an avid reader, excellent in karate, and has wonderful social skills, and he made a 180-degree turn by his fifth birthday, and he is maintaining the personality traits that excel in all fields.

There are more of these cases, but these are typical examples of cases that when we do not incorporate the concepts of ECBD, we are missing opportunities to intervene appropriately.

Chapter VII

Development from Two to Four Months

Truth: two months, facts of the matter

Development has strategies that are dynamic and rapidly connecting. Emotions mature first and then the motor system. That is why infants seem to develop from **"top down"** on the outside; head and face functions develop first and then proceed down to neck, arms, and then the legs as we can see the motor system development. Imagine an upside-down infant, and this is called cephalocaudal development, as we witness development externally. The inner network development with the sensory input starts from the lower brain system functions and connections that are going up to the frontal lobe from **"bottom up."** Motor movements occur later than emotional tagging of experiences inside the brain, and perceptions are formed.

Externally, we see the face and emotional interactions develop from head, and, finally, the legs and motor functions are noticeable by twelve months (cephalocaudal development).

A. At four weeks to eight weeks

1. Infants recognize that their needs are being taken care, develop bonding with the primary caretaker who has been attending to their needs. They develop a social smile by three to four weeks. This becomes cooing by two months, and this needs reciprocity.

2. Very limited focus in the midline, and they still have a basic flexor tone of the muscles, and they cannot move actively. Gaze will be consistent in midline by eight weeks.

3. Head will be kept to one side, called tonic neck reflex, and this disappears by eight to ten weeks.

4. If the caretaker is actively involved with face time, floor time, and gym mat, one can notice a crude hand and leg movement to reach and touch objects on the gym mat.

What can go wrong in this age group for this realization not to happen?

1. An infant never placed down to prevent crying has not met demand and gratification needs. The infant had no opportunity to feel the need to be picked up and be satisfied for being picked up, leading to poor emotional gratification and attachment.

2. An infant who is not picked up, as the caretaker is busy, depressed, inebriated, and neglectful, in dysfunctional settings with abuse and violence, withdraws senses, prevents eye contact, and the social smile is withdrawn.

3. There is poor motivation to develop basic motor skills if the infant is never laid down, touched and was not offered music therapy for directional and motivational sense.

4. Reciprocity from parent is needed for accomplishments, and sensitivity for lacking this starts even as early as two to three weeks of age.

RIGHT ACTION: *What do parents need to do?*

1. The above can be rectified by continuing touch therapy with tummy times and music therapy from six directions as given in the previous chapter. The caretaker has to be gifted with positive emotional stability and inner relaxation and peace to impart this asset on the infant. Infants can feel the tension from caretaker's tone of the muscles.

2. Mother needs to support herself to be relaxed and use the breathing exercises and music therapy with meaningful meditation. Family support is very important. Rest and relaxation are very important in this period.

3. Breastfeeding also helps with relaxation of the mother and bonding with the infant. This is because of many endocrine systems are involved in breastfeeding, with oxytocin being the main relaxation hormone.

4. Professional medical care providers and family members need to pay attention to the needs of the mother-infant relationship, help, and guide properly at this time.

5. For music therapy and touch therapy combination, no more than six minutes of activity each time, six times a day, will get excellent results. Infants need a lot of downtime with sensory stimulation and then a brief stimulus to accept an activity. Allocate three to four minutes prone and three to four minutes supine and do the music, touch and eye contact therapy simultaneously. When done in prone and supine position at each time, the listening and the sensory integration is crossing from right to left and left to right, connecting the functions of both brains. If music is not used and just the tummy times are offered, the efficacy for language development, focus, motivation, and attention span, spatial reasoning, directional sense, discrimination, and motor development opportunities are lost.

6. Same music played will be tuned out by the third time. Therefore, use one tune from the two o'clock position and again from the eight o'clock position. Another tune from the three o'clock and nine o'clock positions. Another tune from the four o'clock and ten o'clock positions. While doing this, the infant is paying attention, listening, motivated to turn toward the music, and relaxed with the parent's touch therapy, besides, as enumerated several times, the language and cognitive abilities that music therapy can confer.

7. Touch therapy includes gentle, soft, and feathery touch in the prone position, while playing music, starting from buttocks up in a fanning pattern toward the shoulders and stroking movements from head toward the shoulders. Circular movements encircling the legs and thighs are important for soothing. For a minute or so, do bicycle movement of both legs, and it helps to have a rolled-up receiving blanket under the stomach. This causes bonding and relief from gases, and movement of legs gets rid of the tensions in the leg muscles and helps the circulation.

8. While listening to music, the infant is connecting to hearing centers, attention and focusing centers, motivation centers to turn toward music, physical movement toward the side of the music, and, by changing the music to come from different or opposite directions, sense of spatial reasoning and discrimination. This therapy when consistently done is creating rich

networks for memory, focus, motivation, spatial reasoning, listening, visual pathways, depth perception, pitch recognition, language acquisition, and physical strengthening of the neck and trunk muscles.

This also helps the use-dependent myelination of nerve fibers. This combination of music from different directions in space, touch therapy, and visual tracking with eye contact and physical exercises helps the myelination of nerve fibers and crossing through the corpus callosum, which is essential for controlling and relaying sensory signals between the right and left brains.

9. Place the infant in the supine position and play music. Do the same from pubis to shoulders and stroking movements from scalp to shoulders with touch therapy, bicycling exercises, chin lift, and eye contact. This gives emotional belongingness, particularly when eye contact is established. It will be brief under four weeks of age, and, progressively, eye contact gets better in the midline. Let the stretching of the muscles make the heel touch the palms on opposite sides for crossing at the corpus callosum, taking advantage of this before the infant can do it by himself or herself at around five months of age. This makes the opposite sides connect internally (right to left brain and left to right brain). More the fibers cross in the midline, more is the intelligence.

10. If placed on the gym mat and the infant makes crude attempts with hands and feet to reach out to the objects, this causes the internal locus of motivation with visual stimulation and visual tracking.

B. At two months

1. Infants by two months can track 180 degrees with the eye movement and need to have this eye movement stimulated. This will create a broad band from eye to brain internally that will be useful in the future for fast reading and comprehension at the same time. The broader the band, the faster is the transmission. Take a bright and light-contrast-colored object like a sponge ball or toy with similar qualities and move them slowly right to left and left to right as the infant tracks, and then vertically and obliquely also.

2. Continue the gym mat exercises and the music therapy, touch therapy, and eye contact as explained above.

3. Motor skills will show the infant to lift chest up movement when in prone position, even in the immediate newborn period with "neck rightening reflexes."

4. Limited fine motor coordination is noted secondary to poor myelination and still needs exercises to promote myelination, which is use dependent and through proper combination of DHA and ARA. These fatty acids are richly available in breast milk (linoleic acid).

5. Socially and emotionally consistent smile for any face. They respond to smiling face better.

6. They develop communication, and the first phonemes are universal—"agoo," "gagoo," and "akhum" (occidental language).

Using the Einstein gym center or any infant gym mat activity has to be done persistently on a daily basis from newborn period to first nine months of life. This floor-time and face-time activity helps the multisensory integration.

TV/iPad applications/iPhone applications cannot achieve this goal of motivation, curiosity, bonding from reciprocity from parent, contentment of mastering a desire, movement, and happiness of accomplishing a task. Music helps to enhance listening skills. By six months, infants would have tried and mastered rolling over both sides and creep to reach for objects and actively reaching for objects and moving objects from one hand to the other.

PEACE

Infants' peace and happiness depend upon the caretaker or parent's happiness. We need a parent who is relaxed and happy. The family support systems need to help the parent or the caretaker. In situations of domestic violence and loud noises, the sensory perceptions get alertness about danger or threat and freeze internally, blocking sensory input, with insecurity and dissociation. Any startling noises can block sensory input. Internal locus for motivation is lost, and there will be minimal external factors for motivating learning secondary to toxic stress in the environment. A parent who is unable to set the infant down and will not let the infant cry is also making the infant vulnerable for sensory deprivation, preventing the need, demand, and gratification cycle.

Touch and music therapy enhances inner peace for the infant and increases caretaker's bonding with the infant. **"Parentese"** helps socially interact and pay attention.

LOVE

With self-respect and love is the natural state of this infant at this age. Parents smile at the infant, and the infant smiles at the parent. They do not know any hate or anger but cry to express discomfort. Even the infants of drug-addicted mothers, when there is a good and loving caretaker, exhibit this outcome from sensory nurture. The self-trust, worth, and love increase as the caretaker's reciprocation increases.

  C. Four months

Gross motor

1. The infant releases the increased tone of muscles by twelve to sixteen weeks of life. The infant learns to get sto-chest up and suddenly can release tone on one side to roll over from prone to supine (front to back). This ideally happens around 3 months of age. Caretakers' or parents' reward or reciprocity is important for accomplishing this milestone for the infant's motivation to continue the effort. By sixteen weeks, the infant rolls over to the supine or facedown position from faceup or supine position. This is called the symmetrotonic release phenomenon and is critical for further gross motor skills.

Fine motor

1. Head is steady on neck to focus on an object, reach for it, and actively grasp it.

2. Tries to reach for objects actively, as the bobbing of the head is not a problem.

3. Develops ulnar-palmar grasp and reaches for objects within reach actively.

Adaptation

1. Social adaptation is by following objects, grabbing, and taking it to mouth.

2. Eye tracking enhances very well and follows a moving object.

3. Prefers playing with toys in sitting position, and it is a good time to get a Bumbo chair and introduce to objects on the tray for exploration, eye-hand coordination, and active grasp with full motivation.

4. More hand-to-mouth activity will be seen, and parents always think of this development as teething for this activity. Infants are pleasure oriented through exploration in mouth and they feel the world through mouth.

Language

1. The cooing becomes a throaty squeal and lets the caretaker know about the excitement.

2. Loud laughing and looks for caretaker's attention (reciprocity)

3. Infants drool a lot at this stage; again, it has nothing to do with teething and is the result of more taste buds stimulating salivary glands to make saliva, and infants have a strong tongue thrust reflex that throws out saliva constantly. Infants are poorly coordinated to push saliva with tongue back and swallow. This is one of the reasons for spitting out food that is offered and is not from rejection of the taste of the food. Infant will get adjusted to new taste as the same food is given till accepted, and it takes a week.

4. One of the reasons why they are not fed till five months is because of this poor coordination.

Personal and social

1. Infants make good eye contact as soon as the caretaker is seen and very happy; they need interaction and reciprocation from the caretaker.

2. Ulnar-palmar grasp changes and they use finger movements to make it thumb side grasp called radial-palmar grasp and get involved in watching fingers.

3. Infants expect to be fed or involved in interactive communication and play as soon as the caretaker is seen.

4. Infants look sad if caretaker is serious; they are sensitive to maternal emotions.

5. Sensory nurture is still the basic floor-time, face-time interaction, reciprocation with a smile and clap, and gym mat activities, but stimulate the eye movements for tracking dark and light objects as well as the toys that hang from the gym center.

6. Engage with pleasant facial gestures in a soothing voice with musical inclination to speech **"Parentese".**

7. One caretaker communicates exclusively in one language and the other caretaker in the other language. Confusion in thematic presentation of a phonemic presentation to the brain happens if one parent switches between two languages. The information gets scattered, and the infant will not pick up any language. Infants are linguists, and they can pick up five different languages.

D. Five months

Gross motor

1. Rolls over both sides easily and tries to get up on knees to creep forward

2. Military crawl may start or at least tries to get up on feet like a bow

3. Rolls over both sides to reach and follow objects out of reach. Motivation for infants is trying to keep toys slightly out of reach to encourage movement. If the infant is frustrated, one needs to step back and try again after a downtime.

4. Bears weight well on feet and prefers being held to stand

Fine motor

1. Consistent radial-palmar grasp and tries to cover face up and explores with fingers and hands aiming for objects

2. Takes objects to mouth and tries to hold a bottle

3. Takes same and opposite feet to mouth

Adaptive

1. Makes throaty noises and expectantly looks at caretaker's interactions for reciprocity

2. Eyes follow objects and indicate wanting a toy through crude hand movements if not within reach. Takes objects consistently to mouth. Expectantly looks at adults eating a meal and follows the hand-to-mouth movement with eyes.

3. More drooling as the infant develops taste buds; salivary glands get stimulated and form copious saliva, and still cannot swallow as fast as the saliva forms.

Language

1. More interactive play with caretakers and less crying

2. More babbling phonemes. Speech and phoneme recognition and discrimination start by five months. Infants need to be spoken to with regular adult talk to stimulate interactive speech.

Social and personal

1. Expectant behavior involves increasing interaction with anticipation of primary caretaker's involvement to soothe the infant and play with the infant.

2. Some very well-nurtured infants do show early signs of stranger and separation anxiety.

3. Facial expression of the infant changes for various caretakers' emotions particularly responds or reacts to sad, angry, and happy faces.

4. It is a time to consider introduction of solid foods to infants.

FOOD INTRODUCTION: Ideally, food introduction by AAP recommendation is to be later, but it is practical to start at five months. This transition discussion by health-care providers is important for future healthy food choices and eating practices.

Doing the food introduction in the right manner is the key for the future development of:

1. Healthy eating habits in the future which includes eating bland vegetables.

2. Acceptance of healthy nourishment;

3. Avoidance of food sensitivities and aversions;

4. Prevention of habits that will lay grounds for diabetes, hypertension, and cancer;

5. The ability to avoid genetically genomic and preserved foods;

6. Training of the taste buds to healthy foods as opposed to sweet foods; and

7. Teaching the brain the right choices now, which will continue to favor the right food choices in the future, and once again, any pathway that develops for the first time stays in the brain as a permanent pathway. Every taste is a new stimulus, and the brain will accept with persistence.

At five months, we can introduce basic foods starting with vegetables first. Give one week to ten days of offering the same food till the infant accepts it. That is the sign of hard wiring for the taste in the brain. Remember that infants have a tongue thrust reflex and will push any food out in the beginning. Offering the same food till the infant accepts the taste is the key to getting them permanently wired to eat vegetables in the future.

First food preparation

The usual parents' complaint is about toddlers not eating greens. But if parents start introducing organic kale as a first meal mixed with two tablespoons of rice cereal, infants will accept all bland vegetables. If apple sauce is given as a first meal, infants will not accept bland vegetables later, as the tongue seeks sweet foods and white carbohydrates. Mind you this is a fundamental life time experiential memory and learning.

For the same reason of hard wiring rapidly, a newborn introduced to bottle and a pacifier will reject the breastfeeding, and it will be a struggle to get them latched on again! This is how fast they can hard wire! Spinach, kale, chards, collard greens, carrots, and green beans have **"Luteins", "Xanthines", and "Antioxidants"** in them and are good for brain development and immune system. Avocado by six months can be introduced.

Natural salts in foods are enough, and no additional salt should be added to foods at this age. Start with kale; after that, spinach, chards, green beans, carrots, and sweet squashes.

Next food group that can be added is protein, like organic lean turkey and chicken added to the vegetable and rice cereal mix. Introducing peanut butter and gluten-containing foods can be later when the intestines mature at around **nine months** of age and will prevent food intolerances and food allergies. Black beans and Blanco beans are also good sources of protein. Vegetarians can offer black beans, Blanco beans, Garbanzo beans, Moong Dal, Toor Dal, and legumes for sources of protein. There are some health-conscious parents, and they are growing in number to change to vegetarian meal plans. Quinoa is a protein grain with nine essential amino acids, and I introduce that at nine months.

Rapidly introducing fruits as the first group of foods with white carbohydrate that is also sweet will be a permanent pathway of food choices trending toward sweet foods. Starting with bland vegetables and gradually introducing squashes and sweet vegetables like sweet potato and carrots, the infant had developed taste buds for bland vegetables and can even eat cucumbers and brussels sprouts as a toddler. These pathways are permanent, called hard wiring for good food habits. There may be some food faddism after two years of age, and they will get back to lifetime healthy eating if the family maintains healthy eating habits.

At any time, it is better to avoid high-cholesterol-containing foods like beef and ham to prevent future cancer chances. Egg yolks alone can be introduced from nine months of age. Fruits also can be introduced by this time. After nine months, it is fair to try peanut butter on and off and some gluten-containing foods to prevent peanut and gluten sensitivity. Quinoa is an excellent grain substitute and has many positive effects on metabolism, brain, heart, and intestines. Flaxseed powder, in very small amounts, gives more amino acid balance. Dry chia seeds can be dangerous, as they go inside the little intestines and swell up and can cause emergencies of the food pipe and intestines. If any of the grains like quinoa causes gastric irritation and loose stools, please do not give that to the infant again, as saponins in quinoa can cause stomach problems with diarrhea and disturbances. If chia seeds are given, better to soak them for over five hours and germinate overnight and in small amounts. By thoroughly washing and rinsing dry quinoa grain, saponins can be washed out.

A consideration for HUD societies and communities

This opens a topic of discussion for poor communities, who cannot afford to buy organic foods; they can all get together and use community vegetable patches and gardening. It will be nice if the government can make arrangements to facilitate this through HUD and school gardening, make parents and community members help learn organic farming, and develop community kitchen gardening. Doing this through the schools with a vegetable patch and tending to the plants teaches good eating habits for growing children and also teaches love and nurture in caring for life and biological systems.

Summarization of developmental milestones by five months

Gross motor

By four to five months, infants reach for objects and roll over both sides. By five months may even creep backward with some forward movement. No bobbing of the head. Steady with neck movement. Infants develop more observation skills and gaze around the house; roll over both sides and have active grasp.

Fine motor

Infants reach for things more with radial-palmar grasp. It is OK to have ulnar-palmar grasp. Infants put objects and feet to mouth. Can have and prefer more eye-hand coordination activities with popping pals and toys.

Sensory

Infants have sense of curiosity and are eager to explore the world with happiness and sense of security and are interested in maternal expressions. Curiosity increases to reach out for objects and explore while lying down or if seated in a Bumbo, more comfortably so. These hands-on activities are needed for spatial recognition, thinking, motivation, and visual tracking. As long as the infant is offered these several times a day, hands-on sensory input goes toward higher cognitive functions. If not done, we are losing opportunities to create a cognitively oriented infant with cognitive and emotional development. A screen will not teach emotions.

Emotional

Infants learn to socially greet the faces, including strangers, with a smile and squealing. Infants can understand emotions of the caretaker or parent and change expression if mother is sad and the smile disappears. This is a lovely time that they smile for a smile and play for a play and most enjoyable moment between caretakers and the infants.

With nurture, many infants develop socially very early by this time and develop separation and stranger anxiety. Social recognition with emotional tag is a better measure of intellectual development.

Problem solving

You give a small object, and they try to keep themselves engaged with the limited skill of hands and feet that they have, and they are happy.

When parents and caretakers do not invest their time to offer and prevent the multisensory integration with hands-on activity, touch therapy, music therapy, eye contact, and hands-on exploration, the infant will have developmental delays in rolling over, reaching for things, and exploring to self-stimulate and self-soothe with happiness. Active grasp gets delayed. Emotions mature before the progress in the gross and fine motor skills. This lag in motor skills can result in future frustration. Language delay also leads to future behavior problems.

Parents and caretakers are the first teachers. Making the infant watch TV/iPad nursery tunes leads to hypersensitivity of sensory stimulation, and there is no scope for sensory integration, and a seed for childhood hyperkinetic syndrome has formed. There is overstimulation from the rapidly changing screen time while active synaptic connections are forming. Let us all focus on preventing future behavioral and learning problems. The rapidly developing synaptic connections are over stimulated from frequently changing screen, almost every five to ten seconds. This leads to hyper responsive motor and emotional pathways of wanting to move and be less reflective. Since an adult interaction is minimal, when there is screen time as a teacher, the reciprocal interaction and laying down a pathway for strategic planning are lost. It is only when a caretaker interacts and makes eye contact, praises, smiles and redirects, and helps that the full learning can be accomplished.

Chapter 7

Six Months' to Nine Months' Development

Eternal facts for this age group

The transition occurring rapidly at six months is critical for future foundations of a secure, socially adaptive, emotionally stable infant, as the neocortex or executive brain centers are making connections rapidly with the world.

Dr. H. T. Chugani's PET scan as given before shows the sparse connections sprouting to the frontal cortex by six months.

At six months, when the environment feeds the senses properly with nurture, perceptions of love, trust, security, attachment, bonding, loving care, meeting the demand, and gratification, the infant's senses send messages via the amygdala and uncus (hippocampus) to the neocortex, where messages are stored permanently. Every sensory input or signal is referenced or judged at the hippocampus level for an emotion of safety and happiness or fear and alertness. This happens without the help of the executive brain to form future states of mind as soon as social awareness develops in the infant.

At six months, infants are just beginning to make connections of first emotions of fear and separation anxiety that are making permanent memory from the limbic system to the portion of the brain that is lying on the eye sockets called orbitofrontal cortex.

The primitive messages and reflexive behaviors are at the subcortical level, or lower brain level. It is very important for the infant to feel happy and safe to make the robust, thick cortical or higher-functioning brain connections that are sprouting visibly on imaging studies by six months.

If at this stage, fear, insecurity, rejection or lack of belongingness, lack of love, inconsistent and chaotic home environment, loud noises, angry parents, custody battles with anger in either spouse, or drug and alcohol addiction and inebriation in parents or caretakers occurs in the proximal (immediate living) environment of the infant, the infant will not connect to the neocortex, which is the seat of human excellence and executive functions.

1. The pathways that connect the hippocampus for emotional learning and intellectual learning get arrested with an emotional tag of fear, insecurity, lack of self-trust, and poor self-regulation or self-soothing permanently.

2. These pathways have dopamine receptors that make dopamine, acetylcholine, and glutamatergic chemical transmitters that are responsible for emotions and learning.

3. Dopamine and serotonin are needed for learning and a state of happiness.

4. Dopamine fires at twice the speed from midbrain to frontal lobe, as compared to firing from hindbrain or lower brain to midbrain. Intellectual learning and cognitive associations get compromised. This will lead to learning and focus and sustained attention span disorders.

Latest studies are under way to find out about the exact role of dopamine in learning and drug addiction.

5. Learning disorders from toxic fear and anxiety on the suppressed neural network pathways creates states of mind that can lead to traits of poor biosocial behaviors and cognitive abilities.

6. Parents need to invest their time and energy on learning the techniques of nurture without any additional expensive fancy toys, gadgets, and equipment, but they need to become the first teachers. They need to educate themselves on the current available knowledge, effective parenting skills without regimental limit setting, and tools and techniques to overcome their own weak points.

7. Quantitative dopamine receptor deficiency as a result of failed and disturbed dispersed pathways from the amygdala and uncus (in general, limbic system) to neocortex at a later stage in life leads to youth health-risk behaviors, including tobacco, drugs, alcohol, impulsivity and hyperactivity, and poor anger management. This is because the body is trying to find happiness and fulfillment from outside the body, secondary to quantitative dopamine deficiency and poor delegation of regulatory function to lower brain centers. This is a lifetime structural and behavioral change. Brain plasticity allows remodeling but not thick fibers like in the zero-to-five-year stage.

8. The brain centers for positive reward system and motivation get desensitized and structurally are replaced with systems that are resistant to reward, seeking more and more substance as a reward or more electronics usage for pleasure rather than having sustained focus on learning.

9. These are because of molecular changes and structural changes leading secondarily to behavioral changes. Given the right path early on, permanent pathways for optimal biosocial behaviors can be established.

All systems mature by the ninth month to eighteenth month, and the roots for future positive or negative behaviors have begun sprouting. This transitional period is a critical period to get all counseling from the providers.

Six months' development

Gross motor skills

At six months

1. Infant are able to move and get into things and, when offered with novelty each time, eager to learn than before. Infants may or may not need support to sit but, in a Bumbo or in a playpen or Pack 'n Play, will reach and exchange object with radial-palmar grasp and will eagerly play with toys in a self-contained safe environment.

2. After a day, another small toy may be needed, as they need new stimulus. Infants can retrieve a toy from a big container and may have difficulty putting it back and, given the chance, will put it down.

3. Infants have learned to exchange objects between both hands and play pat–a-cake.

4. On the floor, they can roll over to places and, given the opportunity, will creep.

5. Can call, first, backward and then forward. This is called military crawl.

6. By seven months, they have expertise on that, and by eight to nine months can actually crawl on all fours.

7. By that time, infant can sit by self and play with toys and get up and cruise around holding on to furniture.

Fine motor skills

1. Infants need to be stimulated by offering matching shapes, little puzzles with pegs, textured toys for feel, scope for pat-a-cake, and rolling objects down from a wide-mouthed container and put them back into a wide-mouthed cup or container.

2. They like to find hidden things and are able to play peekaboo.

3. Plays with popping pals and likes a face and tries to pat for that particular face to pop up.

4. Plays pat-a-cake and knows when clapping is done to reward the infant.

Social adaptation

1. Adaptively, they do develop fear of heights and fall.

2. They become emotionally bonded with primary caretaker and cry when they are out of sight.

3. Separation and stranger anxiety suddenly makes them cry with a shrill cry at night, and this frightens the parents. Infant needs redirection, and the negative cry can be blocked out through redirections and interactions.

Parents should take precautions for no screen time for nursery rhymes but use iPad only for the purpose of hearing rhymes. It is always better if the primary caretaker whom they are attached to does the interactive singing and talking (parentese) and spends that quality time than falling back on electronic gadgets.

Six months is a critical transition phase in child development

This is a critical time for kidney maturity, blood systems maturity, gastrointestinal maturity, social maturity, immune system maturity, cognitive associations, and emotional maturity.

A provider has to teach parents how to address all of the above functions and remove the myths associated with them.

Right action: role of parents in nurture with no expensive toys

What is the role of the parent to stimulate and unleash that intellectual person from the infant (Einstein, Newton, Michelangelo, Picasso, Freud, Jean Piaget, Shinicchi Suzuki, Mozart, and many more)?

1. Caretaker should refrain from TV and any screen device to teach. The sacrifice a parent has to make is to cut out their own TV time while the infant is awake and in their arms.

Activities:

a. Have quality floor time, face time; sit and help the infant to get to hands-on activities.

b. Animated interaction while singing rhymes make them participate with joy.

c. Have pegged wooden puzzle toys with animal, planes, cars, alphabets, shapes, and numbers. This also teaches sequential organization for motor systems.

d. Popping pals with music; one can notice an infant likes a face and, with a memory from previous task, goes toward the same popping pal.

e. Sing melodies, alphabet rhymes, number rhymes; help by making associations. For example: every letter has a sound—*A* says "ah" as in apple, and make the infant touch apple; *B* says "ba," and make the infant touch ball; likewise for many articles that are cheap and sitting around the house and on the body, like *H* for hands, hair, head, and so on. This hands-on association is important, not the flash cards.

f. Flash cards cannot give procedural and declarative memory. The "*H* says 'h' as in hands, hair, or head" is more sensible than showing a horse on a flash card or book. This type of stimulus helps develop language and make cognitive associations.

g. This quality parenting time is critical as the infant responds well to the primary caretaker's teaching to learn. Feeling the alphabet and the object while naming the object is multisensory integration.

h. Read books for many reasons from phonemes presentation to naming parts of the body, social and emotional development, days of the week, and sequential organization of thinking through stories.

i. All information is going into the brain, called "bottom up," and "top down" is the behavioral outcome noticed after two years to three years.

Anxiety guidance

1. The parent has to shift the role from a caretaker to a teacher now and teach a sense of security, self-reliance, and self-regulation to make the infant overcome stranger anxiety and separation anxiety. An anxious brain never learns anything other than being fearful and insecure.

2. To prevent chaotic and inconsistent learning patterns, disciplines of having house rules in eating, sleeping, playtime, consistent home structure and teaching self-regulation and self-soothing are important.

3. The parent or caretaker has to realize that whatever that they are doing is for the good of the infant at this stage, as this is a critical stage when the brain is making rapid connections to the higher brain through all senses dynamically. They have to overcome the weakness of not seeing an infant cry.

4. The crying of the infant seeking negative attention becomes a weak point for parents from all sections of the society.

Understand that the states of self-soothing, self-regulation, cognitive associations, motor and sensory exploration, satisfying curiosity, memory with emotional tagging, intellectual reasoning of space, melody, visual-spatial reasoning, cognitive associations, language, and expression are all connecting dynamically at the same time. With these sensory perceptions is the association of severe emotional bonding; separation anxiety and fear of strangers also develop.

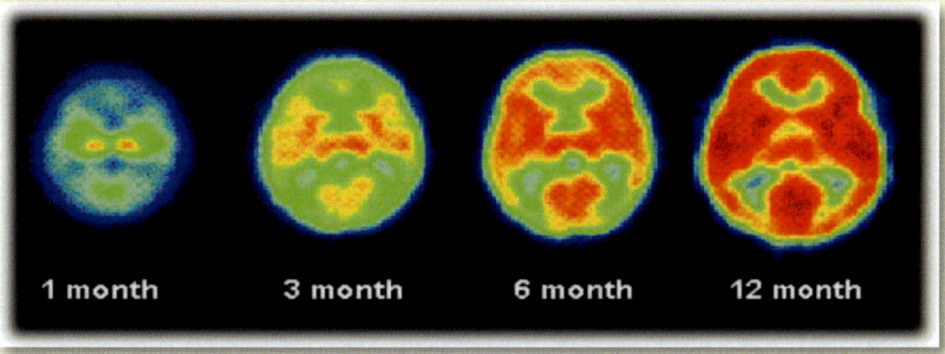

Figure 36: (A repeat for convenience; courtesy of Dr. H. T. Chugani, Nemours Institute, Delaware. The studies are from 1997 at WSU)

At six months, thin frontal lobe connections are visible in this PET scan image

To optimally utilize sensory perceptions, it is the foremost duty of **the parent to become a teacher** to teach that separation is all right, that the parent may disappear but does indeed exist and will come back.

This teaching of self-security is failing in many cultures. As long as the infant is insecure when the primary caretaker is out of sight, they stop exploring and learning but begins to cry genuinely, hoping to be picked up by the parent. Some parents take their infants to the bathroom for their natural needs, as they do not want the infant to cry. Some parents and children co-sleep till five years of age, and this is the cause for later on developing phobias, fears, and sense of insecurity, poor self-regulation, and crying behaviors among school-going children. It may work in other cultures, but in nuclear family situations, in advanced capitalistic countries like USA, this leads to insecurity in the child, leading to school phobia and poor learning.

Sleep training is a right action that is a principle duty of parents now!

Sleep training is critical at this stage. All parents love their infant, and it is their duty to understand that even if the child temporarily cries, sleep training can be accomplished in a matter of two weeks at this age and very difficult after two years.

A child at nine months is afraid to sleep alone, and a child at two years refuses to sleep alone.

Sleep training guidelines

1. Please understand and do not become weak in the heart for an infant's cry, as it is not a cry of pain or illness but of refusal to be independent and being afraid to self-soothe. Infants stop crying day or night as soon as the caretaker picks up the infant.

2. Establish a bedtime routine. If an infant had a routine by two months and maintain the routine; work hard at 6-9 months for self soothing to sleep in the crib; at each visit providers of care have to address this issue, so that the routine can be maintained when it is most needed at six months.

3. Give the last feeding for the night an hour before expected bedtime. It is advisable that all infants during their dynamic growing stages get ten hours of sleep, and bedtime is by 8:00 p.m. at the most. To do this itself takes a little sacrifice in the social life of the parents. Of course, a babysitter is a choice if parents need to go out for social hour, but infant needs to continue the routine habits. In some Eastern cultures, infants are allowed to sleep at 10:00–11:00 p.m. and it is all right from their point of view. It is hard to give proper guidelines counseling when you get a parent who is not concerned about infant sleeping at 11 PM and gets up at 12 noon. They feel it is all right.

4. Start the "white noise" while the feeding is going on and also a soothing bedtime story. Try not to over stimulate an infant at this time. No screen time like iPad or TV or iPhone as a visual stimulation. This prevents formation of melatonin, which is a hormone important for sleep cycle.

5. Take the infant to either a pitch-dark bedroom or a brightly lit room, where there will be no shadows. For this reason, do not use a night lamp or leave open the closet door with the light on. Shadows do scare infants.

6. Do not pick up from crying right away and wait for fifteen minutes before going into the room. Peek through the door and let the infant know that you are still there. Some parents cannot leave for more than five minutes, and this may not work. Anyone can smell a dirty diaper across the room to worry about soiled diaper causing the cry. Do not pick up the infant but rub the hair and walk out.

7. Infants can cry and act choking and can throw up a few times, and their voice can get hoarse. A strong-willed infant will do all of the above. Please be prepared not to panic.

8. For the first two days, the infant can cry for forty-five minutes. By the third to fifth day, it gradually goes down to thirty minutes at the most, and by the seventh day, the infant realizes that their hunger and other basic needs are met and crying will not get attention. Then they happily go to bed without fuss and will have permanent establishment of self-trust, self-soothing, self-regulation, self-worth, and security for themselves and the caretaker. These states are important foundations for the future.

9. Insecurity and poor self-regulation are permanent if they are not trained at an opportune time. Anxiety prevents learning. It is important to work on getting rid of separation anxiety.

10. An infant who self-soothed to sleep will securely sleep throughout the night, and an infant who is not sleep trained will get up half a dozen times throughout the night. This does take a toll on parents to get up several times and go to work in the morning. The spouse relationships also get disturbed.

11. Infants reach out to be picked up, cruise by this time, and are constantly exploring. This is a time when parents need to give space and self-contained places like a Pack 'n Play. This is a good space where the infant can be placed while parents are working and busy.

12. When infants are crying for the primary caretaker, they can be redirected with classical music, alphabets, number puzzles, match-the-shapes puzzles, shapes, cars, objects, animals, abacus, blocks, popping pals, and any musical toy, particularly during daytime in between naps.

13. Please redirect two times and then ignore if they are crying so that the infant realizes to make choices and gets the negative behavior blocked out.

14. Please make eye contact and give a happy clap when the infant calms down with the redirection. With this type of positive redirection, the infant develops a pattern to self-control and becomes positive in approaching the parent, and the parent is helping create pathways of self-redirection and choice making. This choice making comes from the frontal lobe, the seat of human excellence, which is actively connecting now.

15. If the infant is ignored while crying, that reinforces more of a negative high-pitched crying or withdrawal of sensory input. But if the parent gives attention in helping the infant to make a choice that is associated with hands-on learning, like visual-spatial reasoning, motor coordination with eye-hand coordination activities, counting the beads as the beads are rolled on a wire as with abacus, learning names and sounds of animals with puzzles, learning objects, it is a multisensory integration and a positive redirection. That needs to be applauded when the infant is calm with activity. The negative behavior is blocked out.

16. A hard cardboard book that was read to before easily distracts an infant from crying or getting into things. Parents can engage them in conversation while doing their chores.

17. A nine-month-old can get into dangerous situations with plug points and staircase, and parents have to make sure that the house is child safe. Pack 'n Play is a safe place than a bouncer and walker, which passively moves the objects while jumping; Pack 'n Play motivates a movement and a skill.

18. Making the infant sit at the high chair and giving a nontoxic crayon and a paper to write also enhances fine motor coordination and is a good distraction.

19. Singing the alphabet song with phonetic presentation is also a good diversion; the message goes into the brain, and the output comes as early language acquisition by eighteen months with good pragmatics and expression.

Myths about infection proneness from teething and crying with pain

One of the important developmental milestones that happen around six months and more so by nine months is the general maturity from fetal to adult form of systems.

Hemoglobin was fetal type till six months and changes to adult hemoglobin pattern that releases oxygen not rapidly but slowly enough, and oxygen dissociation curve changes.

Gastrointestinal systems mature and can tolerate some sensitivity-producing foods by nine months better than in the first six months. Milk protein casein from yogurt is well tolerated after nine months. It is fair enough to try different food groups now like gluten, peanut butter, cheese, egg yolks (nine months), barley, rye, flaxseed powder, quinoa, and beef and ham products. Still hold off on fish and egg whites till one year of age.

The immune system now loses the passive maternal antibodies that protected the infant against the most common viral infections and starts weaning off by six to nine months from 1250 micrograms/deciliter to 100 or less. As every breath takes in eighty-four thousand bugs through the nasal passages, the prevalent viruses are not neutralized by mother's antibodies anymore. The seasonal viruses invade the body and are multiplied in the tissues. A week later, they are released into the bloodstream to attack the target organs. The most common are the nose, lungs, and stomach.

There will be a fight between the tissue and blood-protecting cells (macrophages, T-cells, histiocytes, tissue necrotic factors, D53, D54, and other mediators like prostaglandins and leukotrienes). All these immunological responses create chemotactic factors that swell up the blood vessels and cause fever. Fever is a protective response that releases more of these factors that will attack the virus. They are not produced till there is a fever for seventy-two hours and keep on fighting the bug for twenty-one days.

While the immune system is busy fighting a bug, another virus invades the system and gets into tissues. There are not enough factors to attack before the virus multiplies. The infant remains OK for seven to ten days and gets invaded by another virus. If there is constant infection every four to five weeks, it is better to get immunological deficiency workup done with the primary care physician's help.

This phase gets better after the first thirty-six months and can happen even if the infant stays home.

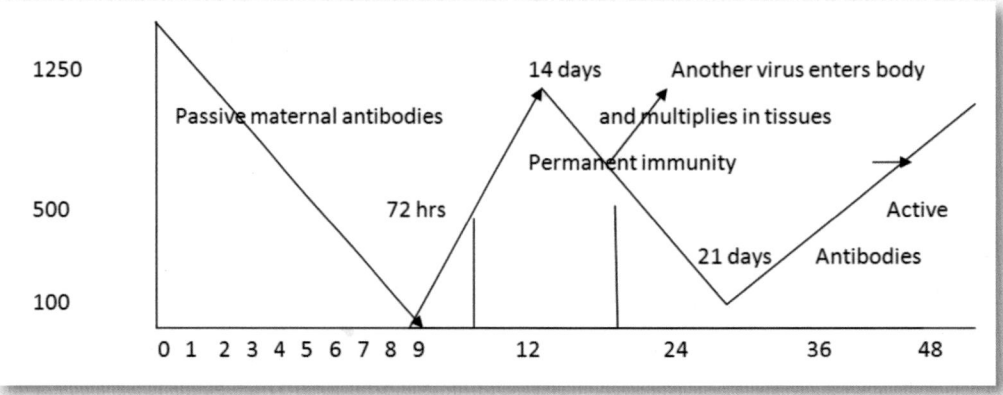

Figure 37: represents visually physiological immunodeficiency.

If the infant goes to a day care or nursery, this is more often than the usual, as an infant incubating a virus sheds it before the symptoms start, and it is a breeding place for viral infections.

Immune stimulants and antioxidants in natural state through fresh fruits and vegetables can give some protection. Teething never causes this fever, and it is physiological immunodeficiency when multiple seasonal viral infections invade the body that causes the fever. Fever helps make own antibodies called as active antibodies.

Many providers call this reoccurring upper respiratory infection phase with chronic runny nose as allergy. Other than food and dust mite, may be cat dander, the body has to be sensitized by exposing itself to a couple of seasons to get nasal allergy.

Teeth start showing up from six months, and infants will get twenty teeth by twenty-four months. That means in an eighteen-month span, an infant gets a tooth or two pop up every month. The infection cycle also is three-to-four-week cycle. Teething and infections happen at the same time, but one is not related to the other. They go hand in hand only. Fever is not from teething. Crying is also not from teething but from social emotional developmental needs.

I am hoping that parents will not use ibuprofen as their first choice, as it can suppress the TNF and other immune factors needed for killing a virus. Acetaminophen will bring temperatures down to one hundred, and low-grade temperature stimulates the immunological factors to fight the virus.

Orajel or any topical anesthetics have no role in teething discomfort, and crying is not from teething but from the social and emotional development of separation and stranger anxiety. Avoiding citrus fruits and juice, massaging gums, and providing ice cold teething ring may soothe the infant if nurture and engagement in other activities suggested do not work.

I personally feel the diagnosis of "teething syndrome" should be removed from *ICD-M (medical diagnostics coding manual)*.

Peace: how can we make an infant relax and be at peace?

1. The mother or caretaker has to be peaceful to know and understand why they are doing certain things at a very young age. Education is the major resource and a responsibility for effective parenting. Flexibility in understanding and to change and break away from old-fashioned thinking is important to create the transformation in the family and the society. Having good children, high achievers making reflective decisions in the long run, creates safe and better communities.

2. The caretaker or parent needs to feel peace within them to give peace to the infant. Infants can certainly realize parent's emotions now.

3. Parents can use music therapy and regulated nasal breathing for six seconds each for inhale, hold, and exhale, while listening to music, before a parent can get agitated. This meaningful meditation technique immediately relaxes the inner mind, and parents can feel that they can make reflective decisions. It will do feedback suppression on epinephrine, norepinephrine, and cortisol, which are the chemicals responsible for reactive behavioral symptoms of agitation and anger. This removes maternal and paternal anxiety and results in calm communication.

4. A caretaker who is always smiling and softly redirecting can make the infant get relaxed and calm.

LOVE

1. Love is expressed with hugs, kisses, and positive reinforcement with an animated clap and smile on the face.

2. This possessive love in the caretaker and parent also needs to make them understand that the need for creating a structure, discipline with love, redirection techniques while the infant is crying is to make one a self-assured individual, growing up with self-trust and respect and, in the future, capable of controlling impulsive behavior and making reflective decisions.

3. When each family unit invests their energies in this understanding and self-education with transformation, the communities get secure and safe with less youth health-risk behaviors. We are spending millions of dollars to fix problems at an age when changes are difficult to happen, while prevention strategies zero to five years are better in preventing health-risk behaviors. That is what geniuses do!

End notes for quick guidance

Twenty-four to twenty-eight weeks' development (six to seven months)

1. **Gross motor**

    Sits with lean-on-hands support

    Radial-palmar grasp; consistently grabs an object. Neat pincer grasp also develops by nine months in some children.

    Can creep or do military crawl. Rolls easily to get to grab or follow an object.

2. **Fine motor**

    Grabs objects from thumb side and tries with one hand

    Infant can push a small pellet and throw things into a big container.

    Plays pat-a-cake and develops peek-a-boo game skills by nine months

3. **Adaptive**

    Exchanges object from one hand to another and able to look up at parent for reciprocity

    Begins to identify self in a picture and shows excitement

    Taps into caretaker's emotions

    Communicates with toys through expression

Indicates pleasure with foods and sitting at the dining table with the family

4. **Language**

    Limited to phonemic recognition and mimics "mmm" sounds

5. **Personal, social, emotional**

    Demands negative attention by crying with insecurity

    Separation and stranger anxiety

    Responds or reacts to mother's emotions

Thirty-two to thirty-six weeks (eight to nine months)

1. **Gross motor**

    From military crawl moves to rocking on knees and finally alternates knees to crawl forward

    Cruises around furniture and gets up with support and can take steps when held by hands

    Some infants walk independently by this age.

2. **Fine motor**

    Uses thumb finger grasp and enjoys more with finger foods

    Explores the abacus and rolls the beads

    Able to put big cardboard and wooden puzzles into the slots and explores shapes and matching and tries to push object through the holes of shapes

    Parents need to take this opportunity to make the infant touch and feel foods and encourage that sensory integration to various textures of finger foods, raw and cooked.

    The natural response is to put food into the mouth. This does not have to be commercial puffs, but food preparations that are offered can be touched, three small portions from the tray, while the caretaker is feeding the rest directly.

    Pat-a-cake is enjoyed more with hand movements.

    Infant likes to play a musical instrument crudely like piano, drums, and violin.

3. **Adaptive**

    Infant identifies objects that are pleasant and have liking.

    Infant is able to match objects and in spatial relationship like match the shapes.

    Looks expectantly at familiar adults to read and play

Puts blocks in big cups and explores the spatial reasoning

Swings and acknowledges rhythm and knows a clap as a reward or praise

Loves self-feeding

4. **Language**

    Social communication is not easy unless the parent prepares the infant. Stranger anxiety precludes immediate social smile but can say "mama" and "dada" and "bye."

    The infant knows parts of the body and points to body parts when asked.

    This is a good time to start reading books with animation or emotional content to the narration.

    Continue adult speech and the musical rhymes, rhythms, and numbers.

    What is going into the brain will be retained.

    Four to five books per day and exposure to music

5. **Social, personal, emotional**

    Stranger apprehension takes over the behavior unless sleep-training and anxiety-overcoming strategies are done.

    Can wave bye-bye and may say a couple of more words

    Happy to identify self in the mirror and communicates with the infant in the mirror

    Prefers to get up several times and wants to co-sleep with parent.

    Sleep training was explained in an earlier chapter with emotional development guidelines.

    Taking the infant to places where there are adult strangers but with the parent securely around need to learn social skills. Typically, public library programs like My Baby Can Read infant and toddlers program, Mother's Day Out program, a two to three half-day care setup, and Barnes & Noble program for reading facilitation are good things to do so that infant gets over separation anxiety.

CHAPTER XIX

Infant Development, Twelve Months to Eighteen Months

Truth: what are the dynamic changes happening? These are not changeable.

At nine months, an infant who barely started crawling and holding on rapidly progresses to repetitiously standing and falling and trying to walk by twelve months. There is persistence despite of repeated falls. Why then is a school-going child giving up easily on task-oriented behavior, and what happened to this persistence?

Something happens in an infant's perceptions by the eighteenth month to either give up or persist after a task. If we can all learn how to nurture the persistence and steer the senses toward a goal, we will have all children in a mold of excellence in all domains of health. It is a challenge for busy parents, but extended family support systems also need to invest time and energy to protect and nurture the inherent talents of an infant and block the negative behaviors in a fun-filled atmosphere.

Dr. Adrian Raine did fMRI studies two decades ago, a prospective study on over thirteen thousand infants. He showed how important it is to develop the social awareness and emotional stability in a strange environment, interacting with an adult stranger with the caretaker present on site, to promote communication and language development skills.

A point to understand here is that the parent will be present and ascertaining that the infant is not leaping into the lap of a stranger but is making the infant comfortable in the strange environment with fearlessness and less anxiety. This is a critical stage of apprehension with separation and stranger anxiety between six and eighteen months, that prevents a child from exploring the environment and learning from the environmental stimuli, unless parent or caretaker teaches the infant to overcome separation anxiety and stranger anxiety. Social mingling and exposure and reading clubs like at public library or Barnes & Noble story time are good for this purpose. There are infant music classes that start teaching from twelve to eighteen months of age, like Gymboree kind of fun places where early school readiness programs are available. Most important aspect is the sleep training. In some Pre-K schools, infants are getting trained in breathing exercises and Yoga/meditation(Tuning In time)

Gross motor

1. The infant crawls at nine months and, given the opportunity, starts cruising around furniture and takes two to three steps alone by twelve months.

2. Squats and runs by fifteen months

3. Can throw a ball overhand definitely by one year

4. Helps the parent dress up by twelve months and definitely by fifteen months

5. Builds a tower with three cubes by fifteen months

6. Feels comfortable holding a crayon and can draw crazy lines but feels content for allowing scribbles on a paper (not on the wall or floor)

7. The infant can walk upstairs one foot at a time without help by eighteen months and comes down creeping or when hand is held, one step at a time.

8. Kicks a ball by eighteen months

Fine motor

1. Can explore small-mouthed containers and develop a pincer grasp to hold a small object and place the object in a small-mouthed container by twelve months. This is an important visual-spatial reasoning technique to foster.

2. Plays with abacus and rolls beads on a wire while learning numbers and counting

3. Self-feeds with fingers and trying to hold and manipulate a spoon

4. Picks up shapes and puzzles to match

5. Tries to draw lines with nontoxic crayons

6. Starts vertical stacking of three blocks by fifteen months, definitely three or more by eighteen months

7. Can place blocks in big cups and explores concepts of in and out as a visual-spatial reasoning game

8. Can use a spoon to scoop by fifteen to eighteen months and fork by eighteen months. Prefers self-feeding.

9. Can put on a shirt or pull up pants by eighteen months. Autonomy is very important.

Adaptive functions

1. By 15 months to 18 months, the infant can learn body parts, numbers one to five, and, through stories and music, days of the week and alphabets (for example, *Bear about Town* and Dr. Seuss's books).

2. These books also teach a pattern of sequential organization, as in *Are You My Mother?* Story, where the bird first went to a kitten, to a dog, and, finally, to the snort.

3. Reading teaches memory and organization and promotes curiosity, sequencing, and motivation to know more.

4. Children learn to point to characters in books and can sit and pretend reading a book by themselves by eighteen months.

5. Points to objects when needed

6. When encouraged, may even develop jargon at fifteen months and to specific thirty words by eighteen months.

7. A simple sentence construction is possible only through parent's constant interaction and exposure to music therapy.

Parents will agree that by eighteen months, an infant sits down, reading the book by himself or herself from rote memory. This motivation is not related to economic background but to parent's investment of quality time. Books are for free from the library, and there are many library programs, free of cost, to be utilized by the public.

If every parent and caretaker gets to utilize these programs with an understanding, won't the whole world be a smart and peaceful place?

For an infant to perform these skills, express them, and show eagerness, a constant mutual reciprocal relationship with positive redirection, guidance, and involvement with the primary caretaker is very important. They trust the primary caretaker. Ideally, if every parent gets to be this primary caretaker, we will have an ideal society.

Rich frontal lobe connections and higher brain functions occur between twelve and eighteen months.

Emotional and social development

1. The infant starts first emotions by six months with fear of strangers and separation anxiety.

2. This leads to crying spells when the parent disappears and is out of sight.

3. The frontal lobe is making associations from the environment very rapidly to create states of fear, trust, security, anxiety, dependency, anticipation, communication through body language, emotional response to caretakers' emotions, acceptance of peer interaction, and vulnerability.

The above emotions are forming rapidly, and we see the behavioral outcomes only after the second year of life. There will be *reactive* behaviors as a first reaction, and it is through authoritative parenting skills that an infant can learn a *responsive* behavior. This mostly is a process of operant conditioning than a reasoning technique now, as the only communication are crying and a temper tantrum. Infants by this time are making the connections to the frontal lobe, which will create executive functions of self-control, but not mature enough to self-control unless they are steered toward making healthy choices and rewarding them. The reward system has to be that of a positive acknowledgement and not a food, like ice cream, candy, or a TV show. A clap, smile, stamp, recognition, praise, and a hug go a long way to bring a smile on an infant's face.

Infant needs to be guided to make choices and remembers the rewards that a healthy choice gets. This stimulates the internal locus, a brain center that exists for a reward system, of an infant to make right decisions. **Reactions come from the lower brain centers like the brain stem and midbrain.** Impulse control, anger control, and self-soothing come from higher brain centers. This happens through a parent who becomes a teacher to teach healthy choices and gives rewards for making the healthy choice. Redirect from anger and crying to motivate an infant to think and be happy in redirecting attention. When redirected with positive response and a good choice, rewarding the infant makes it very pleasant.

Use music therapy, an activity, and redirection with books, rhymes, phonics, and writing on paper with crayons. Music teaches good emotions and language. Pleasant feelings come from pleasing, joyous music.

How to handle some negative behaviors

Prevent mismanagement of attention-seeking eating behaviors

Eating

Eating becomes a concern at this age, as the infant prefers self-feeding. The parent feels that the infant is eating like a bird and losing weight as bones stick out. Infants have a phase from twelve months till puberty to eat to their growth needs. ***They do not grow steadily like ten inches in the first year of life, and triple or gain weight four times over birth weight. They grow two inches per year and gain five pounds per year after their first birthday***. This is ideal growth velocity or growth rate. When they are growing, they eat two meals fairly well; the rest of the time, they dawdle and throw food around. Certainly, they get attention from the parent with an iPad, cartoons, bribes, and substitutions to make an infant eat. If we respect the growth need, we certainly can prevent **obesity** and eating disorders like anorexia nervosa and bulimia.

   a. At this age, no bottles after twelve months, and all food and liquids to be served at the dining table.

   b. Twenty minutes on timer to be set for eating needs, and when the alarm goes off, food is thrown and no substitution till next the mealtime. No threats, no eye contact, and no bribes to be used by parents. Parents should not feel guilty for setting rules and not forcing infant to eat. This is a common weak point for moms, dads, and caretakers.

   c. Cut down the milk consumption to sixteen to eighteen ounces ideally. Do not give milk with a meal. If infant is offered milk with a meal, easy calories are obtained from milk that they have been drinking a lot in the first two months of their life, and the satiety center in the brain tells the body that the calories are filled, appetite goes away, and the infant will not eat. Milk should be given ideally between breakfast and lunch, between lunch and supper, and an hour before bedtime. I usually pick 9:00 a.m., 3:00 p.m., and one hour before bedtime.

   d. Cookies and crackers and cheese snacks will cut the appetite for good nutritious food. Ideally, try to give small fruits like berries, peaches, plums, or nectarines as snacks, as they have good minerals for brain, tissue, and bone growth and immune systems (luteins, carotene, and antioxidants).

   e. Do not substitute foods a little later, as the "poor baby" did not eat food. A very small snack like an inch of a cookie will kill the appetite for the next meal. One-year-olds need only 1,100 calories, and they get it all in small frequent portions on three major meals and two snacks.

f. The eating and toilet training is under the control of the infant, and infants can try to get a lot of inadvertent negative attention if parents are not strong. Infants are usually strong-willed and are born to learn. **Negative perceptions are quickly picked up with a perception of acceptance when parents are not equally strong-willed with love, care, nurture, and dare to discipline. " You give an inch and they take the whole tent"**

g. If there are genes for cancer or diabetes in the family, the poor eating practices are creating grounds through messenger RNA tagging and transcribing it on to the DNA expression. Genes do get turned on from experiences in the environment. This can certainly be prevented if environment and nourishment are carefully planned with good mealtime practices from parents to child.

h. Intensive self-education by parents is needed to make healthy food choices.

i. Proactive parents need to learn more about the role of cur cumin (turmeric), avocados, carotene-containing foods, colored fruits , availability of antioxidants in blue and black berries, pomegranates, calming melatonin from kiwi fruits and dates, kale, collard greens, spinach, zucchini, broccoli and broccolini, cucumbers, protein-rich foods like quinoa, flax seeds, soaked chia seeds (never eat dry chia seeds), black beans, hummus, garbanzo beans, freshwater fish for omegas, and lean turkey and chicken. Heavy greasy foods like ham and beef can cause cancer proneness. Apples and bananas have more white carbohydrates to offset the nutritional content.

j. Forced feeding can cause future anorexia nervosa and bulimia kind of eating disorders.

k. A hungry infant or child will eat, a tired infant-child will sleep, and a child who has to excrete will excrete. This is autonomic and is controlled by brain centers, and as long as the infant is gaining four to five pounds per year, growing two inches per year, and actively talking, playing, and communicating, parents should only set some rules and implement them with love and self-confidence and not with a weakness in the heart.

l. I have seen many desperate parents who resort to iPhone music and cartoons during feeding time, and it has its own negative impact on brain organization, particularly in creating an over stimulated brain and poor communication and poor motivation. It is good to narrate a rhyme, story or engage interpersonal communication. It is ideal if all eat at the dining table at the same time.

Language

An infant who has been babbling and squealing learns to imitate adult speech sounds. Infants learn to know and say specific "mama" and "dada" by nine to ten months, say three words other than "mama" and "dada" by twelve months, have thirty-word vocabulary and simple sentences by eighteen months, and say two hundred words and complex sentences by two years.

Language development should happen through interaction with the caretaker whom they trust and live with rather than through a word application on iPad or TV shows. The contentment with emotional tag with primary caretaker interaction and animation and through floor-time activities makes infants thrive in language and emotional and social development. Not promoting this pathway but screen exposure to make an infant learn leads to more language delay, sleep disorder, and social-emotional developmental disorders. An average infant is watching two to four hours of television, which has become a babysitter while parents are busy with household chores. This can also lead to hyperkinetic child behavior, poor impulse control, apathy, and poor communication skills.

If only a parent can engage an infant to alphabet song, teach them to make associations with body parts or tangible objects, make an eye contact, and teach while working, that relational bonding motivates an infant than a screen that has no emotions. Only a three-to-ten-minute redirection is all that is required. This can be done with numbers, reading books, crayons, music, playing musical instruments, puzzles, rhymes and patterns, which are all educational, and it is critical for the parent to be that teacher or an extended family member as a caretaker to be the primary teacher. This quality time is very effective than the hours spent at day-care centers and in front of TV or iPad.

Problem solving

Many puzzles, Legos, and blocks with hands-on activities are available, from simple blocks and little puzzles with pegs to many wooden educational toys that help create spatial reasoning and self-contentment and build self-confidence. This activity enhances future math and geometrical skills and has a direct correlation for cognitive development. Music is also important for mathematical skills. Building alphabet trains and phonemic associations with daily tangible objects make cognitive associations and learning easier. An example is using "h" sound, as in hands, hair, head, is more of a tangible association than showing a horse on a flash card.

Investment by caretakers/parents: what can parents do?

Truth that will not change

1. The brain is the hardware that is making very rapid programming through the five senses with social awareness, cognitive, intellectual and emotional learning. Every emotional state is a permanent pathway and hard wire in the brain. Senses are the software creating broad bands from outside to inside, from lower centers to higher centers of the brain (bottom up).

2. Unless a parent is aware of their primary responsibility in protecting this phase of development from vulnerability, fear, anxiety, and poor self-confidence to self-control, redirection to making choices, and engaging in happy mood, the infant will hard wire to negative frame of mind and behavior.

3. Autonomy needs to be promoted every step of the way, and it is a rapid dynamic growth. Sleep training is also important to promote inner peace and learning to communicate.

4. Witnessing violence on screen, domestic violence, and brain trauma (psychologically) from any cause are permanent negative prints in the state of an infant's mind. In this state, further connections to higher intellectual brain suffer, leading to future learning disorder and poor self-regulation. Even the brain structure permanently gets altered.

5. Social and emotional stability helps develop communication skills.

6. Parents need to learn effective parenting skills and iron out their differences without using anger as a problem-solving technique. Even if there are two homes, keep a consistent structure in between both homes.

7. Prevent toxic stress on infant's perception.

Right action: this is an overall repetition as a summary of parents' duties.

1. Role of the parents and caretakers after six months, by nine months, is to become the first teachers in a critical rapid transition phase in child development.

2. Structuring the home environment for feeding, playing, sleeping, eating, and doing hands-on activities are important for permanent hard wiring of a certain pattern for learning and living.

3. Chaotic timings for various activities and biological needs lead to confusion in an infant and more unexplained crying, seeking negative attention. Poor sleep and eating habits also confuse the sprouting brain pathways leading to irritability and confusion.

4. Parents do need to understand and implement sleep training as soon as separation anxiety is noticed.

5. Engage in music and activities, free of cost at most of the public library systems, Barnes & Noble, Gymboree (an infant activity center for early school readiness), and similar activity centers, for social and emotional development

6. Music therapy should continue along with small puzzle activities and moving the beads on an abacus. This enhances eye-hand coordination, visual-spatial reasoning, and problem solving skills.

7. Crying should not be ignored, but use redirection by offering a couple of toys a couple of times. When infants crawl to get into trouble and refuse to be redirected for activities, immediately place the infant in a contained area like a Pack 'n Play. Infants usually cry to be in a self contained area.

8. When infant stops crying for attention, immediately pick up the infant. Use a self-contained area like a Pack 'n Play right in the center of the family room. This can happen in some children twenty times a day, and persistence and love pays off!

9. Infants definitely notice the deprivation of free movement in a self-contained environment and learn that the crying did not get any attention, a choice was given, and the good, joyful interaction got attention. This learned feeling becomes a behavioral expression of self-control and choice making later on after two and a half to three years of life.

10. It is ideal for parents to spend more floor time and face time with eye contact, teach phonics by feeling the alphabets, and make associations with daily-use objects that are felt by hands by rolling beads and learning numbers, colors, and counting. Playing with stackable blocks and shapes and matching shapes, pattern recognition, and puzzles lead to better cognitive skills. All of the above activities promote reasoning, spatial recognition, math processing, language abilities, and cognitive associations.

Peace

1. Peace of an infant is based on the environmental stability, parent relationships, and spouse bonding, which is congenial.

2. The immediate surroundings need to promote happiness and relational interaction to make the infant feel stable, particularly with the caretaker's interactions with the infant.

3. Music therapy always is soothing and peaceful even at this age and more so at this stage. Music has to be soft and soothing, not high-pitched metallic sounds.

4. Infants act from brain stem reactive states with aggression, crying, temper, and anger and make connections with prefrontal cortex or higher brain with the help of a peaceful, calm parent who is redirecting to higher brain functions. Infants under four years of age are unable to process but have mirror cells that imitate and learn from adult caretakers. This is a very important function that seems to be missing in autism. Is it the result or the cause?

5. Children exposed to excessive screen time and electronics develop a lot of networks but mostly in the lower brain centers and not the executive brain centers. If a parent is not sitting, watching, and creating pathways of positive responsive development, the synaptic proliferation does not become a pathway of responsive brain but a reflexive, reacting brain and behavior.

6. My main goal of reiterating this information is to make parents and caretakers aware of how important it is for them to be peaceful, calm, and happy and be authoritative in redirecting an infant by blocking negative behaviors while steering the infant into purposeful, happy interactive playtime sessions and games.

Love

1. Love is a Meta energy that is felt through body language, smiles, and tender touch.

2. Caretaker's tension and anger can be felt by the infants through facial expressions, and they become sensitive to a sad face or angry face as young as four to six months. A six-month-old will quiver and pout and cry when the primary caretaker is sad and crying. **This social response is the primary cause for tuning out the sensory input, and stress and fear reactions start**.

3. Love is expressed through a smiling face, through interactive parents, when demands are met in a timely fashion, and through soft voice for communication, tender touch, and playing with the infant on the floor. A soul is seen through the eyes and Meta energy of love is transmitted through **"Eye contact"**.

4. Empathy develops by six to nine months in an infant through the hippocampus area and corpus striatum centers, and if, for any reason, these centers are arrested in stress, fear, or anxiety, the empathy and sympathy will be lost to fear and anxiety. The sense of reward is also lost (Poor sensitivity to reward).

CHAPTER X

Infant from 18 Months to 36 Months

From eighteen months to thirty-six months, there is dynamic socio-cultural, intellectual, cognitive, linguistic, and emotional development. Infants develop some comprehension of consequences of their emotions and actions. Every moment is a dynamic learning process at this stage.

1. Infant have a ***meaningful association*** of themselves in their environment.

2. Infants have established an ***identity of self*** with some pride and possessiveness.

3. This leads to further attaching themselves emotionally with caretakers, demanding their attention even if it is a negative behavior of temper and screaming.

4. Their attachment goes to the extent of ***possessiveness of physical objects*** and not sharing anything that belongs to them.

5. Their reactive brain can unleash on people taking or touching their objects.

6. They also have enough empathy to share with sibling edible treats but not toys or objects.

7. ***This personal ego-filled identity of the self with objects, persons, and possessiveness also makes association from experiences from the environment about loss, grief, anxiety, fears, and insecurity, which will lead to more negative acting-out behaviors and aggression.***

8. If there is difficulty in expressive language development (limited lexicon/pragmatics), poor social adaptations occur.

9. Some common behaviors are biting, hitting, and screaming.

10. This state of ego and superego has its own consequences if pathways of adaptive behaviors are not addressed by caretakers.

A loving, smiling infant who has a natural state of sympathy, empathy, and love can get opposite thoughts, feelings, emotions, in verbal and nonverbal communication, filled with actions of apathy, jealousy, hatred, anger, and avoidance behaviors. They become very sensitive to the aversive sensory stimulation, from foods to social and emotional interactions, language, and communication.

This is a critical time in child development to create the pathways of self-control, autonomy, self-confidence, and trust on caretakers, sensory gratitude of touching and feeling various foods from hand to mouth, motivation, curiosity, inquiry, exploration, social interaction, communication, and a need to live in a state of happiness. This is a period when the infant is totally dedicated to the parent's or caretaker's love and limit setting.

1. ***Positive virtues inculcated through direct caretaker's interaction become the foundation for the future traits of personality development and cognitive development.***

2. Infants learn from a caretaker with whom they have established familiarity and trust, not from a screen without emotional interaction. Parent needs to sit with the child and discuss a positive value from the show or else it is motion, E-motion, action and reaction.

3. Screen time cannot teach a value or a consequence, and the frontal lobe of the infant is not well established to process information.

4. The moving screen of the cartoons over stimulates the synaptic connections, and unless a caretaker has the knowledge and patience to redirect in a positive way, the pathways are not formed.

5. A caretaker creating a positive reward system, helping the child make a healthy choice, teaches how to self-regulate the impulsive emotional reactive behavior.

6. Reflective behavior comes from the executive brain, which is still not well formed in this age group.

Formation of neocortex connections is based on the redirection in a state of calmness with music therapy, redirecting with a positive reward system for a positive choice (it can be a stamp or a sticker; stamp is better, as there will be no peeling and choking).

Authoritative parenting fostering human values and virtues, while nurturing the senses to extract the inherent genius and the inherent strengths in the infant, is a permanent pathway.

With the modern IT knowledge and accessing any books on parenting, it is confusing for the parents to pick a parenting style. The modern IT helps parents download all applications from phonics to games and educational TV shows. The screen time had taken over emotional interaction between the primary caretakers and the infant. Majority of the time, parents are on their iPhone and the kids are playing games on iPad or watching shows before the doctor walks into the room. The waiting time might not have been more than twenty minutes or less.

In the old days, I remember parents brought books; we had children's books that were being read as the doctor walked in. Somewhere along mid-1990, the trend with electronics increased, and we see increased prevalence of ADHD and autism spectrum disorders.

For the last two decades, we have enough neuroscience literature and fMRI studies giving scientific evidence that music and puzzles and caretaker as the teacher have enhanced the inherent strengths in the fields of physical health, emotional, psychological, and intellectual wellness, and mathematical and cognitive development. Screen time seems to have caused attrition of the gray matter and thin white matter, leading to learning disorders, poor communication, hyperkinetic child syndrome, poor processing, poor attention span, impulsivity, and, more than likely, autism spectrum disorder.

Eighteen months' development

Gross motor skills

1. At eighteen months, an infant can walk and run and squat.

2. Kicks a ball and throws ball overhand

3. Walks upstairs one foot at a time, not holding hands
4. Needs help to pull up pants and put on a shirt
5. Prefers to feed self with a spoon and fork

Fine motor

1. At eighteen months, can stack at least four to six cubes
2. Enjoys putting simple puzzles together, like five large pieces
3. Turns a few pages of a book at a time

Language and communication

1. At eighteen months, with a good foundation and with no screen time, infants can pick up thirty words and make simple sentences.

Social-emotional development

1. At eighteen months, infant should be strong and self-assured to play and interact socially while in the presence of parents in a strange environment.
2. They know how to greet and shake hands or give high five.
3. They cooperate when rules are laid down and try to manipulate to test the consistency in expectations from actions and expression. It is the duty of the parent to enforce rule with authoritative parenting skills consistently and persistently.
4. Infants enjoy reading with parent and time spent with the parent even if it is few hours of quality time in the evenings. Those bedtime stories help a lot.
5. If the sleep training is not done, by eighteen months, infants become insecure, which leads to poor self-regulation and poor self-esteem. Fear of separation and anxiety take over, and the brain does not proceed to connect well to prefrontal cortex, which makes cognitive associations, memory, and processing. Attention and focus to task are lost.
6. Like in a symphony, the brain connects from sensory input from lower brain to higher brain functions smoothly. The hierarchical processing and connecting to higher brain gets arrested in the hippocampus and corpus striatum nucleus with fear and anxiety, which leads to poor cognitive development and poor communication skills. Increased irritability and poor sleep patterns are the result of this arrest.
7. TV/iPad/iPhone and any screen time make this worse. There is direct correlation between screen time and poor social behavior, poor communication, and language development behaviors (Lin, Zhou). Ideally, it is better to have caretaker-and-child interaction while teaching with hands-on learning, on the floor with face-to-face interaction. A machine cannot give emotions while narrating a story and judge the emotional development and allay fears that a caretaker can provide.

8. It is nice to prevent ADHD, autism spectrum behaviors, and sensory processing disorders through effective parenting skills and get trained in understanding how the brain and neurobiology, sensory input, and nurture impact personality developmental foundation from zero to three years.

9. In my practice in the last twenty-eight years, I have seen poor improvement of ADHD and autism spectrum behaviors until screen time is stopped and earned back with reward system for no more than twenty to thirty minutes per day (five years and older). References given for the adverse effect of screen time.

10. Parents should focus on the appropriate social development early in life, starting at nine months as recommended in earlier chapter.

Problem solving

1. At eighteen months, all is fantasy and excitement. Reality is accepted with hesitation by three years. Make-believe friends are real for them, and people think they have psychotic disorder.

2. For example, a rope will be considered as a snake at eighteen months and will cause panic, although object is not moving.

3. Infants can put small puzzles together and can try blocks with different designs by the third year of life.

4. Infants can decide on good versus bad choices by the thirty months to third year of life and can start making transactions for self-satisfaction and rewards.

Two-year development

Gross motor

1. Throws a ball through a basket made for children
2. Pulls up pants and puts on a shirt
3. Runs and walks without falling
4. Kicks a ball and throws well a ball overhand
5. Goes upstairs alternating feet but comes down one foot at a time without fear
6. Enjoys outdoors for swinging, slides, and playing ball

Fine motor

1. Turns the pages of a book one page at a time
2. Builds a tower of seven cubes while counting
3. Stabilizes fork and spoon from turning upside down or tilting sideways

Adaptive functions

1. Knows vertical and horizontal concepts but cannot combine both vertical and horizontal
2. Builds a horizontal train with blocks and vertical separately stacked up to eight or more blocks

Language and communication

1. Has a two-hundred-word vocabulary and a complex sentence with a subject and a predicate
2. Knows prepositions well
3. Reads books from memory. Make-believe and role-play activities and expressions are more common.
4. The imaginative, creative play is so real that they are some experiences picked up from real life and used to allay the fears and anxieties. They talk to these figures.

Personal social

1. Still insecure to leave parent and play independently
2. Requires parent nearby to learn in a relaxed fashion
3. Able to have basic understanding of emotions and is able to comprehend and express emotions of sadness, fear, joy, and anxiety
4. Very ego filled to get all attention and unable to share objects and becomes more possessive of people, objects, and personal toys.
5. At twenty-four months, still it is easy to believe rope as snake, although some reality concept occurs. Reality is still a partial creative imagination, and they can easily believe in unrealistic expectation.
6. Fairies and elves exist, and animals can talk. Humans can fly, and horses can have wings and fly.
7. Darkness and shadows create fears now. Night terrors happen and are normal.

Three-year development

Gross motor

1. Goes upstairs and downstairs, alternating the feet
2. Can ride a tricycle as infant and can alternate the feet on pedals
3. Can do bunny hops with both feet

Fine motor

1. Can have a good crayon and pencil grip
2. Can draw a vertical line and horizontal line
3. Can imitate or draw a circle

Adaptive function

1. Makes a tower with ten cubes
2. Can combine horizontal and vertical lines concept
3. Can make a bridge with three to five cubes if shown
4. Has a concept of face on drawing and gives it a name
5. Can play basketball well
6. Knows small and large and makes associations with objects and real-life situations
7. An infant who can look at cathedral ceiling and explains that as a triangle is smarter than one who simply identifies shapes. The three-dimensional concepts are well developed at this stage.

Language

1. Completes comprehensive sentences with expression
2. Uses plurals and very clear correct grammar of first person and second and third person (subject, predicate).
3. Obeys commands by comprehending expectations
4. Able to answer questions when read to clearly
5. Able to explain actions in picture books and reads from memory
6. Can sound out the phonemic presentation of alphabets and make association of letters with real objects (like "o" for orange, "k" for kiwi, "h" for hands, head, or hair).
7. Can count at least up to ten, but some infants can even count up to one hundred.

Social personal

1. Looks for peer interaction and play
2. More realistic approach like believing in a rope to be a nonmoving object and not a snake but not confident enough

3. Can feel that humans can really fly like Peter Pan, Tinker Bell, and Batman. One fortunate child dressed up as Batman for Halloween and dived off a five-foot deck, as he thought he could fly. He did not get injured by some divine intervention or supreme luck of the infant boy or his parents. Instead of trick or treat, he was in the ER getting checked out with CT scans and X-rays.

4. Likes more autonomy in feeding and dressing. Buttons and unbuttons and puts on shoes without laces.

5. Willingly takes turns with peer group and still will be possessive of own toys, objects, and parents

6. Sensitive to parent's emotional state and makes perceptions of fear and can get very angry and stressed out or anxious and fearful.

7. Can easily play independently when parents are away.

Chapter XI
4-Year Development and Summarization

Gross motor

1. Walks and runs upstairs and downstairs
2. Can imitate dance steps with feet wide apart, like in ballet and other types of dancing
3. Does broad jumps , hops on one foot, and can play hopscotch

Fine motor

1. Good pencil grip and can write some letters and numbers
2. Can write own name and draw a person with at least four parts
3. Dresses and buttons well
4. Can draw a square and a cross (+) sign and may copy the shapes. Some children can eve draw a very good triangle when they have had nurture.
5. Can hop on one foot
6. Knows right and left well enough and is not expected to have ambidexterity till seven years of age, which is accepted.

Language

1. Completes construction of sentences with some adjectives also in expression
2. Language is used to express feelings and will be used as a tool of communication for daily needs, wants, and learning.

Personal Social

1. Self-regulation and autonomy
2. Prefers brushing teeth and hair and taking bath by self
3. Knows sex identity and realistic—a rope is a rope and ketchup is not blood—at this age
4. Can alternate feet while jumping and good on bike with training wheels
5. Have needs and expectations with willingness to work toward a reward system. Positive rewards have a meaning.
6. When good habits are taught, they are respected and respond to praise and rewards, like stamps, stickers, stars, and tangible points.
7. Intentional peer play and interactions. They are ready for school.

By the fifth year of life, the child is ready for school, with good autonomy, respect for rules, and good fine and gross motor coordination with pencil grip, is fully toilet trained, stays within lines while coloring, has good drawing, ties shoelaces, has excellent expression of feelings, asks for wants and needs, knows how to take care of bathroom needs, has personal cleanliness, and is motivated to learn in all areas; may even know how to add and subtract small numbers.

A four-year-old boy in my practice did a three-digit subtraction from a story problem that the father gave during the physical checkup. The credit goes to his parents who really brought him up with the five domains of health per the WHO definition. He is now in high school, as a straight "**A**" student in all advanced classes. He is fluent in 5 languages and is a pleasant individual socially. Both parents work, but they gave quality time, and to this day, he is a computer genius and uses electronics only for learning. Many are fluent in two to three languages.

Every parent can create a genius like this, and genes that are bad will not get expressed if the nurture overcomes the fearful, toxic, and aversive influences on development.

Summarization and Reiteration

What do parents need to remember?

Truth

1. Infants learn from the external influences from their immediate environment.
2. Adults in their environment play a major role to influence and set a role model.
3. Quality time is more important than the quantity of time.
4. Everything the infant observes will be imitated by them.
5. Infants have excellent memory and are born to learn with natural curiosity.
6. They love themselves more and have respect for authority and need direction to make choices.
7. Emotional maturity comes before we see them walk or talk. Wiring had happened about perceptions and emotions before gross and fine motor skills are seen.
8. Infants are very persistent till they master a skill.
9. They are ever looking for guidance, soothing, love, sympathy, and empathy.
10. Infants are sad when parents are sad and offer a bag of bandages as a fixer-upper for a parent when crying or anyone crying. They come to wipe tears. Infants are very sensitive to parent's emotions.
11. Why and how then that we have violence among children and youth?
12. Violence is a learned behavior.
13. Where are the societies going wrong without any intentions of creating violent children?

Meena Chintapalli, M.D. F.A.A.P.

Right action: what can parents learn and do to help healthy brain growth

Parents have to know that they are the first teacher for the infant, and they are empowered to create a better world with global peace. This war against violence and youth health-risk behaviors is a silent acceptance of responsibility by every individual in the society to acquire the twenty-five years of neuroscience knowledge that is linking the daily lifestyles to optimal or suboptimal biosocial behavior and mental health learning disorders.

When and how does this responsibility start?

1. The first responsibility starts when planning for pregnancy and an infant or as soon as pregnancy is found.

2. Intimate partner violence should not exist, and the mother's mental status should be of inner peace, contentment, and joy and free of stress.

3. No liquor at all during pregnancy, and many medicines are toxic, including aspirin, antihistamines for allergy, and cold and cough medicines.

4. Healthy meal plan is very important, which is filled with fresh produce, preferably organic fresh fruits; green, red, and orange/carotene-colored fruits and vegetables, which are good for luteins, antioxidants, vitamins, minerals, immune proponents; legumes, freshwater fish, vegetable proteins, and omegas through diets like flaxseeds, soaked chia seeds, quinoa, brown rice, and balanced with fresh nuts and meats.

5. Taking multivitamins is essential, as B10 deficiency causes neural tube defects. Physical exercise in pregnancy helps general well-being.

6. Listening to soothing music and not high pitched, high tone, and rapid music like rap and death metal.

7. Parents need to get ready to understand the concepts of dynamic brain growth and the need to move away from the concept of how they were raised to what is the essential aspect of current literature and concerns on shielding the newborn till three years from toxic stress and aversive influences on the biological, psychological, emotional, cognitive, and social growth of the unborn infant and child.

8. Parenting education should be available equally to the poor and rich sections of the communities.

9. At zero to thirty-six months or the first one thousand days of life are very critical to experience expectant growth, and the training should incorporate screen time controls, music and touch therapy learning, feeding right from the beginning with good food practices and meal plans that prevent later morbidity for various eating disorders. Music is essential along with social and emotional development and language development.

10. Exposure to dance, music, and learning a musical instrument is important. Exposure to fine arts at a very young age, before they are verbal, is essential for good executive brain network development. Physical activities from the time of birth are essential, pertinent to their age.

Infants learn to read so that they can learn by reading. Puzzles and pattern recognition play and toys are more important than the electronic games and doing things online.

The following few behaviors need to be handled well before three years of age and are summarized:

A. To prevent eating disorder and power struggle over eating

1. Parents need to understand about authoritative parenting skills.

2. Parents need to create consistent and persistent structure.

3. When crying in a store for wants, please leave the store with the child and deprive an opportunity of outing with parent for groceries or mall, even if it has to be repeated a dozen times.

4. When resisting eating breakfast, ask for two choices and prepare the choice taken and remove the plate if dawdling after twenty minutes. No substitution of foods till the next meal and give sips of water for whining. I recommend buying a timer or setting up the oven buzzer. A hungry child eats within ten minutes, and the rest of the ten minutes is for parent satisfaction.

5. Do not give food and milk or juice with a major meal. Infants grow two inches per year and gain ideally five pounds per year after their first birthday. As a result, infants eat to their growth needs. In the first twelve months, infants grow ten inches and triple and quadruple their birth weight. After the first year, the growth needs are one-fifth of the first-year needs. They fill up with one thousand calories plus age times one hundred calories per year after the first year of life.(1000cals+age x100)

6. Not realizing the above needs, parents have expectations of consumption of a certain quantity in their mind that leads to a power struggle over eating. This leads to forced feeding that will result in future eating disorders like anorexia nervosa and bulimia (binge eating and vomiting).

7. The orifices that parents cannot control are the oral and the excretory systems.

8. Make sure that all liquids and food are offered at the dining table. No TV, iPhone, or iPad screen is necessary to make an infant eat. No running around, as it can prevent choking hazards. Screen time is proving to be toxic to brain organization.

9. Offer water with major meals. Cut down the milk to sixteen to eighteen ounces per day, ideally in between the major meals.

10. With small milk feedings of six ounces each time, give small fruits like few blueberries, strawberries, peaches, plums, nectarines, apricots, kiwi, and black grapes. Ideally, colored fruits and vegetables have luteins and antioxidants, which are good for brain growth and immune systems. Apples and bananas do cause more bowel irregularities because of pectin in them, and they have no luteins. Papaya is an excellent fruit that is not so much favored.

B. Temper tantrums and how to handle

1. Next comes the limit setting and crying spells. An opportunity for parent is to steer the crying spells into purposeful activities of phonetic presentations, numbers, days of the week, months of the year, puzzles and word building, and writing with crayons on paper, stories, and rhymes with music therapy. This teaches an infant about making choices and teaches self-soothing.

2. This technique helps making a hard wiring to the frontal lobe from the midbrain emotional centers. In these pathways are the dopamine receptors for making dopamine as a learning hormone for future school readiness. Unused, there is loss of 600,000 cells/minute x 10,000 connections between nerve cells (neuron); if used, 250,000 cells per minute x 10,000 connections from neuron to neuron.

3. Engaging in an activity that is teaching something educational prevents a power struggle, teaches self-control of emotions, and is pleasant. Temper should not be rewarded with anger and threat of going into a corner. Spanking teaches it is OK to hit. This self-regulation becomes a permanent part of the brain and is teaching thinking before reacting.

4. Language and communication is rapid. Parents need to talk like they are talking to an adult and help make good decisions. Reading at least four to five books per day leads to communication skills, which is very dynamic at this stage. Public library programs like infant and toddler reading programs enhance communication skills. Any social interaction with other adults under parental supervision is good for self-trust and emotional stability, which will be good for communication. Social mingling with peer group is important through large muscle activities like gymnastics and swimming and social and motor development through participation in therapy places like Gymboree or a play place with adult supervision. By the third year, many children are ready for team sports like soccer.

5. If the infant refuses to sit in a car seat, stop the car and pull off into the alley till the sobbing stops. Cancel the trip and come back home. Start classical music like Suzuki music CDs of violin and piano prior to strapping the infant into the car seat. Explain the rule of the trip prior to bringing them to the car. The rules are generally respected by the infants.

6. I know of toddlers who panic when the car engine starts and the parent had not strapped them, and they make noise loud enough to be heard about strapping. Children do respect rules and if the adults are persistent.

C. Toilet training concepts

1. Parents get eager to toilet train an infant by the time they are running, around eighteen to twenty-four months. This is a complicated neuromuscular and social development. The infant needs to stay dry for five hours, hold the orifices and control the need till in a socially acceptable place is reached, and then open the orifices and make the deed, feel empty, and then clean. This is an intricate motor and neurosensory balance that cannot be conditioned.

2. Infants try to hide behind couches and curtains, seeking their privacy, and then come and tell the parent to change their diaper. A consistent pattern of this is an indication of neuromuscular maturity. Socially and emotionally, infants need to feel comfortable sitting on a potty chair. If this potty chair is an adult attachment, and in the rare chance of the infant slipping into the

Early Brain Sprouts from States to Traits

water, it will prevent the infant from ever trying to use the potty chair. Some kids do fine with step stool support and adult seat attachment, as they do not get scared seeing the excreta in the bowel.

3. Try to get the infant training potty chair where the feet will touch the ground and it imitates an adult potty chair. Adults at this juncture can take the infant to show what they actually do on the potty chair so that the infant can imitate the adult. Then if the infant is sitting on the potty chair, instead of running behind furniture and curtains, then it is wise to put them in pull-ups. If they consistently sit on the potty chair with pull-ups, then it is an indication to pull down the pull-ups and do the excretion into the potty chair, which is trainable. This is a gradual process.

4. Operant conditioning in the developing countries for toilet training works, as that can happen on the ground anywhere, but for advanced countries with rigid rule for aesthetic reasons, pushing toilet training before the infant is ready leads to poor controls and regression in the future. Any child trauma incurred at this stage, like assault, violence, abuse, or witnessing violence, will lead to poor toilet training, fecal soiling, or bed wetting in the future.

5. Redirection all the way to make good choices and tangibly rewarding with a stamp or star or sticker is important to steer the infant to make healthy choices. This is a permanent part of the brain structure.

D. **Role of minerals, fiber, and antioxidants in meal plan: body and mind are sustained by what goes into mouth**

   1. Organic foods, quinoa, and polycomplex carbohydrate diets, and minerals through healthy organic fruits and vegetables make permanent pathways for future traits of healthy eating habits. It prevents cancer proneness and prevents type II diabetes and obesity.

   2. Packaged foods with preservatives are also toxic to brain cells and immune systems. The nutritional value is poor, as compared to fresh produce. Many preservatives give migraine or headache, and other things that happen internally are difficult to assess—how much pollutants are going in along with heavy metals from juice drinks, preservatives in packaged foods, and nonorganic meat products.

   3. The above discussion is a briefing on what parents can do to prevent poor eating habits, poor communication and language, learning disorder, and discipline problems through love, nurture, and redirection; and it includes tips on toilet training. Parents have to become creative in creating novelty—pull out toys and reintroduce after they have been forgotten.

E. **Role of the communities, legislation, and society**

1. *The only way to pleasant parenting is to accept their role as investors of time and energy with full understanding, love, patience, nurture, and self-education, always reflecting on thoughts without a reaction*. Parents and adults raising infants and children need to develop tools for balancing their own emotions to positive and reflective thinking, spiritual practices that are conducive to replace innate negative emotions with positive reflective thinking.

2. Parents need to help the communities spread the education on nurture and facts on ECBD to build a strong, intelligent, spiritual child in the society and create global peace.

3. Communities need to create a strong parent support system for zero-three-year child development in a positive way.

a. The peace in an individual is a state of mind that has adjustment, change of attitude and contentment, self-regulation, fluid shift change of emotional balance to pleasant, and reflective thinking. Parents certainly can fall back on some relaxation courses for stress relief.

b. Infants are not capable of processing information that is presented to the senses. Infants are totally dependent upon the adult in their life helping them to synthesize and balance the emotions.

c. If the adults in their life have issues of pride, maladjustment, poor homeostasis of emotional challenges, poor coping skills, poor judgment, poor self-refinement, and poor self-audit and are not able to break away from old-fashioned parenting practices, it will reflect upon the infants' behavior in the future.

d. Infants are rapidly absorbing everything they perceive from their environment; social and emotional learning is laid down into the brain structure, and the actions are later on expressed as behaviors with at least 354 variable expressions of personalities.

e. Parents need to learn what authoritative parenting skills are and block the styles of parenting skills from their own learned experiences on how they were raised.

f. Spouses need to bond and stay on the same structure and consistency, even if they are in two separate homes. The communication gap does make the child get exposed to a chaotic environment that leads to confusion in expected behaviors from the infant or child.

g. If the parents are separating, it has to be an amicable separation, with love for the child, and they have to come to an understanding on how to raise this infant and incubate him or her from picking up toxic anxiety and stress from their environment. Stress creates hormones that burn the brain cells. The scarring is true at a critical age, and the rewiring is a poor synaptic thickness at a later age (after five years).

h. Music, communication, and touch therapy always calm an infant. Little children two years and above can also do deep nasal breathing as given at websites like www.leftbrainbuddha.org.

Love builds self-respect and trust

1. Love is a state of happiness and respect for authority.

2. Love makes an individual control aggression through redirecting thoughts, words, and actions. This comes from parent's guidance. There are many tools for anger management both for parents and children.

3. Love also means respecting oneself and building self-trust and confidence.

4. Love is an imitation from adults in the infant's life till the infant can process and argue or disagree with parents. This happens typically after the fourth year of life.

5. Adults should foster the natural state of love, sympathy, and empathy more cautiously from the eighteenth month of the child's life when he or she tends to become possessive of objects, persons, and emotions. The natural state of an infant is to love with eagerness to belong and attach themselves to a caretaker.

6. Adults should train themselves to move this attachment to teaching autonomy to their child with love, guidance, discipline, and redirection as addressed above till so far.

I am giving a few cases from my practice, and they are real cases. The names are changed per HIPPA guidelines, protecting the identity of patient. The cases improved along with chemical management. The five SAI Educare teaching techniques were taught and implemented through parents for children zero to five years old, children older than five years , and all teenagers.

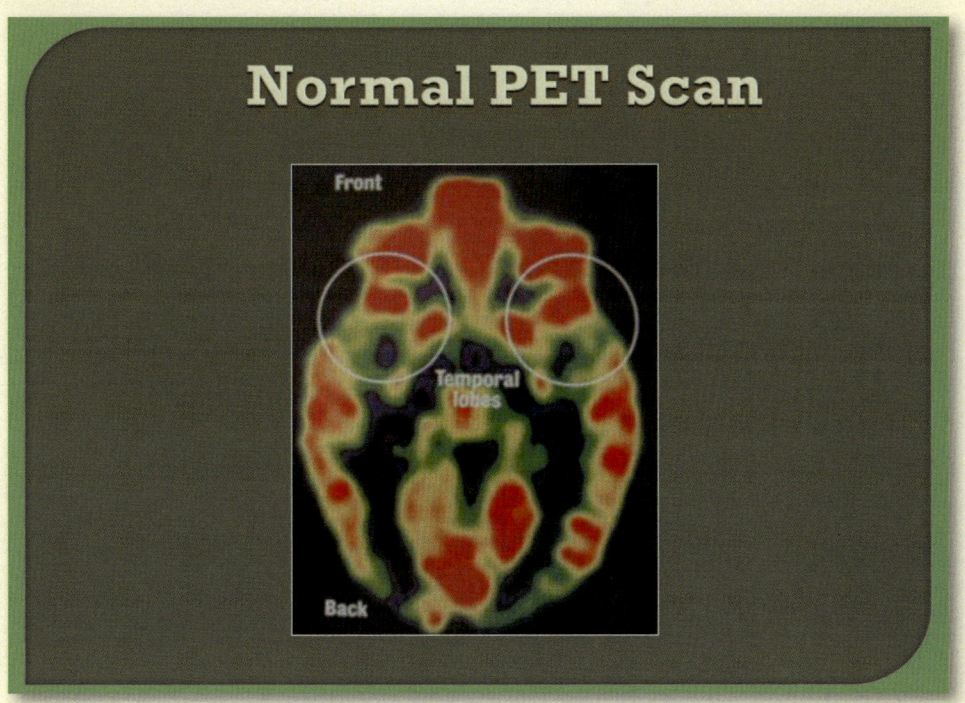

Figure 38:Normal 4 year old

(Courtesy Dr. Harry T.Chugani, 1997at WSU and now at Nemours Institute, Delaware)

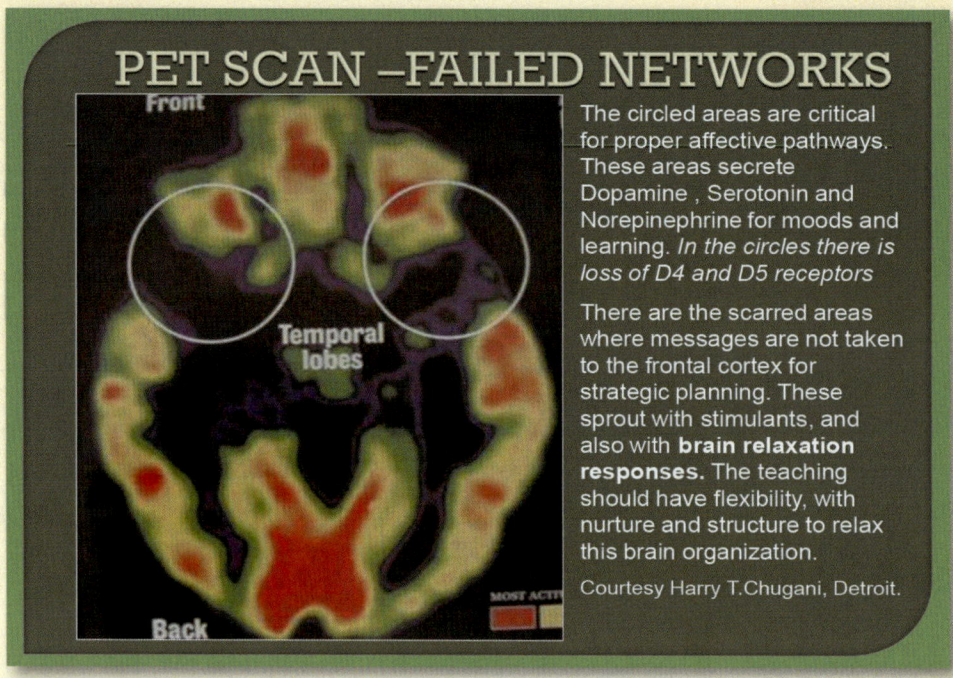

Figure 39: A PET scan of 4 year old abused victim (Courtesy Dr. Harry T. Chugani, WSU, 1997, at Nemours Institute, Delaware)

Chapter XII

Case Presentations

There are many cases in the last twenty-eight years, with accumulated prospective follow-up and with ECBD knowledge for the last twenty-three years.

Case 1: psychosocial dwarfism

1. **1979:** During my ambulatory fellowship in the child development clinic, my first experience was that of a three-year-old male brought by the mother, who was a single parent, for poor growth velocity, short stature, illegible speech, food hoarding and night walking, random movement, and not sitting still. He was a product of FT pregnancy and normal delivery and no trauma. He was eating too much, sometimes raw meat, and he was the only child. Mom did give history of depression, and there was disturbed spouse relationship. Child was clinging to the mom. After thorough examination, few labs were ordered including TSH and bone age. The results showed some growth arrest lines and normal TSH. After exploring the differential diagnosis, his description was classic for psychosocial dwarfism with a folie à deux parent.

   Home assessment and prior records indicated a need for placement of the child. He was sometimes disciplined for hyperactive and aggressive behaviors in the bathroom or locked up in the closet. He did receive corporal punishment with belt when he did not listen. Within four to five months in foster care, the child started talking and grew four inches in linear growth, and there were no food hoarding and night pacing. The case was followed for eighteen months, and he was already talking. I thought and developed a concept of unopposed alpha-adrenergic stimuli intracranial, in the central nervous system that caused this inhibition globally, to prevent executive functions and cognitive skills. The stress seems to have suppressed the hypothalamic pituitary system also. From my personal thought process and concepts, I came to the conclusion that the reason for growth velocity failure and poor frontal lobe functioning, getting arrested in fright or flight, was from constant fear and excessive stimulation of the alpha-adrenergic receptors in the brain as a result of cortisol, epinephrine, and nor epinephrine. I developed a protocol to use alpha-adrenergic blockers to treat the anger and aggression. We had not many of those in those days in 1979. In those days, there was just a small discussion of minimal brain damage, causes undetermined. ADHD was not a major diagnostic condition. The patient was in therapy when I left for Wisconsin in 1980. I could never follow up and do the research protocol.

2. My curiosity grew as I saw more children having difficult cognitive skills and language delay when there was a divorce or angry custody battle, and they were not doing well in school. The concept of attention deficit disorders came in mid-1980s, and I never had a chance to stay at one place for more than four to five years to follow cases and invest more time into ADHD and behavior disorders other than follow protocols. By 1989–1990, I had enough number of ADHD cases, and all of them had some issues within the families, and the expression of children was one of hyperkinetic syndrome and poor academic performance. With medicines and the family was helped to see how they can bring communication and limit setting with love

back into their life—I personally taught the SAI Educare five teaching techniques to parents and patients above five years of age—the children started to improve, and their attention span increased at school. There was a lot of attention paid on heavy metals like lead toxicity in Milwaukee, Wisconsin, and the lead levels in the air were high, and many inner-city children had high levels that needed chelating. How much of heavy metal consumption is happening from eating animal meat that might have lodged heavy metals in their meat from fodder fed soaked with pollution from environment, acid rain, and air pollution? How many people can afford organic meals from vegetables, animal meats, and sea and freshwater fish?

3. Computers were making their entry to children's life by early 1990s, and many three-year-old children became wizards in unlocking the computers, playing cartoons, maneuvering the mouse, and web searching, and the rates of autism spectrum disorders started increasing progressively and peaking now at one in sixty-five. ADHD with inattention, hyperactivity, and impulsivity started rising also. When I read the Johnson & Johnson Institute roundtable, all made sense to me, and I became more rigorous in parenting skills training that I already was implementing in my private practice, incorporating the knowledge and parent awareness education on the brain plasticity, malleability, early child brain development (ECBD), formation of neural pathways that determine behaviors, intellectual learning, and emotional, cognitive and social development. I started showing the PET scans of abused and normal brain during this teaching. I could see positive results when I advised parents to get involved with music therapy from birth along with eye contact and touch therapy. From the time I was practicing pediatrics in 1984, I always discussed spouse bonding issues and how to solve problems amicably so that the children will not face fear and anxiety. I got a tool that is backed up by scientific data now, since 1997.

Case 2: attachment disorder and separation anxiety leading to depression

1989: I used to be the pediatric chair and a team leader in management strategies at a neuro-psych facility in San Antonio for a short period of two years. One case study I can never forget is about a fourteen-year-old girl admitted for therapy and medical management for phobia of school, somehow in eighth grade, and every day, the parent needed to bring her home by noontime for abdominal pain and crying with fear and anxiety. The precipitating cause was never known. Her IQ was at borderline mental retardation level. She looked very well and had no other medical illness. She told therapists that she did not know why she was afraid and gets a tummy ache at school daily. One day, I was talking to her about trees, nature, and balance in nature; how the five fingers work together, and one finger cannot do all the work unless all fingers of the hand work together—unless we as a team come together and try to solve her problem, no one could help her.

Then something prompted her to tell me that she was afraid that she would lose her mother permanently when she was at school. The reason for her fear was that her father drank and beat her mother up while she was very young. She grew up in fear then that something would happen to her mother. She always slept with her mother because of the same fear. Her father died because of alcoholic cirrhosis, and now she was worried that she would lose her mother too, although there was nobody to hit her or bash her against the wall. ***This is a classic case of***

getting arrested in fright and flight with long-standing toxic effect on the brain, arresting the pathways from sprouting to frontal lobe from the amygdala and uncus. In the state of fear and anxiety, the pathways do not go to the portion of the brain that makes strategic planning, memory and recall, motivation and critical thinking.

Mother did not let her get sleep training at 6-9 months to develop autonomy, self-confidence and self- soothing. She required a lot of therapy, and so did the mother to understand the role of teaching self-regulation and autonomy to the child. The individual and family therapy and speech and rehabilitation therapy continued. She took her GED three years later. No further follow-up.

Case 3

SB was an IVF infant, first male, born to elderly couple at forty-one years of age. Both parents were executives and back to back had another girl infant within two years. The parents followed all the knowledge that was imparted to them, and he was somewhat colicky. His milestones were accelerated in gross motor, fine motor, speech and language, and had very few infections that needed antibiotics. He was a straight A student till seven years of age, and the behavior became as a classic definition of ADHD, combined type, when he entered the second grade. He came for assessment right after the summer vacation; he was aggressive at times, and the worst was the oppositional defiant disorder. The parents were against any medical management, and we did optimal cognitive behavior management, which was failing. No overt abuse or dysfunction in the family, and both parents came for each visit. We even did the alpha wave neuro stimulation program for a while at the parents' request, a form of neuro-bio-feedback. Parents were under the impression that the aggression was related to Adderall.

One day, as I was talking to him, I had him draw what he liked, and he drew a rocket ship that had pockets on all three wings at the end, and he called them detonators. When a predator comes close to him in the rocket, the detonators would blast off and fight the predator from getting closer. He wanted to be a lion if he were to be an animal and would get rid of any animal that will try to cause him injury.

The parents tried many therapies outside the insurance that would create alpha waves and delta waves for learning and relaxation, but in vain. He needed up to 30 mg of Adderall XR to keep him from getting into trouble at school with drug holidays.

When he was going into seventh grade, that summer, I offered my five teaching techniques of curriculum that will transform at heart level. I taught the family yoga, meaningful meditation with regulated nasal breathing exercise and with music and guided imagery, inhaling for seven seconds, holding for seven seconds, and exhaling over seven seconds. I gave him four positive thoughts to practice with life application for the week; he was already in physical activities, and he would do a declaration form attested by his parents every day. I developed a Y chart with tangible cognitive behavior modification with specific goals, consequences with response gains, and reactive costs. He had a declaration chart to fill daily on how he implemented the positive thoughts as a journal, at school and at home. Value-based story was read at each session, and thoughts pertinent to that story were discussed and developed as a journal guideline.

After we started doing this, the family was more relaxed and opened up on some issues. The parents took a little bit more of a drink daily at dinner and, later on, were too inebriated to talk with the kids, and the kids watched a lot of TV shows, mostly with fights like *Star Wars*, guns and shooting like *FBI, Rockford Files*, besides kid shows like *Batman and Robin*. The family stopped TV and electronics, did meaningful mediation three times a day with guided imagery and soothing classical music, and discussed the life application of the assets that were assigned daily after supper, and the mom and dad stopped drinking. The family changed after five sessions, and SB decided to stop all meds and use meditation with nasal breathing to relax and redirect. Love and attachment grew in the family. Relationships improved, and they had the best loving Christmas that year without alcohol to relax, but love replaced the needs of external factors for happiness. That patient is a twenty-five-year-old naval engineer and keeps a job, and never did he need medicine to control his ADHD after these five sessions. The internal relaxation, love, bonding, happiness, and family human values are essential for a healthy society. Mostly the transformation helped.

A family is a biological unit of the society, that is happy with love, peace, order at home through individual character building.

Case 4

JJ was a six-year-old male, middle of three children, the last two being the boys. The mom and dad grew up in a rigid background, and they both decided to let the rooster run the roof. It only got worse when the youngest brother came along and was two years old, getting into JJ's things. JJ stopped responding to time-outs and would go and sit himself in a corner and start playing with his toy or sing. He would continue to misbehave at home, and his grades were good at school. He distracted a lot of kids after finishing his work. Teachers sent home Conners scales and ACTeRS that showed (1993) ADHD with hyper and impulsive behavior and no learning disorder, as his grades were good. As his grades were good, the parents did not want an evaluation. Upon obtaining a thorough history, it was obvious that JJ got away early on in his life with a lot of things. He was watching a lot of cartoons and action figures shows. His sister, being the only girl and oldest, was busy with school and helping their mom and had less interest on TV, and she was expected to live up to family values, and she was nice, gentle, and loving. The younger brother was also watching TV and was becoming aggressive at two years of age.

I sat down with the family, the mom and dad in particular, and laid down the reasons why the TV should be off till the kids slept, gave guidelines on effective parenting skills that are authoritative, and assured them that the parent who controls the child will be respected more. Both parents should be on the same page and do the persistent, consistent, love-filled structure with consequences spelled out for all three children for making wrong choices. I had five teaching techniques that I implemented since I was practicing medicine, which are explained in detail in my other book, *Brain, Mind, SAI Educare*.

The school was instructed to make him responsible at school that if he completed good work rapidly and correctly, he would receive badges, commendation, and leadership awards. JJ grew up since then with no discipline problems, and no ADHD medicines were needed. He became a very good student and is now in college and is a good sportsman also. He became a good son and a good citizen with loving and sharing nature. The parents followed everything that I taught them and did not need many counseling sessions.

"Peace is a shore less ocean—it is the light that illuminates the world."

"Virtue is the sign of the educated person. This is what makes education worthwhile."

—Satya Sai Baba

Case 5: how the brain needs to be protected among preterm NICU graduates.

Brain connects more outside the uterus postpartum.

An infant was brought to me by 2 concerned parents an anxious mom and dad with serious concerns on their one and only infant daughter who was five months old postpartum by that time. She was born at 24-25 weeks gestational age and was in the Neonatal Intensive Care Unit for 5 months with many life threatening complications. The parents were told that she would possibly have a vegetative life, and no guarantees were made for her neurological status. Mom was a special education teacher, and the dad a police officer, and this was their very first child. She was twenty-five weeks preterm female who needed respiratory support, umbilical vein catheter, PIC line for nutrition support, and an incubator. She needed daily transfusions. She developed grade IV intraventricular hemorrhage on one side and grade III on the other side, developed bronchopulmonary dysplasia grade that required oxygen supply at the time of discharge from the hospital. She had grade IV retinopathy of prematurity and developed catheter-induced infections, which included viral and bacterial meningitis. She had Vancomycin-induced cardiac arrest (accidentally she received ten times the needed dose in NICU) and needed to be resuscitated for three minutes. At the time of dismissal, she had home oxygen therapy, apnea monitoring, a huge lepto-meningeal cyst on the right side, and left hemiparesis. Gray matter on CT scan was thin. There was grade IV retinopathy of prematurity.

Besides taking care of all complications and getting her off the oxygen, I worked almost every three days with the parents on infant brain nurture with the curriculum that I gave in the earlier chapters. This included the meal plan therapy also as enumerated in the early chapters. She still has minimal hemi-paresis and walks independently. She went to regular school with no learning disabilities and passed on the top twenty-five list at her high school and is now going to nursing school to become an RN. She never had any bacterial infections that required antibiotics. She might have had a couple of strep throat infections. No allergies and no food intolerance. One time she had migraine, and we controlled her cheese intake, and she got better. Parents were very careful with food choices, and she was given more homemade meals than the commercial foods since infancy. She was referred to a neurosurgeon to see if leptomeningeal cyst was causing a problem with severe headache, and the neurosurgeon did not want to touch her, as she was doing so well.

This is a classic example to show that most of the brain connections happen outside the womb, from the environmental stimuli, in a safe, secure environment with details from food that sustains the body to what we are feeding through all the senses.

Case 6

Concerned mom and dad brought a preterm infant who was twenty-four to twenty-five weeks gestational age after a five-month NICU stay. He had respiratory distress syndrome that required prolonged respiratory support, developed bronchopulmonary dysplasia, grade IV intra-ventricular hemorrhages, grade IV retinopathy of prematurity, two episodes of meningitis, both viral and bacterial, and very thin sheet of gray matter on brain CT scan. He was discharged with grim outlook for future learning capabilities, as he had a very difficult course.

I gave my curriculum, nurture, and personally trained every step of the way on the therapies given in my curriculum, including gradual introduction of food that has antioxidants, luteins, and omegas. He never had difficulties at school and now is teaching math at college and is also using that money to become an engineer. Math is his greatest strength. This patient also did not have any major infections, and I never had to give him antibiotics at all. He had one episode of RSV that required admission and was given Ribavirin mist therapy in the tent and nebulizer with beta2-agonists. After that, he remained healthy, and the parents were very careful with food choices early on.

Food is essential for the body functions, and is fundamental to body's functions, like Oxygen. It is essential to pay attention and eat healthy foods. Eating herbs, greens, and vegetable proteins, having less packaged foods, and using as much fresh produce and homemade meal plan always have been an integral part of my infant examination sessions. Another strong policy is no screen policy till two years, and only using thirty minutes a day, supervised by an adult, has been a strong teaching in my practice from 1990. Parents who trusted this teaching and followed the instructions 100 percent reaped similar rewards. I have many preterm infants today going to college and doing very well in high school with no morbidity.

Case 7

A nineteen-year-old mom brought a thirty-eight-month-old male for getting assessed for autism spectrum disorder. He had classic impulsive, hyperactive behavior, no communication at all, and poor eye contact and he never sat still to work with him. She moved from Oklahoma to get better help and got an admission to go to school after her GED. She had no family, and he was unable to be tolerated at Head Start programs. He was kicked out of two programs.

The mother was a 15 year old teenager and did not do alcohol or drugs during pregnancy. She broke up with her boyfriend, and the father was given visitation rights. She as a teenager needed family help, and her sister with four kids accommodated her. Her biological mother also stayed with them. She felt she needed to be out of that house and moved to San Antonio, as the boyfriend was stalking her. In addition, the history also was given that the infant at fifteen months did not come home on time, and the police were sent. The infant was locked up in the closet, and the father was having fun with his girlfriend. Again, the same SAI Educare program teachings and multisensory integration techniques were given to the mother. I saw the family every two weeks. In about five to six months, he was talking and making good eye contact, but he still was hyperactive. We worked with natural foods that have calming effects like quinoa and more minerals from fresh fruits and vegetables and gluten-free diet and no packaged foods. He somewhat improved. It was very tempting to use ADHD meds, and he was barely four years at that time. Physical, occupational, and speech therapies and PPCD through public school were given. With music, he would sit still to learn and got interested in story time for five to nine minutes.

The mother went back to Oklahoma for the summer and came back with a very hyperactive child. The maternal grandmother came for the visit, and after listening to the ECBD lecture from me, she let out more secrets. Her brother-in-law had a very loud voice, had an explosive temper, and was abusive verbally and physically to all the children and wife. It was sometimes scary. He regressed after going there, and the maternal grandmother was willing to work with him from then on. By the fifth birthday, he was totally out of the box, and the only condition he needed to be treated for was ADHD and minor learning disabilities. He subsequently moved out of town. He was good with communication, had good emotional expression, and was very loving. The fear and anxiety are so toxic, and the cure for current community violence globally is to promote self-respect and love through different healing programs suitable to every child. It should be a tangible multi sensory integration.

Chapter XIII

What Are My Relaxation Techniques in a Nutshell for the Caregivers and Children Four Years Old and Older?

These are the five teaching techniques I use with ADHD and behavioral disorder patients. I use the same for parents to calm themselves.

Yoga and meaningful meditation

1. Yoga and meaningful meditation techniques with music, guided imagery, sitting quietly in a comfortable position, and focusing on nasal breathing (inhaling through nose, holding breath, and exhaling through nose for six seconds each while playing classical, soothing music and with guided imagery at the same time). This should start with ten-minute sessions and gradually build it up to twenty minutes, ideally done three times a day. The meaningful meditation increases attention span (tuning in) and internal relaxation, enhances motivation, increases the strength of the immune systems, balances the autonomic dysfunction by reducing the heart rate and blood pressure, enhances the longevity of life, cuts down the effects of vasopressin, nor epinephrine, cortisol, and adrenaline as the oxytocin rises in the blood, and suppresses the stress hormones. The NO (nascent oxygen) levels increases blood flow to the brain and helps regenerate the white and gray matter thickness. The immune system responds and helps control infections.

   I incorporate into this guided imagery to think positive through the sensory commands of the five cognizing senses, sound, taste, touch, visual, and smell, and hands, feet, and mind.

   An example is like this for guided imagery:

   Imagine visiting Grand Tetons in spring. There is a nice golden sun arising in the horizon. Take a deep breath as you enjoy staring at the golden sun and hold the brightness in your heart. After six seconds, release gradually to your eyes as you exhale. Eyes have a choice to see only good and not the bad. Pull this golden light and love, fill your heart with this light and love as you inhale nasally, hold it for six seconds, and release through the nose to the ears. Ears are listening to the beautiful wind chimes and the birds chirping. Ears make a choice not to hear bad like tattle tales. Pull the light and love back into heart as you inhale nasally and hold it for six seconds and exhale nasally to release love and light to tongue. The fruits here are delicious from their natural state, and the tongue is given for good, gentle speech and eating right. Pull the light and love back into your heart as you inhale nasally and hold for six seconds and gradually release as you exhale nasally for six seconds and understand that hands do their duty to help yourself first and help others. Repeat the command likewise for legs and, finally, release the light and love to all of the body. Body is filled with love and to help. As you open your eyes, understand that the whole body is like that sunlight that gives life's resources to good and bad alike. It is important to keep breathing till one can calm down.

Early Brain Sprouts from States to Traits

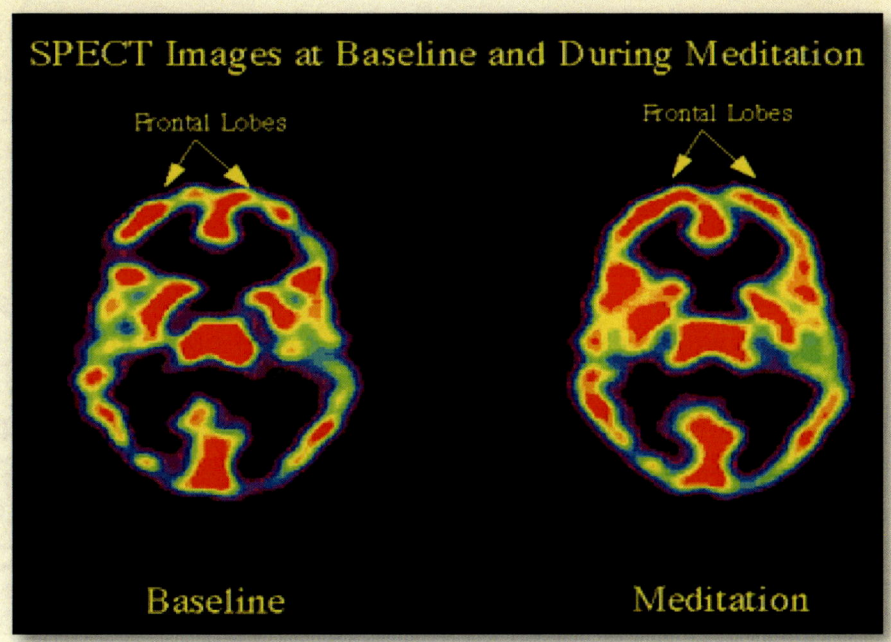

(Figure 39 Courtesy of Dr. Andrew Newberg from Buddhist Monk Studies)

How to do the basic breathing technique??

a. One has to sit straight in a comfortable position on a chair or cross legged on the floor.

b. Both feet should cross if sitting on chair and spine straight.

c. Try to take slow regular breaths before starting meditation, wiggle the body's tension, rotate the eyes clockwise and anti clockwise, rotate the neck as long as there are no spine problems.

d. Make the thumbs of each touch the index finger and rest them on lap.

e. Another way is to rest the right hand in the left hand and press the thumbs together directed upward making a triangle with the thumbs and hand and rest that position in the lap.

f. Pull in air in a relaxed position over 6-seconds and fill the larynx, windpipe, push diaphragm down and push abdominal muscles out to accommodate as much air

g. Hold breath for 6 seconds.

h. Exhale over 6 seconds through the nostrils only. Not from mouth.

i. Follow the same for 10-15 minutes and increase to 20-30 minutes sitting time.

j. Playing soothing music initially helps before the guided imagery can be started. This is a very basic technique and other techniques need a GURU and GUIDANCE.

k. Duration is usually 1 minute per age up to maximum of 60 minutes of sitting. Usually 10- 20 minutes three times a day and when stressed out.

2. **Positive thoughts:** At least pick three to four positive thoughts from on line or from www.saicdp.org Educare calendar for life application and practice to live along those values

for that day. I developed calendars with stories and positive values that I give parents. **I call them human asset management strategy**. Parents and family will discuss that day how they practiced those values that day, while facing day-to-day life's challenges. This enhances family bonding and communication with good family time, which is missing in many families unintentionally because of stressful lives making both ends meet. Guided imagery helps with the positive thoughts also over time.

3. **Stories:** with positive human values (like *Chicken Soup for Kids' Souls* for older age group and makeup values with common stories like Dr. Seuss books). I have given a few stories at the end of this book for a creative lesson plan format for parents to use, and many more can be created by parents in a similar fashion. The story create ideology, enhances family communication, teaches temporal sequential organization, stimulates critical thinking, teaches abstract reasoning, creates association formation toward cause and effect, promotes expressive language, and confers emotional maturity and creativity.

4. **Physical activities:** are very important for relaxation responses, and these stimulate positive reward networks. The circulation to brain increases along with oxygen supply, causes internal relaxation, builds teamwork and comradery and social and emotional maturity, and teaches disciplines of posture, self-regulation, and emotional balance. Dance, martial arts, drama and music, and learning a musical instrument are all important to stimulate executive function brain connections and improve motivation, sustain attention span, and get the child out of his or her shell. In younger age groups, these same activities offered to two- to five-year-old children prevent morbidity in psychosocial and psychosomatic problems, conferring higher cognitive and intellectual development.

5. **Learning music** vocally or with an instrument has a very positive effect in transformation at the heart level. Music not only teaches communication but also confers emotional balance. Music teaches feelings of joy, relaxation, inner peace and motivation, expression, and language acquisition. Music does a lot more than just increasing auditory cortex stimulation for listening. Choir or group singing is good too.

It is easy for the provider to succeed in endeavors and life application of knowledge gained if parents listen. Having parents like in the above enumerated families is my asset.

This is head, heart, and hands connection, and the heart needs the transformation. Love, self-respect, and respect for others are seated in the heart, and that heart valve needs to be opened up through life application of positive human values.

No matter what area of the reward system is damaged by toxic effects of anxiety and fearful stress, it causes perception of insecurity in a rapidly growing mind. The dopaminergic redirection through the tools that are available in the healing arts curriculum of SAI Educare (implemented in my practice since 1992) seems to increase the activity of executive function networks and increases sensitivity of the positive reward response systems.

When the environment exposes the rapidly growing zero- to five-year brains to fearful toxic stress and anxiety, reward systems get desensitized, network activity reinforces negative reward seeking, and poor motivation occurs. The electronic addiction has the similar negative effect on brain networks. The dynamically growing brain is very vulnerable to these effects.

None of this can be accomplished if the family feels medicines will quickly help and are the only solution to quickly fix a problem. Medicines may control, but rewiring the broken connections internally through family education, love, bonding, and relational transformation within family members is the key to behavioral changes and getting back on connecting to the positive reward systems and motivational sensitivity to connect to cognitive executive networks.

Chapter XIV

What Can Parents Know about Their Own Skills and Where Are Their Parenting Skills Coming From?

SAI Educare parent self-audit

SAI Institute of Educare always focuses on the patho-physiology of disease processes. The thoughts precede words and actions and lead to structural and electrophysiological states in the brain. Statistics that are given show that 40–45 percent of adults in the childbearing age seem to have emotional and behavioral problems that seem to need attention. The current behaviors of the adult caretakers originate from their learned experiences, and it is hard wired into their memory at a subconscious level from their infancy. Unless parents can understand the deficiencies that they have in their outlook, willing to let go of their thinking, and willing to learn the latest knowledge on brain neuroplasticity and the opportune time to create permanent pathways of optimal child development, the cycle of violence and the toxic effects on the brain continue with increasing prevalence of community violence and escalating spectrum disorders, ADHD, and youth health-risk behaviors.

We have 25 years of research and experience on the adverse effects of modern technology and screen time on the neural pathways during dynamic growth 0-5 years. Teaching parents acceptable nurture and effective authoritative parenting skills will definitely will help cut down the prevalence of the youth health-risk behaviors, ADHD, language delays, learning disorders, and autism spectrum behavioral outcomes. The community partners and parents need to participate in this global movement to create a peaceful home, nation, and world.

Current trends in getting training in parenting skills are from a legal standpoint through the intervention from either Adult or Child Protective Services for problem solving in the family and interactions. Most of the trainers are lacking knowledge on neural plasticity, the opportune optimal brain nurture period, and the patho-physiology of toxicity on the developing brain from domestic violence, witnessing violence, and the relationship of current adult behaviors to what happened zero to five years in their life. As a result, regimental time-outs and alternate old methodology are being used.

In general, all parents, not just the high-risk parents with legal needs, need to know about the neurodevelopment from birth to five years to create a good foundation for an individual to grow up with strengths. Communities need to rise to let this knowledge disseminate, not just for parents in the legal system and in addiction rehabilitation facilities but for all parents and caretakers involved with child care.

Communities worldwide need to realize why children grow up and need drugs or anger or explosives to satisfy their personal needs. Why did their heart and mind scar?

Why are they not thinking of consequences of their thoughts, words, and actions?

Why does a parent need to beat a child or shake an infant?

Why do people have to carry guns in the first place?

Why is there racial discrimination and retaliate type of mentality?

If a child is misbehaving, did the parent realize in opportune time that the behavior is misbehavior?

When did the parent realize the misbehavior, and what has been done?

Are there other members in the family with similar behavior?

Is there a problem in the family with drug and alcohol use and abuse?

Are the family members seeking any help to curb this substance abuse?

Is there a problem with explosive temper in the family?

Has the family been going through the typical "cycle of adult violence"?

How involved is the family with a faith system, human values, and social adaptation?

How is the interpersonal relationship within the family members, adults and children, community involvement, peer interaction, and academic performance?

These many basic questions need to be addressed before a set of behavioral rating scales can assess a child or adult of having learning disorders, depression, anxiety, phobias, ADHD, or any form of maladaptive behavioral disorders. Currently, we make an assessment of behavior disorders from the behavior checklist, which does not address the underlying factors for the psychopathologies to have occurred.

The root cause for the current adult parenting techniques is from their learned behavior in their infancy and childhood.

The SAI Educare Parenting intervention includes six sessions for training the adults and children in understanding brain activity and multisensory processing and integration. It incorporates the neuroplasticity, resilience of early infant and child developmental experiences, and pathways of neurodevelopmental organization and uses the asset management of five human values. SAI Educare Parenting also adapted the research material from the Search Institute of the definition of human nature, 1999 report from the research triangle. The six intervention sessions were constructed from the latest information about brain organization and psychological multisensory perceptual influences and took into consideration the responses from families that attended the pilot training sessions. During the dialogue with those present in the training sessions, they were guided to conduct self-evaluations about the questions that were enumerated above.

The five main assets on which the discussions included are below:

Truth

Love in speech is truth.

Human beings are the only species in the whole creation that can speak and can change their behavior from bestial qualities of various grades to the realization of the highest intellectual capabilities filled with love, sympathy, and empathy. Human beings are capable of expressing this love, sympathy, and empathy through thoughts, words, and actions. Indeed, we have great intelligence to send unmanned spacecraft to Mars and Jupiter. We invented the technology, and we are falling prey for the same technology by losing human connection and depending on a robot to teach the infants and children.

Right action

Love in action is right action.

Human beings are the only ones who can perform a deed to make others happy, make them-selves happy, and share the happiness with others and the family.

Human beings are the only ones who can respect themselves and attain a meaningful education, hold a job, and support the family and community as they care about themselves as much as they care about others. They can show their respect toward elders and the children. They can respect the earth and take care of the elements in the universe. By understanding themselves, the human beings play a role in respectfully taking care of their surroundings, earth, home, family, and the community. This love and respect in action prevents injury to others, while the person with self-confidence and self-respect will climb the ladder of success without hurting others. Social, ethical, moral personal responsibilities make all actions as Right Actions.

Peace

Love in feeling is peace.

Peace is an internal locus, and so is motivation to be peaceful within.

All efforts should be made to control the emotionally altered electrophysiological state of aggression to peace within, and only human beings are capable of this asset.

When one can self-audit their thoughts, words, and actions that are aggressive against others, objects, and property, it is the wisdom that comes from the prefrontal cortex of the brain that, when used, will direct right actions.

Animals do not have this portion of the brain that sits on the eye sockets, the higher brain called the neocortex.

If one fills their thoughts with feeling of love before they speak, it is reflective of their inner peace. There are tools that can help change the altered electrophysiological changes from aversive emotions to a feeling of peace through neuro-sensory pathways.

Love

Love begets love.

Love is a state of tolerance, endurance, and forgiveness without any hooks attached to the service done to others and the environment.

Love is for love only and is unconditional.

Love for oneself is self-confidence, which is the foundation for future strengths of an optimal personality.

If one respects themselves, they respect others and the needs of others.

Nonviolence

Love in understanding is nonviolence.

When an individual has long-term goals, persistence, **dedication, devotion to duty with discipline, and determination (the 5 Ds)**, to accomplish these goals is the highest understanding of human life and its purpose. There may be obstacles created by people and circumstances, but understanding that the others cannot be responsible for one's failure or success but using the 5Ds to succeed with passion for worthy goals will prevent one from resorting to violence and will succeed through individual effort.

One should have an understanding that the success should be accomplished with self-confidence and industry but not at the expense of hurting others. Every being has a right to be successful in his or her own passionate field. Universal love will not hurt others, as the understanding of the highest energy in all is same.

Examples of such human beings are many, like Abraham Lincoln, Mahatma Gandhi, Martin Luther King, Florence Nightingale, Maria Montessori, Rosa Parks, Nicolaus Copernicus, and many more. No one could stop their good work, and they faced the worst challenges in life. They left their legacy because of their understanding about the highest purpose of human life and worked toward that goal.

The six parenting sessions were divided to teach the brain plasticity and hard wiring that originated from birth through adulthood, through the experiences from their external environment, and adaptations for survival, leading to the current adult parenting techniques and emotional balance. Healing was offered through the five teaching techniques of SAI Educare programs, and touch therapy and eye contact were given for parent to child bonding.

In each of the six training sessions, human developmental asset management teaching was conducted through sensory training of silent sitting, tuning in, guided imagery, theme of the week, positive thinking, quotations or prayer, storytelling or group discussion, group singing, and group activity. These human values teachings were included with the children as well as with the adults attending the training. Lesson plans were created for the children. All of the lesson plan formats have positive neurodevelopment effects and stress relief.

The following training sessions were based on the latest information on brain activity, developmental assets, and sensory input influences (Barnes 2000; Benson 1997, 2001; Rabin 1999). The multisensory integration training program that incorporated the five teaching techniques given in an earlier chapter was constructed using this information. The children's training sessions were one hour in length, with volunteers' help.

First session

Aim: To introduce the impact of multisensory experiences on human development and understand the neuroplasticity and opportune time to make changes for permanent brain wiring through sensory experience.

Objectives: To provide the participants with information about brain structural organization from the sensory experiences and the hierarchical brain networks and synaptic proliferation that result in actual structure of the gray and white matter of the brain.

Goals: At the end of the session, the participants should have an understanding of the human development per the brain organization and the impact of experiences, good and aversive, on the brain organization and architecture. Parents should be able to use multisensory integration to balance their emotions for the subsequent week.

Introduction

The goal of the first session is to let the trainees understand the difference between human and subhuman development with the help of PET scan data.

Dr. Harry T. Chugani's 0-12 months PET scan is used in every training session.

The colorful PET scans explain how the brain has no red activity even at one month of age but just enough activity to express basic needs. How rapidly the brain connects and forms pathways that show activity in the form of yellow and red emissions, showing of pathways that are laid down as a result of sensory input, recognition of signals to the senses, and wiring for the first time from outside to inside by twelve months.

If there is fear and trauma from emotional to physical deprivation, the senses quickly will tune out and withdraw. In applications and actual cases from patients seen by the presenters for the development of imagery processing of brain activity, the PET scan explains how sensory input from the caregiver and the needs of the infant because of the human desire to meet physiological, physical, psychological, and biological reflexive behavioral needs to be addressed. A lived experience causes the activity.

A happy face is pleasant to look at. Infants' cry to get picked up is a demand and needs gratification. A flat affect with no emotions from depression or a frowning or inebriated toxic look does not carry pleasant sensory input for the infant and can affect the infant's development through sensory withdrawal.

An infant with limited facial input, touch input, environmental input, chaotic feeding, and changing routines leave the child with a creation of adverse memories within their demands and gratifications of needs of hunger and soiled diaper. Chaotic routines will escalate in crying and exaggerated body movements until the infant perceives that engagement will not occur. After escalated crying and exaggerated body movements to try to engage the caretaker, the infant withdraws into sensing of the self. An adult needs to understand how children of depressed mothers are considered wonderful children to take care because of their limited crying and activities. This inactive, quiet child's condition is a perilous sign. The brain activity is being slowed down to basic lower brain fight-or-flight functions and infant withdrawal or disengagement at an early developmental age. A continuous state of this nature will cause psychopathologies, impulse control problems, or social deviation in the later development of that child, all related to attachment and bonding.

The sense of security, trust, and bonding makes smooth connections from basic brain stem needs to good connections from the brain stem via the midbrain to uptake by hippocampus by the third month. There is attachment and bonding established by this time. When this is established by six months, the early signs of signals processed reach the neo cortex or the prefrontal lobe of higher brain functions. This is a very important structure for cognitive associations, processing, intellectual gathering, and math skills, and is a seat for permanent memory. It rapidly and richly connects by twelve months from the external influences from the immediate environment. ***Any disturbances, like domestic violence, no music exposure, poor touch and interaction, and screen time, can have adverse effect and failed hippocampus-to-frontal-lobe connections. Therefore, there is a good chance, as early as twelve months, to create architecturally a brain that has broken connections leading to hyperkinetic child syndrome, poor language development, poor cognitive associations and processing, poor social interaction, and possible autism spectrum disorder.***

Nurture to prevent this comes from educating parents on parenting skills.

Activities

In the last hour of the first session, the participants are guided in real-life applications for themselves and their children through purposeful activities.

1. One of the first activities is called tuning in. In this activity, a regulated nasal breathing exercise for six seconds in, six seconds hold, and six seconds to exhale, meditating on the breathing timings with classical and soothing music, guided imagery, and socially appropriate action guidelines for the above, will be provided. This releases NO, which will supply increased blood flow to the brain by dilating the blood vessels and also create the hormone Oxytocin, which has negative feedback suppression on stress hormones. After relieving the state of anxiety and agitation, the rest of the role-play activities would be lined up. This also helps the immune responders. Guided imagery of golden sun and light and love was practiced every session. (A sample description was given in earlier chapter).

2. Another activity involves role-playing human trends and animal trends. In this, the participants are assigned to one group of humans and another group of many animals, and one will be the Lion King. All animals will try to convince the lion, monarch of the forest, that they be declared as far more superior to humans and give a description on how their hide, meat, and

horns and tusks are helpful even after the death. They argue that humans need to be buried or cremated, and they stink and are dangerous if they are not cremated or buried after death. This group tries to convince the Lion King how they are better or unique; examples will be comparison of behaviors and usefulness of fox, elephant, tiger, lion, and deer versus human beings. They even declare that human beings kill each other and animals without a cause and a mouse may run by, and the animals like the tiger will not even touch the mouse if it is not hungry. After listening to all complaints, the lion makes a statement that the human beings may behave like animals upon instinct, whereas animals cannot change their instinctual behavior; human beings are the only ones capable of changing the instinctual behavior to responsive behavior. Animals only know how to exhibit their instincts and cannot change.

3. In training sessions, participants are guided to discuss instinctual behaviors versus higher-order thinking. A discussion and dialogue that needs to be engaged in is to develop skills and tools to change reactive, impulsive, instinctual behaviors to responses that are not aggressive that can inflict injury. Discussion ends in recognizing that the transformation and change can occur only in human beings through wisdom and discrimination, whereas animals cannot change and act upon instinct.

4. Assigned activities are to maintain a journal, selecting two situations throughout the week before the next session that reflect thoughts, words, actions, and results in regard to reacting behavior versus reflecting behavior (reactive, brain stem–mediated animal behavior to reflective and responding frontal lobe behavior). The values, brief quotes, and possible spiritual reflections of the diary homework are recommended from the *www.saicdp.org* website, which gives quotes and a sample calendar. The website was designed and started in 1998 for positive or dynamic thoughts for parents, teachers, and children. The second part to the homework is demonstrated through the participants' active participation. When the children are returned to the participants, the primary caretaker and the child volunteer for the demonstration and learning.

Demonstration

The caretaker is guided to think loving thoughts about the child before him or her. Next, the caretaker and child look into each other's eyes. Then, while holding hands, they are guided to express their love for each other. The session touch exercise has been modified and demonstrated to the participant on how to use a fanning massage movement on the back of the child for calming the child as a relaxation technique and also as an option when the child is about to escalate as a method of diversion and to enhance release of Oxytocin.

After the first session, a teen mom, whose hand used to shake when her boyfriend called, who was very abusive to her and was a stalker, told me that she could not even hold the phone. She practiced the guided imagery with tuning in and meaningful meditation techniques and felt very self-reliant and relaxed and, within the week, felt confident to talk to him without shaking. Her anxiety totally got under control with five days of practice. Her three-year-old son, who was crying and was trying to get negative attention with hyperkinetic activities, also relaxed with eye contract and maternal touch, and giving those ten minutes after work made a difference.

Second session

Aims: Guiding the participants in understanding the impact of their own childhood memories; impact of storage and retrieval of those memories.

Objectives: To process how brain storage of certain childhood memories impact present-day choices and behaviors, how memories include multisensory information and understanding where certain memories may be stored.

Goals: At the end of the session, the participants will be able to identify how certain memories from their family experiences impact their choices for raising their child. Also, the participants will be guided in the "tuning in," and child focusing exercises began at the first session.

Discussion

The second session begins with a review of the previous session to make sure that the participants understood neurobiology, early childhood experiences, and development of a personality. The major areas include brain development, environmental stimuli, and experiences that create a behavior.

Review the intervention strategies from the previous session and the use or application of at least three to four techniques discussed and how they impacted their life this past week. All will do tuning in and positive thoughts for the day and move on to the next session.

The first step of the second session is to review what steps worked or did not work for them. Guiding them through their own nuclear family experiences expands upon this information. An open dialogue of their routines, what skills are performed without planning when a parent was going through challenging behaviors, what skills or tools were used to handle the situation needs discussion. This opens up the understanding of the participants' knowledge on different areas of the brain that have different functions.

PET scan images of appropriate pathways from nurture in a calm environment and experiences from inappropriate presentation from environment to the senses.

Breathing exercise, yoga and meditation, or "tuning in" with music or guided imagery calm and shut down the agitation of the right brain with environment and open up the activity of the left frontal lobe, parietal lobe, and prefrontal cortex, which is important for executive functions.

Activities

1. Parents need to sit down quietly and write down three actual memories from their own experiences of their caretaker's interactions, both good and bad, in childhood that involved sight, sound, smell, touch, and feelings. Parents really need to relax and recall the memories from a long time ago, understanding how those memories have stayed with them after many years. These are the multisensory experiences, which include sight, sound, and feelings reinforced into the permanent memory repository that they are not aware of at the current moment. Repetitious multisensory activities can create a strong storage and retrieval of that information. One may have had a difficult time writing down three memories from their

childhood experiences, if the memories were suppressed secondary to unpleasant moments, and it is all right not to remember. An explanation is that if childhood experiences were in the constant "fight-or-flight" states, then the brain would have been in a survival mode using the lower brain functions. In using the lower brain functions for survival, the person may not have complete recollection of his or her childhood memories because the survival was based upon those suppressed memories either with built-in anger around the experiences or with poor self-image. This phenomenon is not bad. Their understanding was that these types of memories existed and could be processed and "rewired" with present-day multisensory information for creating alternative behaviors or reactions. If retrieved, they can be faced with courage and efface the bad memories. This is because body makes internal Opioids (Opium) that results in poor memory and fainting at times.

2. These childhood family experiences impacted the current choices for raising their child.

3. Tuning in and guided imagery causes internal relaxation and help face the retrieved information. The techniques were discussed earlier.

Parents should maintain a diary of the personal experiences by selecting two situations that reflect thoughts, words, actions, and results in regard to reacting behavior versus reflecting behavior. Parents continue the practice of loving thoughts about the child before him or her. Caretaker and child look into each other's eyes. Then while holding hands, they express their love for each other. Continue to practice touch therapy as demonstrated on how to use a fanning massage movement on the back of the child for calming the child when escalated or when there is a refusal to calm down before going to sleep.

After this session, while I was conducting a pilot project with an elementary school in San Antonio Independent School District with a parent of a child who has ADHD that was not at all responding to Ritalin, Adderall, and other name brands. He was in counseling, and things were not getting better. He would dart out of the class rooms and had explosive temper.

I discussed situations that can cause toxic effects, and if they are not removed, the response would be poor. He was in school counseling only. The mom told me that she practiced the recommendations, and the child was relaxing with expression of love. The mother thought she needed spiritual counseling, and so did her husband and they went to church after several years and sought forgiveness and made confessions. She then told me that she thought about forgiving herself, and so did her husband. They felt that they no longer needed the alcohol every day.

Their story did stir me in my heart. Mother was seduced at five years of age, and her mother made her feel guilty and pushed her to a corner in her house and beat her up and blamed her. She did not know why she was beaten up. She could barely remember a few other times that she was beaten up similarly. She remembered feeling dirty and unsafe. Later on, she felt good while drinking as a teenager and started drinking so that she could sleep without worries. Till that day that I talked about hidden memories, she did not remember. Now she remembered and realized that she was not at fault, as she was so young and knew nothing, and she was vulnerable. I made her recall how Jesus had forgiven Mary Magdalena, who later became a saint, and all are capable of that through love and forgiveness.

Her husband had a similar story. He remembered being raped till twelve years of age, sodomized, and he felt very dirty and hated himself. To forget the ill feeling, he resorted to booze since twelve years of age and ran away from home at sixteen years of age. He never went to church till after the parenting sessions and now feels lighthearted with God in his heart.

This love and forgiveness are the healing elements in all spheres of life.

> *"I'm selfish, impatient and a little insecure. I make mistakes, I am out of control and at times hard to handle. But if you can't handle me at my worst, then you sure as hell don't deserve me at my best."*—Marilyn Monroe

> *"Being deeply loved by someone gives you strength, while loving someone deeply gives you courage."*—Lao Tzu

> *"Life is a challenge—Meet it! Life is a song—Sing it!*

> *Life is Game—Play it! Life is a Love—Enjoy it!"*—Satya Sai Baba

Third session

Aims: Some theories about birth order positions and selecting a partner based on these positions and expectations.

Objectives: To process how choice of partners comes from own family experiences and importance of understanding partner interactions' impact on raising children.

Goals: At the end of the session, the parents will be able to identify how certain memories from their family experiences impact their choices of a partner for raising their children.

Discussion: The parents need to write down three memories from childhood, adolescence, young adulthood, or adulthood that can describe the interactions from their lived family experiences from caretakers or other significant adults in their lives. After this recollection, the parents will write down the sights, sounds, smells, feelings, or possible tastes involved with those memories.

Leman's (1998) work on how birth order in the family dictates the type of interactions and expectations required of a child in the United States society is discussed first. Birth positions are explained from over twenty years of experiences with families in treatment with the presenters. Birth positions are a combination of biological birth, family expectations of that birth position, family life cycles, the family's community influence, and historical influences impacting the family's community.

Birth positions are explained as expectations from the family placed on a child, according to the child's biological and social birth history and values of the family.

The first birth position is explained as the rules, roles, and values of the family being carried on into future generations by the person in this position. The child is expected to advance, succeed, and promote the family's name and heritage and cultural rites and rituals. This birth position is expected to take the lead in decisions and the construction of guidelines in accordance with the family.

The second birth position has the child advancing in skills for determining who has the power in the family system and forming coalitions with that power. Who the person will become and how this person will behave will be determined from the types of coalitions that are formed with those in power within the family.

It is the third birth position that can be considered the family's emotional barometer. This individual is highly sensitive to the family's and other persons' nonverbal behaviors for determining emotional state. This person tends to be a mediator and possible peacekeeper of the family. Furthermore, they will try to avoid conflict at all costs. The family sometimes identifies this birth position as the problem child or the emotionally over reactive child.

The fourth birth position has more-relaxed family rules, guidelines, and expectations. This birth order position allows for family rites, rituals, and values to be challenged. The importance that the family places on the last child born to this family system will determine how much latitude this birth position is allowed for challenging or changing family guidelines. This birth position is allowed to explore different rites, rituals, values, and life choices when compared to the other birth positions. This position relies on others as the final word that will dictate guidelines, rules, and choices.

Open dialogue

Parents need to go through their experiences with family values and self-assess if they were influenced in choosing life partners based on this information.

Depending on the agreed-upon functions, roles and rules, and their desired balance within their own family, community, and society, the family may have different birth position roles assigned to the children that may surpass their biological birth order in the family. For example, in a family system where males are expected to be the primary persons for carrying on family rules, values, and success, a second biological birth male would be given first birth position over a biological firstborn female. The female would then be guided to the second birth order position role even though she was born biologically first in the family.

Understanding own birth order position will allow the individual to understand partner functions. Different birth order position roles in a long-term relation will generally involve less conflict. If both spouses are from first birth order, there will be conflicts, when both try to enforce rules, values, rites, rituals, and roles strongly bestowed upon them by their family systems. A first birth order with a fourth birth order would generally produce less conflict, as the first birth order would enforce rules, values, rites, rituals, and roles from the family system, while the fourth birth order position would expect the enforcement of new rules, values, rites, rituals, and roles. First birth order with second and third birth positions would be less conflicting if there is an agreed-upon position that the firstborn position's own family rules, values, rites, rituals, and roles will be the primary guide for the family. Second birth order positions will be less conflicting if there is the perception that the partner is one of authority or exhibits competency in the agreed-upon success of the family. Third birth order positions will be more stressed and anxious with partners that create constant conflict, while more capable with partners that can compromise on situations and are emotionally aware of the interactions in the family.

1. Parents will reflect on the choices and analyze their decisions in reference to the known and unknown experiences from early infancy that determine current decisions. If good, keep them, and if bad, understand and erase with positive memories.

2. Next, **"Tuning in"** is introduced again like in the first session and internal relaxation.

3. Write down the conscious application reflecting and referencing based on birth order position in challenging situations.

4. The caretaker is guided to think loving thoughts about the child before him or her. Next, the caretaker and child look into each other's eyes. Then while holding hands, they are guided to express their love for each other. Another exercise demonstrated is how to use a fanning massage movement on the back of the child for calming the child when escalated or when there is a refusal to calm down before going to sleep. This opens up the love for the child and expression of love and bonding. Internally, if love is replaced with anger, these moments really open up the gates in the heart and flood them with love and forgiveness.

Fourth session

Aims: To explore strengths, weaknesses, traditions, and values from caretakers, family, and community.

Objectives: Critical processing of memories during childhood, adolescence, young adult, and adulthood about the way they were taken care of, identification of current parenting style attitudes that can be attributed to different developmental experiences of childhood to adulthood, and exploring strengths and weaknesses of current parenting style.

GOALS: Parents understand the five parenting styles and realize the best effective parenting style, understand the weaknesses of various parenting styles, and understand that their current parenting is from their long-term subconscious memories of how they were raised and will be able to reflect on making changes to effective parenting skills.

Discussion: The first thirty minutes of the session is spent conducting a dialogue with the participants about the fourth session's applications of at least two areas of focus from the previous session's homework. During the dialogue, the presenters guide the participants in a review of the previous session's aims and objectives. Furthermore, the previous session's aims and objectives are connected to the fourth session's aims, objectives, and what they will be able to do at the end of the session.

Activity

Parents will write down at least three skills or tools that they hold important in parenting and, in another section of the paper, write down the skills or tools that are not helping in their present parenting. Examples of skills, like hardworking, or limit setting, love in discipline, spanking, controlling, token and rewards, and the amount of rules placed on children. If there were memories from childhood, put a C next to that value; or AD for adolescence, YA for young adult, or A for adult. Mainly because these parenting skills were learned parenting skills from their own experience.

A. In rigid parenting, the caretakers have clearly defined rules, roles, expectations, and family-to-community interaction guidelines. This type of parenting style believes that

rigid adherence to the defined rules, roles, and expectations of the family-to-community interaction are essential for the family. Rigid adherence to the caretakers' beliefs is rewarded with conditional love and acceptance. This means that the family member is loved conditionally through adherence to the caretakers' expectations. When there is deviation from the caretaker's expectations, the family member receives aversive feedback and is left out of family interactions, physical reprimands, and strong verbal reprimands or through the use of guilt.

1. **Rigid parenting does not accept developmental adjustments in their parenting.** 2.)

2. **Rigid parenting does not accept feedback or guidance from extended family members or others in their community**.

3. **A rigid parent would resort to corporal punishment, belting the children when they talk back. Some parents wash the tongue with soap and water**.

4. **Another characteristic of rigid parenting is that the caretakers' desires and decisions must surpass the children's desires and decisions.** The children are not allowed to make their own choices, and there is no compromise when it comes to their wishes or decisions. The children have a very difficult time making decisions without caretaker input. They are clingy and unsure of themselves as autonomous human beings when they venture outside of the family system. This follows through all developmental cycles into adulthood. This type of adult will seek rigid adherence that should be followed in their own new family system. Children also freeze and withdraw their senses with fear.

B. **A permissive parent provides for the necessary clothing, hygiene needs, and biological needs such as food and shelter. Permissive parenting provides limited rules and guidelines. These parents cannot withstand a crying child and will give in to the child's wants. They fail to sleep train and leave the child in anxiety states, clinging to parent, and indecisive. The children later on develop school phobia. In early infancy, parents fail to redirect them for self-regulation, and after the early infancy, these children grow up with no self-regulation or self-control and tend to become impulsive and demanding. The children become very autonomous and do not adhere to rules or guidelines that are not to their liking. In early childhood, they set their eating, sleeping, and activity schedules. When caretakers are required to provide rules and guidelines by the community, because the preteen children are wandering the streets past midnight or watching inappropriate television till early hours in the morning on a school night, the children are not flexible to the feedback and continue with the balance that is formed in the permissive parenting system. The children from this system defy adult guidance and social rules in the community. Many children from this system are reported to have conflicts within school from the pre-kinder years and with peers from early childhood throughout adulthood. The children from this system are more likely to establish criminal behaviors and be "street smart." An example is from my own case report of a mother who will not allow a twelve-year-old bed wetter to take the responsibility of changing the sheets and laundering them. This child has poor academic performance and peer relationships.**

C. Another parenting style is neglectful parenting. This type of parenting is similar to the permissive parenting in rules and guidelines. In addition to this, the caretakers do not provide for the necessary clothing, hygiene maintenance, and biological needs such as food and shelter. These family systems usually include caretakers with severe mental psychopathologies and/or substance abuse. Physical abuse, sexual abuse, and extreme neglect are evident in these systems. The children from this type of system exhibit a limited desire for appropriate social interactions and social success. The children may be observed with oppositional defiant disorder and have severe behavior problems, or with limited energy and extreme social withdrawal with learned helplessness as a major feature. The caretakers from this system are not open to extended family or community feedback. Neglectful parenting systems are closed from outside interactions or feedback to keep the "secrets" of abuse and neglect in the family going.

D. The last parenting style presented is effective parenting or authoritative parenting. These caretakers have clearly defined rules, roles, and expectations, and the family has good community interactions and expectations to give back to community. This type of parenting style has clearly defined rules and guidelines that allow for appropriate activities and rewards during the family life cycles and changes in childhood development. At the breakfast table, two choices of foods are given. When throwing a temper, consequences of poor self-control are well defined. The child is informed to make a choice within the next couple of minutes before the caretaker makes the choice. Usually, the child will make the good choice. This enhances the frontal lobe processing of making the decision through discrimination. If there is resistance to the selected bath timeline, the child is reminded that this was his/her selected choice. The caretakers are involved with providing constant feedback and interactions that allow for choice and autonomous development while safety and appropriate understanding of developmental cycles are also included. Effective parenting with open arms involves other extended family member interactions promoting loving and caring relationships. The family system surrounds themselves with the children's developmental effective autonomy. This family system has clearly defined rites, rituals, values, and cultural identity within the community. By cultural identity, it is meant that sets of norms are provided that guide behavior and help shape the identity of the family groups. The children from these family groups are sought out by their peers because of the clarity of their positions, clearly defined identity, purposeful activities, and success within the school system.

There is the combination of two or three styles of parenting at different times that leads to massive confusion in a growing child. This is the need-based mixed-parenting style. The child will not know what to expect and becomes what they want to be. Parents now need to process their own family of origin of parenting styles. One condition was that memory experiences may have been from a developmental period before higher cognitive processing of the information could occur. The other possible condition was that the person was in a **"flight-or-fight"** lower limbic processing for survival, and survival mode may have been the organism's primary brain activation. Furthermore, whichever condition was in existence, the adult would be able to recognize those unconscious memories' impact by the person's present-day responses and reactions to their children and other adults. For example, if they found themselves overreacting or staying escalated in a certain emotional state more than the circumstances merited, then it was very possible for those unconscious memories to impact the present-day functioning. Next, the participants were assigned homework to form a plan to identify strengths of their own parenting style and manner of addressing weaknesses of that parenting style.

Activity

For the last half hour of the session,

1. Next, "tuning in" was introduced again like in the first session; the method for tuning in was explained in previous chapters.

2. Another exercise demonstrated is how to use a fanning massage movement on the back of the child for calming the child when escalated or when there is a refusal to calm down before going to sleep.

Fifth session

Aims: To explore differences on how the participants were raised when compared to how their children are raised.

Objectives: To describe brain development and behavior at different developmental ages; describe maximum conditions for multisensory learning at different developmental ages; and introduce how values can be integrated with the multisensory interventions.

Goals: At the end of the session, the participants will identify parenting styles that influence peer choice, peer influence, partner selection, school functioning, and value formation from their experiences, and develop effective parenting style or interest to become an effective parent.

Open dialogue

Review the information presented in the entire sections on neurodevelopment and the parenting.

Activity

The participants were then assigned three groups labeled A, B, and C and given writing instruments. The A and B groups were instructed to read the instructions silently and write responses.

   A. Was given papers with instructions to process what a wedding ceremony meant to them and to write a message to the groom and the bride at the bottom of the paper.

   B. Was given papers with instructions to write down what birthdays meant to them and to write a birthday message at the bottom.

C. Was guided in a hands on exercise that involved construction of an oil lamp using a lime cut in half, squeezing the lime pulp and juices out, turning the lime inside out, filling the lime skin with lamp oil, and placing wicks within the oil. For one of the lamps, some participants of C were instructed to squeeze the excess oil out of their oil-saturated wick, while other participants were instructed to leave their wicks saturated.

After the participants in the assigned groups were finished with their tasks, dialogue was begun with the wedding assignment group. An example is a woman who was very depressed during a wedding ceremony and cried a lot, which was addressed from her memory. During our memory exercises with sights, sounds, smells, and feelings for the next twelve sessions, the woman was able to discover her memories of being thrown out of the house in her diapers during the breakup of her father and mother, and the father was getting remarried. She was ignored while she was screaming through the window to be let back inside while gazing at the father and the family. Processing these memories allowed the woman to be aware of the memories and then to "rewire" her responses to the wedding ceremony and she was able to get over the ill feelings and forgive her father for his weakness. She could even express her aversion toward men in her life and the anger she held for any harsh talking by her spouse to the possible trauma at a very young age.

The next dialogue was conducted with the birthday assignment group. During the dialogue with both A and B participants, the focus was maintained about the meaning of shared rituals with family memories that included sight, sounds, smells, and feelings. Also, the strength and impact of certain shared rituals such as birthdays and Christmas provide strong evidence of the type of parenting and childhood experiences that formed present-day parenting parameters within the areas of love, truth, nonviolence, appropriate conduct, and peaceful existence.

After the dialogue with A and B groups, C was requested to explain their task. Several participants were encouraged to provide information so that those who wish to participate were given an opportunity. Next, group C was requested to light their lamps with a match provided by the presenters. One lamp stayed lit longer, while the other stayed lit for a shorter time with a small flame. When asked what the difference between the two lamps was, the participants reported that when the excess oil was squeezed out, the lamp burned longer and brighter. The presenters guided the participants in a metaphorical dialogue using the oil lamps and their memories of shared rituals from their family of origins.

The activity was explained as a guide to understand human behavior. A sour bitter person was much like the lime filled with sourness and bitterness. Then that person has to work hard to squeeze that sourness and bitterness from their lives with an attitude of love and forgiveness to prevent stress from "fright/flight" effect on the brain and brain scarring to improve themselves and the relationships with the family. In this same process, the person turns his or her life inside out by getting rid of desires, anger, and bitterness of jealousy, and hatred, which had been hidden in unconscious memories, and is now conscious and able to comprehend. Next, the person fills his or her life with a new substance, "rewired" memories for addressing his or her life situations, interactions and parenting, filled with love, sympathy, empathy, which is the natural state of every human being. The wick represents the will that allows memories and thoughts to be transformed into actions and behaviors that will enlighten everyone. The caution presented is that the saturated wick represents the pride saturated in pride of selfishness and difficulty in letting go of the unwanted emotions and behaviors. An explanation for the short-lived light from the saturated wick and oil is that the pride and lack of change in emotions, attitudes, and behaviors lead to selfishness, anxiety, frustration, anger, turmoil, and ineffective problem-solving skills.

However, the wick that was squeezed out represents the removal of pride and "rewired" with good thoughts and memories; one can expect the creation of lasting memories that will present effective parenting parameters within the areas of love, truth, nonviolence, appropriate conduct, and peaceful existence. The long-lasting fire represents the enlightenment. Unless the selfishness and self-fulfilling thoughts, attitudes, and actions are not squeezed out forcefully, the harshness in words and actions can be reflected. This transformational approach in SAI Educare programs constructs interventions for school contact and issues. Furthermore, SAI Institute of Educare will continue to construct interventions for peer influence at the different grade levels of elementary, middle school, and high school.

The last hour focused on group processing of issues, concerns, possible obstacles, and possible options in the participants' selection of partners, parenting styles, and possible area of "rewiring." At this time, the construction of quotes or prayers that apply to their changing "rewiring" of their memories is explored. Strengths and weaknesses of the caretaker roles in parenting and desired objectives for their children are explored. At the end of the session, the participants will be able construct effective interventions for home and school use. Specific conscious choices to construct effective parenting will influence the type of peers selected, peer influence, partner selection, school functioning, and value formation.

At the end of the session, the participants are given the task to bring their children and their experiences of the five sessions to the last scheduled session. The participants are instructed to select two situations throughout the sessions before the next session that reflect thoughts, actions, and results in regard to reacting behavior versus reflecting behavior. The second part of the homework is to demonstrate to the other participants what active participation in the sessions will require continued practice in order for the "rewiring" to become part of the conscious memory.

Sixth session

Aims: The participants and the children were informed that the aims of the sixth session were for them to explain the use of knowledge of brain activity, multisensory information, and value information from own family of origin for raising children.

Objectives: How to continue the process of multisensory interventions with values for specific situations in parenting; continue to present effective parenting parameters within the areas of love, truth, nonviolence, appropriate conduct, and peaceful existence; continue to construct interventions for school contact and issues; and continue to construct interventions for peer influence at the different grade levels of elementary, middle school, and high school.

The participants were guided in their dialogue to stay within the aims and objectives of the sixth session. Participants usually reflected how useful knowledge of brain activity and developmental milestones allow them to modify their perception of self and of their children's capacity. Another area of focus included the determination of unconscious reactive memories being "rewired" to a more effective parenting style. Participants share how their past struggles in parenting were modified. They now understand how the multisensory process training improved the family functioning. The children of the participants also shared their experiences at the caretakers' sessions. The majority of the participants were grateful for the opportunity to be trained in optional methods of calming self and parenting. The participants were reminded that what had begun to be put into practice would disappear like the saturated wick of the lime if they did not continue the process for at least six months.

After these sessions, one family was able to pull their life back together by getting rid of the anger they held toward their father whom they felt abandoned them. The mom went back to LVN school. The son and daughter are rid of encopresis. They now are much older and are college kids in Oklahoma. No ADHD after our initial sessions. One boy who was on medicines for ADHD and not responding did not need meds when the father controlled rigid parenting and the tone of his voice changed to softer tone. He developed authoritative parenting skills. A teen mom developed courage to talk to a stalking boyfriend and faced the challenges. With guided imagery, she relaxed, and when she relaxed and developed authoritative parenting skills, her three-year-old started behaving well.

A case presentation (not a fiction)

A child was brought for misbehaving at five years of age with impulsivity and hyperkinetic child syndrome. His parents recently separated from a very stormy and angry relationship, and the divorce was finalized four months prior to this visit.

Parents and child were interrogated, and the situation of fright and flight was explained, as the child was angry and confused and was misbehaving to get parties together. Individual and family therapy were advised. Multisensory integration was taught, and the parents were asked to at least be congenial to each other and talk without anger.

The parents took notes and did not come till seven years of age, with the school ADHD and parent ADHD rating scales seeking medicines. They have not been in therapy, and they have not ironed out their differences. The child was at the mom's house for two months and the dad's house for two months. At both places, it was impossible to manage his anger, explosive temper and impulsivity, apathy, and cruelty to pets. He needed psycho-pharmacotherapy and was recommended cognitive behavior modification and insisted on family and Individual therapy.

He disappeared till he was nine years old, and this time, he was hearing voices. This can happen with extreme freezing dissociation in fright-and-flight reaction and indicates moderate to severe withdrawal of senses, trying to make his own internal dopamine for pleasure or paregorics that make one have flight of ideas. He was urgently admitted to a neuropsychiatric facility. He again came at thirteen years of age with history of several suicidal attempts.

He came for medical treatment of asthma a13 years in a critical state. After hospitalization, he was given maintenance protocols and advised home monitoring of respiratory status and to come back in two weeks. He wanted to leave the world by not taking medicines and ended up in the pediatric ICU and struggled for life for a week. Three weeks later, he swallowed fifty Tegretol pills. He wanted to die, as he felt that no one cares about him. After a lengthy discussion, he explained why. Here was the conversation:

"Ma'am, tell me why I should live."

"Why not, son? You are the one and only one in the whole creation who can make a difference for yourself and others. You can tend to nature, birds, animals, and other beings!"

"What for? Nobody cares about my feelings."

"It is hard to believe. I know your parents always came together for your visits! They seem to love you!"

"No, ma'am. They are interested in their own life. They do not talk to each other. I was pushed around between two homes, and I wanted both in one home. They broke up anyway, and I could not stand it. Then they fought all the time. My mom remarried, and the guy and Mom were smoking pot, and I started doing the same at ten years. I had to light the pot for my stepdad, whom I hate. My father is never around. He is not remarried, but he does not seem to care. I have nobody to be mine. Why should I live, and for whose sake?"

After this heavy conversation, both parents were called, and it was explicitly discussed how and why the brain got disorganized and their role as parents caring for him—to go to picnics and be civil and communicate. The father took a vow to be a daily part of his life. He does love his son, but he said he would move closer to the mother's house and promised himself to be involved. They tried to change for the sake of their child after almost a decade of anger as an inferno between them.

He came weekly for a month and once in two weeks afterward and, eight months later, once in three months. At each visit we practiced guided imagery, meditation, and nasal breathing exercise. A diary of human values with life application was given, and he was asked to read fun stories and pick positive values from them. The parents maintained reward system and communication with each other and went to lunches together periodically, and he felt that he had both parents and was OK to have two homes. At sixteen years of age, he gave up all habits, stopped all medicines like Tegretol, Lithium, Adderall, Clonazepam to calm nerves, and he smoked only three cigarettes per day. He went to regular school and graduated. It took him eighteen years to rebuild trust, self-worth, confidence, autonomy, and ambition to be somebody in life. We had many human values discussions and the highest purpose of human life. He started going to church with his father and to church activities like Habitat for Humanity.

By nineteen years, he came to give testimonial that he conquered anger through building self-respect, human values of self-respect, peace, and effective anger management, and tried to understand that there is a higher purpose for human life. He was the second child but the first boy in the family, and he was loved and pampered. But he grew up with domestic violence and misunderstandings, which led to poor orchestration of brain networks to be in "fright and flight," leading to the challenging behavioral outcomes. When he could identify how he connected to those behaviors as a result of experiences and memories that he was not even aware of, and subsequent understanding by parents of the cause for the current behaviors on the basis of neurobiology training, all parties could break this cycle of violence and lead a normal life.

This case presentation summarizes the evolution of behaviors that incorporate into the structure of the brain from molecular, neurostructural, neuroarchitectural, cellular, social, intellectual, humoral, immunological, neuroendocrinal, neurophysiological, biological, organizational, psychological, and biosocial behavioral outcomes from perceived stress, anxiety, poor nurture, and aversive environmental forces and experiences.

The proximal environmental stability assures a healthy life fulfilling the definition of the five domains of health as defined by the World Health Organization.

We are still fragmenting the knowledge that is available enough through neuroscience research, and with the most recent imaging data with DTI and ability to measure the activities, there is such an overlap between autism spectrum disorders, ADHD, ODD, OCD, LD, and ED. There is enough current data about the profuse synaptic proliferation, dispersed mini columns of neuronal organization with dispersed pattern, and increased glial cells that are inflammatory, GABA associated inhibitors of neuro proliferation, as a result of which small axonal connections are made and long-distance axonal myelination and connections not seen during the stages of dynamic brain growth of first four years of life. Later on, inflammation and degeneration are seen in the same area where there is profuse synaptogenesis, as compared to normal infants.

Excessive exposure to electronics, besides the family dysfunction, feeding habits, aversive environmental experiences, and lack of nurture with multisensory integration can be a major factor to prevent the spectrum disorders, ADHD, learning disabilities, and emotional disorders. From the current data and from the good results I personally had with a wide variety of case presentations, inflammation and neuroendocrine disturbances have been the underlying causes of the current health-risk behaviors and psychological and biosocial behavioral disorders.

The person in the case study above survived the cycle of violence through his own effort but after extensive education on how he became what he was. He was taught through his self-inquiry to become a wholesome individual, and he succeeded. The brain is malleable and plastic.

I am giving a diagrammatic presentation of definition of health, the 5 main tenets of human personality or character development, and the 5 teaching techniques that are internal relaxation exercises and cause multi sensory integration.

A TABLE FOR THE FIVE TEACHING TECHNIQUES OF SAI EDUCARE RELAXATION RESPONSE AND MULTISENSORY INTEGRATION FOR LEARNING

Intellectual wellness	Physical wellness	Intellectual wellness	Psychological wellness	Spiritual wellness
Truth is that we can change; animals can't.	**Right action** is good action.	**Peace** is our original state.	**Love** is balance in everything.	**Nonviolence** is our natural state.
Integrate this in all acts in schools and at work. (Positive Thinking)	Directly, we discuss the facts and actions. This is relaxation response	We plan to synthesize, balance emotions of and peace with contentment.	Do activities to overcome various learning disorders.	Enhance group and social milieu from a very young age.
POSITIVE DYNAMIC THOUGHTS AND LIFE APPLICATION OF THE ASSETS AND DISCUSSION OF ASSET MANAGEMENT, VERY DAY IN LIFE. Asset means a value like Maslow's assets for human evolution. These are non religious, human values.	TUNING IN FOR ATTENTION, FOCUS, MINDFUL MEDITATION, NASAL BREATHING IN-HOLD-OUT, SIX SECONDS EACH	GROUP SINGING LIKE CHOIR OR AT SCHOOL. LEARN CLASSICAL MUSIC AND HOW TO PLAY AN INSTRUMENT.	STORIES OF IDEOLOGY, POSITIVE HUMAN VALUES. DISCUSS THAT DAY EVENTS, STORY, AND ORGANIZE. THIS HELPS SEQUENTIAL ORGANIZATION AND REASONING AND CRITICAL THINKING.	ACTIVITIES THAT ENGAGE AND ARE EDUCATIONAL AND FOR RELAXATION ARE BETTER WITH SPORTS. ARTS LIKE DANCING, YOGA, WRITING, WORK ON SPATIAL REASONING AND PATTERNS, DRAWING, PAINTING, CROCHETING

The first line is the definition of health, and adults and children above four years can do this, and parents need to practice the contents of the table that will help raise children without stress. These are integrated, direct approach and indirect approach.

The second column defines the assets that are fundamental and cannot change. In the whole creation, human beings are the only ones who can change from basic aggressive and somewhat subhuman behaviors to the highest sainthood and self-respect and self-realization.

The emotions of peace, love, understanding, and adjustment are our properties, and they are inside of us. We are searching for thing that gives pleasure and happiness, and desires are never ending. So we are losing mental balance with the tortuous thinking to hurt ourselves and others. Newborns are always in a state of peace and love and basic in the demands for survival. Ambitions are all right as long as we can control and not hurt the body by secreting too much of the hormones of stress that will destroy health in all five domains.

Nonviolence is understanding everything in reference to love and positive outlook. It is a process and needs practice and better started at a very infantile state. The foundation will be strong and will be like a tree that is not usually knocked down with the usual rains and blustery winds. The roots are the character that we need to develop every moment while it is an opportune time.

The third column refers to have Direct, Indirect or Integrated approach in core curriculum subjects and in life application of positive thoughts and values.

The fourth column shows a few suggestions how we do not even need to go anywhere and spend any money on expensive gadgets and therapies, but intensely practice multisensory integration for one-self, and it is good for children to teach them sequential and temporal organization to enhance visual motor coordination, social involvement, and expression through narration. Self-esteem gets better day by day with the accomplishments. The catch is daily practice and life application of the given table.

A sample of 156 positive quotations are given on SAI Educare Calendar www.saicdp.org

Sample of the above Taxonomy implemented through stories

Goldie the Goldfish

Asset: Peace.

Sub Assets: endurance, patience, change in attitude, adjustment

Once upon a time, several fish lived in a glass aquarium in a little boy's house. Like many people have different names and personality, the fish had different kinds of thinking. Goldie the goldfish enjoyed his aquarium. But Maisie, Banger, Flyer, Lenny, Dreamy, and Mopey all had bad thoughts about staying in the aquarium.

What did they do?

Maisie wanted to get out by getting attention by making noise. It banged itself against the wall of the aquarium and got hurt and collapsed.

Banger wanted to get big to draw the attention of the owner so that he would be dropped off in a big pond. He overate and became very ill because of eating too much.

Flyer wanted to escape by flying out of the aquarium, and it did that, fell into the garden, and was never seen again!

Lenny was an angry one, and nobody wanted to be friends with Lenny, who became a loner and sad.

Dreamy became bedridden, not doing anything, and was sad too. And so was Mopey.

Goldie was always happy and played joyfully. One day, the owner felt that Goldie was too big for the aquarium and dropped Goldie into a big pond in the garden.

The cool breeze and the butterflies made Goldie ecstatic. He was too happy to see the birds. He enjoyed the fresh air. He could see the mountains, the sun, the stars, and the moon. He enjoyed the smell of flowers and the colors. He felt "life is so wonderful and Earth is so beautiful."

Quotation assigned to this story

We become what we think we are. Positive redirection is so important for children to extract the positive pathway and redirection rather than creating emphasis on being action oriented to complete a thought that comes to mind. Strategic planning and endurance give better results than a half-thought-out action.

Explain the meaning of these many positive redirections on the same story to be understood by different age groups. Discuss how all sub assets or values are reflected in the story.

"Slow and steady wins the race."

"Haste makes waste."

There is a nice Education in Human Values song that can be sung, or create your own tune with the following:

"If at first you don't succeed, try, try, try, again.

Don't despair, don't give up, and in the end you win, you win,

In the end you win."

An EHV song

"If you think you are fat, you are fat,

If you think you are short, you are short,

If you think you are sad you are sad,

If you think you are mad you are mad,

If you think you are crazy you are crazy,

If you think you are dizzy, you are dizzy,

But, but

If you think you are pretty, you are pretty,

If you think you are tall, you are tall,

If you think you are friendly, you are friendly,

If you think you are smart, you are smart

If you think you are helpful, you are helpful

All you think you are and you become

Make this world a happy place to play, sing, learn and help." SAI Institute of Educare

Make all kinds of fish in different colors and different sizes or cut out from a foam board or carve small fish from foam blocks and color them. Float them in water and recreate the story and discuss how rude thinking had damaged the fish that were rude and how patience paid off for one little fish that grew in its own time and ate well.

Talk about how each child will learn to do their duties and not demand what they want but can be compliant like that little fish and grow to be somebody who will be recognized in the end through their good character.

Character is not seen, but others feel what we are inside through our thoughts, words, and actions.

Make a declaration of that and make sure parents mark the recognition of practice for the following declarations.

Meena Chintapalli, M.D. F.A.A.P.

		Monday	Tuesday	Wednesday	Thursday	Friday	Saturday	Sunday
1.	I will not demand but listen.							
2.	I will eat right and not the junk to make this body healthy.							
3.	I will be good to get recognized and not be bad to be recognized by my family.							
4.	I will ask if someone needs help and will help.							

Good Tongue And Bad Tongue

Main asset or value is   Truth

"Truth never changes and always stays the same."

Sub Asset: Faith, accuracy

Faith: "Steady faith in you removes doubts."

Accuracy: "Every person has a reason to be born."

Guided imagery and meditation for ten minutes with tuning in classical music

Once upon a time, a king wanted to have an exhibition of articles that would make people happy. A lot of articles were brought like flowers, fruits, books, musical instruments, sweets, expensive diamond ornaments, models of expensive palaces, silk robes, and so many more things. The king went through all of them, but his attention was caught by a clay model of a tongue called **Good Tongue**. The face was a happy, smiling face with a pink tongue well within the mouth. The face and the tongue looked so beautiful. The king sent for the sculptor and said "I am very upset that the exhibit is so cheap, and why did you put it there? How dare you take the exhibit so lightly? Let me know why you put that there in the first place?"

The sculptor did not get scared with the anger of the king, and he very politely replied, "Sir, all other things give momentary happiness. Good tongue through speech of soft-spoken words of love and sympathy gives happiness forever, gives hope and cheer to the people suffering with grief and fear, and gives strength and confidence to the weak-minded people and even the homeless. Love and sympathy can be expressed only with soft speech and make one feel like a king or god."

The king was very satisfied with the reply, all his anger gone, and gave him a lot of gold. The same king wanted to have an exhibition of the things that make people unhappy. The hall was filled with sticks, whips, knives, swords, thorny plants, bitter fruits, poison, liquor, barking dogs, cawing crows, and a clay model of big red eyes with a black tongue abusing a poor lean and hungry man called *Bad Tongue*. The king called the sculptor again. The sculptor explained to the king.

"My lord, bad tongue can kill others' happiness and joy, destroy their hope and courage, and push them into the pool of misery. It wounds the heart forever, and it is the worst enemy of man. When tongue remains behind the teeth, it helps enjoy the food, can talk effectively, and become useful. Out of boundaries, it cannot function. So are the human beings when they cross their boundaries."

The king gave him another bag of gold and took him as a minister in his court so that he could be a good ruler.

Please discuss the above quotes so the children between two and a half and five years can understand and make a statement how they can be used in daily life.

Discussion for example

1. Do animals have tongues? Can their tongues talk?

2. Can animals say how they feel? Can we say how we feel?

3. Can we talk about good foods and bad foods? Can we choose good foods even if the tongue does not like the taste?

4. Unless you put the food on the tongue and chew it, taste does not come into the mouth. How can we say we do not like food till we tasted the food?

5. When you talk, you have to use your tongue. Did you feel great and good when you were praised and some told you they love you?

Adults in child's life have to be unbiased about various foods to make a child eat healthy foods. Discuss about using tongue for good speech and good food so that the body grows strong and with good personality.

Choose a song of good values from *Zootopia* or create your own song like I do.

>**When you are angry, you are not pretty**
>**When you are happy, smile is pretty**
>
>**When you are angry, words are not pretty**
>**When you are happy, words are lovely**
>**When you are angry, feelings are ugly**
>**When you are happy, feelings are holy**
>
>**When you are angry, body gets hot**
>**When you are happy, body feels cool**
>
>**When we are angry, we lose our friends**
>**When we are happy, we make more friends**
>
>**Oh, what a good thing to be happy**
>**Life is filled with love and joy**
>**Our circle grows**
>**Happiness is ice cream**
>**We can share x 2**
>
>**—Meena Chintapalli**

One can create music or rhyme with their creativity or just hum and make a rhyme.

Declaration: I will use my tongue for good speech and for eating good food.

This declaration is monitored by parents for the whole week with the following table:

		Monday	Tuesday	Wednesday	Thursday	Friday	Saturday	Sunday
1.	I will speak gently and softly.							
2.	I will eat good food and not junk.							
3.	I will try all new foods.							
4.	I will talk to make people happy.							

Parents or caretakers have the responsibility of giving points for each day of the week for following this chart. Tangible rewards are gold stars or smiley faces.

Man And Animal Dilemma

Main Asset: Right action

Sub Asset: Morality, cooperation, humility

Morality: "There is no morality than the highest truth that human life takes care of everything on earth."

Cooperation: "Do not discriminate by color, race, or riches."

Humility: "Feels happy to unite and work with others."

Guided imagery and tuning in classical music for ten minutes

Once upon a time, all the animals were very much concerned about the claimed superiority of the human race over the animals and the sovereignty over the entire universe. They felt that, given a certain chance to speak up, they will prove how inferior human race is! They went to the king of the forest, Lion King, and asked him to hold a conference. Lion called for a conference of all the animals big or small. On the first day of the conference, the fox represented the animals as a spokesperson for the day and made the following points.

1. Men and animals are alike in being born through the mother. Why are we animals and they human?

2. We cannot accept that we are foolish and they are wise.

3. We have no speech, and they do! Of what highest purpose speech does if they are using it for small talk and hurt people? What are we losing by not having it?

4. We are called as cruel. We do not harm anyone till we are hungry. No injustice or corruption is done against any creature to make our fill. We are less cruel than men. Mr. Tiger won't even touch a mouse if he is not hungry. We are not sly. Cows give hide and meat. Foxes give fur for coats to keep everyone warm. Elephants give expensive tusks, lift weights, and give hide. After animals die, our meat and skin are useful, but if human beings die, they are not useful.

5. Dog got up to say how faithful, loyal and loving they are compared to the human beings. In return, human beings feed them cheap leftover food usually, and this is their ingratitude.

Second-day conference

1. Tiger got up to say how the skin of most of the animals is used after their death and how useful the nails are as jewels.

2. Elephant got up to say how majestic they are and how every part of their body is useful for man and how elephant's ivory tusks are expensive.

3. Fox got up to say how the meat of the animals feeds the other animals and humans after death, whereas human body rapidly decomposes and stinks right after death and need to be disposed of quickly.

At this wise old Lion King got up majestically, fully agreeing with the facts brought forth by the animals, and made one last statement to all the animals. "My friends, I agree with all that you are saying. Please do not forget that we act on our instincts, and human race is the only race that helps the forest and water systems, moves things around, builds dams and protects forests, and keeps the balance in nature through their good thoughts. They can control their reactions. They are the only race that can change their behavior from bad to good and act like God. We cannot change our behavior."

All animals quietly acknowledged what the Lion King just said and did not declare war on human beings.

Activity: Create a role play for fun with the kids and create how each animal is good in their behavior—what can happen when they are angry, and how human beings can use music therapy and breathing exercise to control their anger and behavior. Do the guided imagery and meditation.

Song: From Education in Human Values

"If you are feeling angry, you need a change of pace

Take away that ugly frown and put a smile on your face

Smile, smile, smile, smile all day through

Smile, smile, smile, and the world is smiling too."

Declaration: We have all a gifted body to be useful

		Monday	Tuesday	Wednesday	Thursday	Friday	Saturday	Sunday
1.	I will try to be a good person.							
2.	I will think before I speak bad or hurt anyone.							
3.	I will breathe with my nose to control.							
4.	I will change to be good every day.							

Poor Man's Wealth

Main Asset: Peace

Sub Asset: Contentment: "Contentment lies in few needs and not on money."

Adjustment: "Accommodating other's views and being humble."

Guided imagery with classical music for ten minutes

Story

John and Jay were friends and neighbors in a big city where crime and casualties are a common occurrence, like New York. They grew up together. John used to be a very happy, easygoing, calm, and relaxed individual. He used to work very hard during the day. He spent nice times with his family and kissed his children good night. When he hit the sack, he used to be out like a light and slept like a log. He lived in a small home. Jay became extra lucky through his business ventures and became a millionaire and lived in a big house! He could not sleep well at night. He had to worry about his children when they went out shopping, as rich kids got kidnapped. He was restless till they got home safely. He had to make certain that all doors and windows were closed at bedtime and all the time! He checked the burglar alarms a couple of times. He used to get exhausted in the morning because of lack of proper restful sleep at night. One day, Jay had a lot of compassion and, overtaken by love and friendship, gave a big chunk of money and jewelry to his friend John. John was overwhelmed with this gift and talked about it all day. When the night came, he was troubled by the insecurity of protecting the wealth. He closed all doors and windows. He forgot to spend story time with his children. He had the worst insomnia protecting the jewelry and the cash.

He felt very agitated every day in the mornings and could not focus on his work.

After going through this for a week, John ran to Jay with a big apologetic hug and returned the jewelry and cash. He said, "Your friendship is valueless. But this gift took my peace and happiness away. Please forgive me for returning it." Jay understood and did not get angry.

"Money cannot buy happiness. Self-respect and love are inside of you to be happy. Having a few wants is good. Having a good life is what you make of it."

Sing the song "He's Got the Whole World in His Hands."

Declarations: Happiness is not wealth but a healthy body that has satisfaction

		Monday	Tuesday	Wednesday	Thursday	Friday	Saturday	Sunday
1.	I will listen to music and cool down.							
2.	I will pay with what I have.							
3.	I do not need new toys every store visit.							
4.	I will share my toys with a friend or family.							

Activities

1. Create origami With papers that are recyclable: boats, birds

2. Hide toys for a few days and see how new they appear after missing them for a few days.

3. Take a walk and teach about how plants grow and how they are content with the gardener and give a lot back like fruits, wood, seeds for more plants, shade for birds and people, home for birds, and take our carbon dioxide and give oxygen for our life. Without trees and plants, we cannot build a house.

4. They are majestic and peaceful, as they give and never ask anything at all. They have life, and they are dependent on human beings to plant and take care of them with love.

5. Human beings are destroying nature by using too much paper that comes from trees, like using paper napkins, paper plates, copying paper, paper bags, paper towels, and throwing them everywhere,. We can all protect nature by using reusable, scrubbable, and washable items in the house. We can prevent cutting down the trees to get ozone layers back. It starts with *you*.

Poor Tailor's Luck And Love

Main Asset: LOVE

"Love never seeks reward. Love is its own reward and award."—SAI

Sub Asset: Thoughtfulness

"All good thoughts create ripples of good words, visions, and actions."—SAI

Tolerance: "Be silent yourself; that will induce silence in others."—SAI

Guided imagery with classical music for ten minutes and nasal breathing

Story

Once upon a time, there lived in a small town a very poor tailor. One day, he had just enough cloth to make one coat. While he was cutting the cloth, he said, "May God help me survive from tomorrow." He cut the cloth to make the coat, got tired with hunger, and went to sleep. When he woke up the next morning, to his surprise, a beautiful coat was stitched with glittering buttons, ready to be sold. He and his wife were surprised, puzzled, and amazed. The couple put it up in the showcase, and soon after he put in the showcase, it got sold for a good price. Now he could afford to buy cloth for two coats. He cut the material and slept, like the previous day. By next morning, the two beautiful coats were ready-made, and the tailor got twice the money by quickly selling them. Likewise, his business grew. People from far-off places came to buy these beautiful coats. One night, both the tailor and his wife wanted to see who was responsible for these beautiful coats. They silently walked at the stroke of midnight to their shop. At the stroke of midnight, many dwarfs entered the workplace and started stitching the coats while singing with joy. They all worked together as a team to make as many coats as they could from the cloth that was there. The tailor and his wife were filled with joy, as his effort was graced with God's love to send his elves to help him grow in business. When Christmastime came, the tailor and his wife stitched neat coats as Christmas gifts for the dwarfs and pinned a note, saying, "Thank you, gentle elves, for helping us grow in business, and this is our gratitude and thank-you for all that you have been doing for us. Please accept our love to you too." The next morning, there was a note instead of the coats pinned to the cloth that was cut and ready to be stitched. "Dear sir, we are very happy that our dedication and compassion helped you. We do not expect anything but love to multiply. Thank you for your generosity. We will now go and help another needy person."

"Love always gives without expectation, and selfishness gets and forgets. Gratitude is an important quality."

Discuss the story and moral of the story with children. Discuss how they can show love for themselves and others. Share and not expect anything. Here, money came as the result of sharing work with love, and they did not leave money but shared with joy the hard work the tailor was unable to do.

A SONG

Love is a circle that keeps growing; Love is an expansion in unity

Love is joy and team work, Love for self is your courage

Love is an ocean with no limits; Love in you is so joyful

Love in others is your strength, Love the love for goodness sake x 3

Activities

1. Discuss various leaders who had self-confidence by respecting themselves and did great things, like Abraham Lincoln, Mother Teresa, and Florence Nightingale, because one who respects themselves also respects others.

2. Expecting something after helping anyone is not true love. Love does not ask back anything but helps others when they need help.

Declarations diary

		Monday	Tuesday	Wednesday	Thursday	Friday	Saturday	Sunday
1.	I will help Mom and Dad.							
2.	I will do my work and not give a hard time.							
3.	I will not hurt my sister or brother.							
4.	I will share my toys with a friend or family.							
5.	I will cooperate in getting daily work done.							

Parents have to create their own tangible reward systems. Music, silent sitting with tuning in music, and guided imagery have a critical role in attention and focus.

References

1. The Autistic Brain in the Context of Normal Neurodevelopment:
   Mark N. Ziats, Catherine Edmonson, Owen M. Rennert:
   Frontiers in Neuro Anatomy, 2015; 9: 1
   http://www.ncbi.nlm.nih.gov/pmc/articles/PMAC4548149Ziats@bcm.edu

2. 2. How music helps brain development in Infant : By Cara Batema Education Oasis: Building Baby's brain: The role of Music
   http://www.educationoasis.com/resources/articles/building_babies-Brain

3. Cognition. http://www.cml.music.edu/research-programs-in-the-center/infant-perception-and-cognition
   Neuroscience /ScitechPosted August 15th 2016 (Assal Habibi)

4. Music evolution and Neuroscience NIH public access article Biosocial Influences on the Family: A Decade Review Brian D. Onofrio and Benjamin B. Lahey: J. Marriage Fam. 22010, June 1; 72(3):762-782. Doi:10.111/j.1741-3737.2010.00729.x. Dept. Psychological and brain sciences, Indiana University, Bloomington , Indiana
   Tel: 812-856-0843, bmdonofr@indiana.edu
   Epidemiology and Psychiatry Department of Health Studies, University of Chicago
   Tel 773-702-2582. Email; blahey@health.bsd.uchicago.edu

5. Internet and Gaming Addiction: A Systematic Literature Review of Neuroimaging Studies
   Daria J.Kuss and Mark D. Griffiths
   Brain Science: 2012, 2(3),347-374;doi:10.3390/brainsci2030347.
   International Gaming Research Unit, Nottingham Trent University, Nottingham NGI 4BU, UK.
   Tel: +44-789-111-9490

6. Gray Matter Abnormalities in Internet Addiction: A voxel based Morphometry Study Yan Zhou, Fu –chin Lin, Ya-song Du, Ling-di Qin, Zhi-min Zhao, Jian-rong Xu Hao Lei Department of Radiology, RenJi Hospital, Jiao Tong University Medical School, Shanghai 200127, PR China State Key Laboratory of Magnetic Resonance and Atomic and Molecular Physics, Wuhan Institute of Physics and Mathematics, Chinese Academy of Sciences, Wuhan 430071, PR China Department of Child & Adolescent Psychiatry Shanghai Mental Health Center, Shanghai Jiao Tong University, Shanghai 200030, PR China Corresponding author at: Department of Radiology, RenJi Hospital, Jiao Tong University Medical School, No. 1630 Dongfang Road, Shanghai 200127, PR China. author at: State Key Laboratory of Magnetic Resonance and Atomic and Molecular Physics, Wuhan Institute of Physics and Mathematics, Chinese Academy of Sciences, West No. 30 Xiao Hong Shan, Wuhan 430071, PR China.
   E-mail addresses: clare1475@hotmail.com (Y. Zhou), fclin@wipm.ac.cn
   (F.-c. Lin), yasongdu@yahoo.com.cn (Y.-s. Du), flyingfool838@hotmail.com
   (L.-d. Qin), zmzsky@163.com (Z.-m. Zhao), xujianr@hotmail.com (J.-r. Xu),
   leihao@wipm.ac.cn (H. Lei).
   These authors contributed equally to this work.

7. Early Brain development Research review and update Pam Schiller Review article, Brain Development, exchange November –December
8. The Integration of Cognition and emotion during Infancy and early Childhood: regulatory Processes Associated with Development of Working memory
   Wolfe, Christy D; Bell, Martha Ann
   Brain and Cognition, v65 n 1, p3-13, October, 2007
   Descriptors Elsevier.6277 Sea Harbor Drive, Orlando, FL 32887-4800
   usjcs@elsevier.com
9. Persistent Fear and Anxiety can Affect Young Children's Learning and Development: working paper 9: Feb. 2010, National Scientific Council on the Developing Child(2010). Persistent Fear and Anxiety Can Affect Young Children's Learning and Development: working paper No. 9
   http://www.devlopingchild.net
10. How Musical Training affects cognitive development: rhythm, reward and other modulating variables Ewa A. Miendlarzewska and W. Wiebke J. Torsi Department for Fundamental Neurosciences, University of Geneva, Switzerland Publication in Frontiers in Neurosciences. 2013; 7:279
    On line publication: 2014, JAniary20. Doi:10:3389/fnins.2013.00279
    Email: ewa.miendlarzewska@unige.ch
11. Gray Matters: Too Much Screen Time Damages the Brain Review article by Victoria L. Dunckley, M.D https://www.psychologytoday.com/blog/mentl-wealth/201402/gray-matters-too-much-screen-time-damages-the-brain
12. Phonological Processing Skills of Children Adopted Internationally: Kathleen A .Scott, Karen Pollock, Jenny A. Roberts and Rena Krakow: American Journal of Speech-Language Pathology.673-683. DOI: 10.1044/1058-0360(2013/12-0133)
    Email. Kathleen.scott@hofstra.edu
13. Radiological Society of North America. (2016, November 21). Musical training creates new brain connections in children. *Science Daily*. Retrieved December 20, 2016 from www.sciencedaily.com/releases/2016/11/161121180403.htm .
    Radiological Society of North America. "Musical training creates new brain connections in children." Science Daily. www.sciencedaily.com/releases/2016/11/161121180403.htm (accessed December 20, 2016).
14. Musical Training creates new brain connections in children and may be useful in ADHD and Autism treatment: November 21, 2016, RSNA Journal Reference: C.J.Steele, J.A.Bailey, R.J. Zatorre, V.B. Penhune
15. Early Musical Training and white Matter Plasticity in the Corpus Callosum: Evidence for a Sensitive Period Journal of Neuroscience, 2013;33(3):1282 DOI: 10.1523/JNEUROSCI.3578-12.2013
    Early music lessons boost brain development Science daily 12 February 2013 Concordia University
16. Abstract: music has origins in emotion
    Music is communication with emotional expression

Charles T. Snowdon, Elke Zimmerman, Eckhart Altenmuller
Department of Psychology, University of Wisconsin, Madison
Tel: 608-262-3974 E.mail: snowdon@wisc.edu
Elke Zimmerman from Institute of Zoology, Tierarztlitche Hochschule Hannover, Hannover, Germany
Eckhart AltenMuller: Institute of Music Psychology and Musician's medicine (IMMM) University of Music, Drama and Media, Hanover, Lower Saxony, Germany

17. A Diffusion Tensor Imaging Study in children with ADHD, Autism Spectrum Disorder, OCD, and Matched Controls: Distinct and NON DISTINCT White Matter Disruption and Dimensional Brain-Behavior Relationships.

18. Journal Reference Stephanie H. Ameis, M.D., M.Sc., Jason P. Lerch, Ph.D., Margot J. Taylor, Ph.D., Wayne Lee, M.Sc., Joseph D. Viviano, M.Sc., Jon Pipitone, M.Sc., Arash Nazeri, M.D., Paul E. Croarkin, D.O., M.Sc., Aristotle N. Voineskos, M.D., Ph.D., Meng-Chuan Lai, M.D., Ph.D., Jennifer Crosbie, Ph.D., Jessica Brian, Ph.D., Noam Soreni, M.D., Russell Schachar, M.D., Peter Szatmari, M.D., Paul D. Arnold, M.D., Ph.D., Evdokia Anagnostou, M.D.
http://dx.doi.org/10.1176/appi.ajp.2016.15111435
American Journal of Psychiatry, 2016; appi.ajp.2016. 1 DOI: 10, 1176/appi.ajp.15111435 Source center for Addiction and Mental Health

19. Of the National Academy of Sciences of the United States of America, 108(32), 13281–13286. [Paper]

20. Huttenlocher, P. R., & Dabholkar, A. S. (1997). Regional differences in synaptogenesis in human cerebral cortex. The Journal of Comparative Neurology, 387(2), 167–178. [Paper]

21. Mills, K. L., & Tamnes, C. K. (2014). Methods and considerations for longitudinal structural brain imaging analysis across development. Developmental Cognitive Neuroscience, 9, 172–190. [Paper]

22. Lebel, C., & Beaulieu, C. (2011). Longitudinal development of human brain wiring continues from childhood into adulthood. The Journal of Neuroscience: The Official Journal of the Society for Neuroscience, 31(30), 10937–10947. [Paper]

23. Tamnes, C. K., Walhovd, K. B., Dale, A. M., Østby, Y., Grydeland, H., Richardson, G., ... Fjell, A. M. (2013). Brain development and aging: Overlapping and unique patterns of change. NeuroImage, 68C, 63–74. [Paper]

24. Blakemore, S.-J., & Mills, K. L. (2014). Is Adolescence a Sensitive Period for Sociocultural Processing? Annual Review of Psychology, 65(1), 187–207. [Paper]

25. Blakemore, S.-J. (2008). The social brain in adolescence. Nature Reviews. Neuroscience, 9(4), 267–277. [Paper]

26. Barnes, L.L., (2000). Spirituality, religion and pediatrics. *Pediatrics*, 104(6), 899-908.

27. Benson, H., (1997). Timeless Healing - The power and biology of belief. New York: Fireside.

Benson, H., (2001).The Relaxation Response, New York: Morrow.

28. Field, T., Healy, B., Goldstein, S, et al., (1988). Infants of Depressed Mothers show "depressed" behavior even with non-depressed adults. Child Development, 59, 1569-1579.

29. Field, T., (1992) Infants of Depressed Mothers. Development and Psychopathology, 449-66.

30. Field, T., Fox, N.A., Pickens, J., & Nawrocke, T. (1995). Relative right from EEG activation in 3-to-6 month old infants of depressed mothers. Developmental Psychology, 31, 358-363.

31. Field, T., (1999). *Early Interventions for Infants of Depressed Mothers.* In Warhol, J., (Ed) New Perspectives in Early Emotional Development. Johnson & Johnson pediatric Institute.

32. Kaplan, P.S., (1999). Child directed speech produced by mothers with symptoms of depression fails to promote associative learning in 4 month old infants, *Child 33. Development*, 70(3), 560-570.

33. Leman, K., (1998) The new birth order: Why you are the way you are. Fleming H. Revell.

34. Rabin, B.S., (1999). Stress, Immune Function, and Health, the Connection. John Wiley and Sons.

35. Search Institute (1999). Pass it on! Ready to use handouts for asset builders. Search Institute: Minneapolis, MN. *Developmental Assets for Preschoolers.* Retrieved May 2nd 2001, from www.search-institute.org/assets/preschoolers.html

36. Acta Neuropathol. 2006 Sep;112(3):287-303. Epub 2006 Jul 4.

37. Minicolumnar abnormalities in autism.
    Casanova MF[1], van Kooten IA, Switala AE, van Engeland H, Heinsen H, Steinbusch HW, Hof PR, Trippe J, Stone J, Schmitz C.
    Author information: Department of Psychiatry and Behavioral Sciences, University of Louisville, 500 South Preston Street, Louisville, KY 40292, USA. m0casa02@gwise.louisville.edu

38. Minicolumnar pathology in autism
    Manuel F. Casanova, MD, Daniel P. Buxhoeveden, PhD, Andrew E. Switala
    Email:Address correspondence and reprint requests to Dr. Manuel F. Casanova, Downtown VA Medical Center, 26 Psychiatry Service, 3B-121, Augusta, GA 30910; e-mail: casanova@np2.mcg.edu doi: http://dx.doi.org/10.1212/WNL.58.3.428Neurology February 12, 2002 vol. 58 no. 3 428-432

39. Neuropathological findings in autism
    Saskia J. M. C. Palmen, Herman van Engeland, Patrick R. Hof, Christoph Schmitz DOI: http://dx.doi.org/10.1093/brain/awh287 2572-2583 First published online: 25 August 2004
    almen, Herman vEngeland, PatrickR. Hof, Christoph SchmitzDOI: http://dx.doi.org/10.1093/brain/awh287 2572-2583 First published online: 25 August 2004

40. The minicolumn hypothesis in neuroscience
    Daniel P. Buxhoeveden, Manuel F. Casanova
    DOI: http://dx.doi.org/10.1093/brain/awf110 935-951 First published online: 1 May 2002

41. Development and specification of GABAergic cortical interneurons

Corey Kelsom andWange Lu
*Cell & Bioscience*20133:19 **DOI:** 10.1186/2045-3701-3-19
© Kelsom and Lu; licensee BioMed Central Ltd. 2013
Received: 25 February 2013.**Accepted:** 28 March 2013.
Published: 23 April 2013

42. From Best Practices to Breakthrough Impacts
Suggested citation: Center on the Developing Child at Harvard University (2016). From Best Practices to Breakthrough Impacts: A Science-Based Approach to Building a More Promising Future for Young Children and Families. http://www.developingchild.harvard.edu
May 2016, Center on the Developing Child at Harvard University

43. Mapping Early Brain Development in Autism
Eric Courchesne,1,2,* Karen Pierce,1,2 Cynthia M. Schumann,1,2 Elizabeth Redcay,2,3 Joseph A. Buckwalter,1,2
Daniel P. Kennedy,1 and John Morgan1,2
1Department of Neurosciences, School of Medicine, University of California, San Diego, La Jolla, CA 92093, USA
Autism Center of Excellence, School of Medicine, University of California, San Diego, La Jolla, CA 92093, USA
Department of Psychology, University of California, San Diego, La Jolla, CA 92093, USA
Correspondence: ecourchesne@ucsd.edu
DOI 10.1016/j.neuron.2007.10.016

44. Bandura, A., (1977). *Social learning theory.* Englewood Cliffs, N.J.: Prentice-Hall.

45. Barratt, E.S., Kent, T., Bryant, S., & Felthous, A., (1991). A controlled study of phenytoin in impulsive aggression. *Journal of Clinical Psychopharmocology*, 11, 388-389.

46. Binder, R.L., & McNeil, D.E., (1990). The relationship of gender to violent behavior in acutely disturbed psychiatric patients. *Journal of Clinical Psychiatry*, 51, 110-114.

Chugani, H.T., & Phelps, M.E., (1986). Maturational changes in cerebral function in infants determined by 18 FDG positron emission tomography. *Science,* 231, 840-643.

47. Chugani, H.T., (1999). Metabolic imaging: A window on brain development and plasticity. *The Neuroscientist.* 5(1), 29-40.

48. Chugani, H.T., Behen, M.E., Muzik, O, Juhasz, C, Nagy, F., Chugani, D.C., (2001). Local Brain Functional Activity following Early Deprivation: A study of Postinstitutionalized Romanian Orphans. *Neuroimage,* 14(16), 1290-1301.

49. Coccaro, E., (1992). Impulsive aggression and central serotonergic system function in humans: An example of dimensional brain-behavior relationship. *International Clinical Psychopharmacology*, 7, 3-12.

50. Costa, P., McCrae, R., & Dye, D., (1991). Facete scales for aggreeableness and conscientiousness: A revision of the NEO personality inventory. *Personality and Individual Differences*, 12, 887-898.

51. Cummins, J., (1985). The construct of language proficiency in bilingual education. In: J.E. Alatis (Ed.), Perspective on bilingualism and bilingual education (p.209-231). Washington, D.C., Georgetown University Press.

52. DeCasper, A.J., & Spence, M.J. (1986). Prenatal maternal speech influences newborn's perception of speech sounds. *Infant Behavior Development,* 9, 133-150.

53. Diamond, A., (1994). Faculties of Learning by infants, a summary. *Behavioral Neuroscience*, 8, 659-680.

54. Estroff, S.E., & Zimmer, C., (1994). *Social networks, social support, and violence amongst persons with severe, persistent mental illness.* In. Monahan, J. & Steadmand, H.J. (Eds.), Violence and mental disorder: developments in risk assessment (p 259-295). Chicago: The University of Chicago Press.

55. Farver, J. M., Natera, L. X., & Frosch, D. L., (1999). Effects of community violence on inner-city preschoolers and their families. *Journal of Applied Developmental Psychology Special Issue,* 20(1), 143-158.

56. Fox, N.A., (1991). If it's not left, it's right. *American Psychologist,* 46, 863-872.

57. Haydon, P.G. & Drapeau, P., (1995). From contact to connection, Early in synaptogenesis. *Trends in Neuroscience,* 18, 196-201.

58. Hernandez, R.M., (1999). Touch therapy for children and adolescents: Innovative psychotherapy techniques in child and adolescent therapy. 2nd edition. 435-453.

59. Hofer, M.A., (1994). Changing parental roles, hidden regulators in attachment, separation and loss. In. Fox, Nathan, ED. The development of emotion regulation: Biological and behavioral considerations. Monographs of the society for research in child development, 59, 2-3.

60. Huttenlocher, P.R., (1990). Morphometric study of human cerebral cortex development. *Neuropsychologia,* 28, 517-527.

61. Huttenlocher, P.R., (1999). *The role of Early Experience in Infant development.* Johnson & Johnson Pediatrics Round Table, 15-28.

62. Kaufman, J., (1997). *Characteristics of emotional and behavioral disorders of children and youth* (5th ed.) Columbus, OH: Merrill/ Macmillan.

63. Kingery, P.M., (1993). Violence, drugs, and victimization among young African males. (Race and ethnic studies, research and policy report No. 3&4), Texas A & M University.

64. Kingery, P.M., Coggershall, M.B., & Alford, A.A. (1998) Violence at school: Recent evidence from 4 national surveys. *Psychology in the schools*, 35(3), 247-258.

65. Kolb, B., (1999). Role of Early Experience in Infant Development. Johnson & Johnson pediatric Round Table, 5-14.

66. Kolb, B., (4th eds.) (1996). *Fundamentals of Human Neuropsychology.* New York: Freeman.

67. Kreutzer, N.J., (2001). Song acquisition among rural Shona-speaking Simbabwean children from birth to 7 years. *Journal of Research in Music Education,* 49 (3), 198-211.

68. Kuhl, P.K., (1999). Language Acquisition. Johnson & Johnson Round table, 101-125.

69. Loeber, R., & Farrington, D. (1998). Serious and violent juvenile offenders: Risk factors and successful interventions. Beverly Hills: Sage.

70. Mayer, G.R., (1995). Preventing antisocial behavior in the schools. *Journal of Applied Behavior Analysis,* 28, 467-478.

71. Mazel, B., (1983). Nine temperament dimensions of Thomas and chess, New York.

72. Miller, A.B., Cohen, M., Galvin, D.M., (Eds.), (1996). C.S.A.P. substance abuse resource guide: Violence. National Clearinghouse for Alcohol and Drug Information, Development: Center for Substance Abuse Prevention.

73. Mooncey, S., Giannakoulopoulos X., Glover V, Acolet D, Modi, N., (1997). The effect of mother-infant skin-to-skin contact on plasma Cortisol and B-endorphin concentration in preterm neonates. *Infant behavior and Development,* 20, 553-557.

74. Monahan, J., & Steadman, H.J., (Eds.). (1994). *Violence and mental disorder: Developments in risk assessment.* Chicago: The University of Chicago Press.

75. Perry, B.D., (1995). Childhood trauma, the neurobiology of adaptation and use-dependent Development of the brain: How states become traits. *Infant Mental Health,* 16(4), 271-291. D. Cohen (Eds.), Manual of developmental psychopathology.

76. Pliszka, S., (2002). UTHSCSA News on ADHD Study.

77. Ramirez, J., Pasta, D., Yuen, S., Billings, D., & Ramey, D., (1991). Final report: Longitudinal study of structure English immersion strategy, early-exit and exit transitional bilingual education programs for language-minority children, Vol. I & II, San Mateo, CA: Aguirre International.

78. Ratey, J.J., (2001). *Users guide to Brain.* New York: Pantheon books.

79. Rothbart, M.K., Posner, M.I., & Hershey, K.L., (1995). Temperament, attention, and developmental psychopathology. In D. Cicchetti

80. Rutherford, R.B., & Nelson, C.M., (1995). Management of aggressive and violent behavior in schools. *Focus on Exceptional Children,* 27, 1-15.

81. Swanson, J.W., Holzer, C.E., Ganju, V.K., & Jono, R.T., (1990). Violence and psychiatric disorder in the community: Evidence from the Epidemiological Catchment Area surveys. Hospital and Community Psychiatry, 41, 761-770.

82. Wiand, L., (2003). Sacred/Shamanic music and its effects on Trauma Related Disorders. Poster Presentation at the Integrating Research on Spirituality and Health and Well-being into service Delivery [ICIHS], April 1-3, Bethesda, MD.

83. Volavka, A., (1995). *Neurobiology of Violence.* New York: American

84. NIMH grant 2-ROI-MH36840 awarded to REFERENCES

85. E.C.Alexander, A.L., Lee, J.E., Lazar, M., Boudos, R., DuBray, M.B.,

86. Oakes, T.R., Miller, J.N., Lu, J., Jeong, E.K., McMahon, W.M., et al. (2007). Diffusion tensor imaging of the corpus callosum in Autism. Neuroimage 34, 61–73.

87. Anderson, A.W., Marois, R., Colson, E.R., Peterson, B.S., Duncan,

88. C.C., Ehrenkranz, R.A., Schneider, K.C., Gore, J.C., and Ment, L.R. (2001). Neonatal auditory activation detected by functional magnetic resonance imaging. Magn. Reson. Imaging 19, 1–5.

89. Araghi-Niknam, M., and Fatemi, S.H. (2003). Levels of Bcl-2 and P53 are altered in superior frontal and cerebellar cortices of autistic subjects. Cell. Mol. Neurobiol. 23, 945–952.

90. Aylward, E., Minshew, N., Goldstein, G., Honeycutt, N., Augustine, A., Yates, K., Barta, P., and Pearlson, G. (1999). MRI volumes of amygdala and hippocampus in non-mentally retarded autistic adolescents and adults. Neurology 53, 2145–2150.

91. Aylward, E.H., Minshew, N.J., Field, K., Sparks, B.F., and Singh, N. (2002). Effects of age on brain volume and head circumference in autism. Neurology 59, 175–183.

92. Bailey, A., Luthert, P., Dean, A., Harding, B., Janota, I., Montgomery, M., Rutter, M., and Lantos, P. (1998). A clinicopathological study of autism. Brain 121, 889–905.

93. Barnea-Goraly, N., Kwon, H., Menon, V., Eliez, S., Lotspeich, L., and Reiss, A.L. (2004). White matter structure in autism: preliminary evidence from diffusion tensor imaging. Biol. Psychiatry 55, 323–326.

94. Baron-Cohen, S., Allen, J., and Gillberg, C. (1992). Can autism be detected at 18 months? The needle, the haystack, and the CHAT. Br. J. Psychiatry 161, 839–843.

95. Bartholomeusz, H.H., Courchesne, E., and Karns, C. (2002). Relationship between head circumference and brain volume in healthy normal toddlers, children, and adults. Neuropediatrics 33, 239–241.

96. Bastuji, H., Perrin, F., and Garcia-Larrea, L. (2002). Semantic analysis of auditory input during sleep: studies with event related potentials. Int. J. Psychophysiol. 46, 243–255.

97. Bates, E., Thal, D., Finlay, B., and Clancy, B. (2003). Early language development and its neural correlates. In Child Neuropsychology, Part II, S.J. Segalowitz and I. Rapin, eds. (New York: Elsevier), pp. 525–592.

98. Bauman, M.L., and Kemper, T.L. (2005). Neuroanatomic observations of the brain in autism: a review and future directions. Int. J. Dev. Neurosci. 23, 183–187.

99. Belmonte, M., Cook, E.H., Jr., Anderson, G., Rubenstein, J., Greenough,W.,Beckel-Mitchener, A., Courchesne, E., Boulanger, L., Powell, S., Levitt, P., et al. (2004). Autism as a disorder of neural information processing: directions for research and targets for therapy. Mol. Psychiatry 9, 646–663.

100. Ben Bashat, D., Kronfeld-Duenias, V., Zachor, D.A., Ekstein, P.M., Hendler, T., Tarrasch, R., Even, A., Levy, Y., and Ben Sira, L. (2007). Accelerated maturation of white matter in young children with autism: a high b value DWI study. Neuroimage 37, 40–47.

101. Bloss, C.S., and Courchesne, E. (2007). MRI neuroanatomy in young girls with autism: a preliminary study. J. Am. Acad. Child Adolesc. Psychiatry 46, 515–523.

102. Boger-Megiddo, I., Shaw, D.W., Friedman, S.D., Sparks, B.F., Artru, A.A., Giedd, J.N., Dawson, G., and Dager, S.R. (2006). Corpus callosum morphometrics in young children with autism spectrum disorder. J. Autism. Dev. Disord. 36, 733–739.

103. Buxhoeveden, D., Semendeferi, K., Buckwalter, J., Schenkar, N., Switzer, R., and Courchesne, E. (2006). Reduced minicolumns in the frontal cortex in patients with autism. Neuropathol. Appl. Neurobiol. 32, 483–491.

104. Campbell, D.B., Sutcliffe, J.S., Ebert, P.J., Militerni, R., Bravaccio, C., Trillo, S., Elia, M., Schneider, C., Melmed, R., Sacco, R., et al. (2006). A genetic variant that disrupts MET transcription is associated with autism. Proc. Natl. Acad. Sci. USA 103, 16834–16839.

105. Campbell, D., D'Oronzio, R., Garbett, K., Ebert, P., Mirnics, K., Levitt, P., and Persico, A. (2007). Disruption of cerebral cortex MET signaling in autism spectrum disorder. Ann. Neurol. 62, 243–250. Carper, R.A., and Courchesne, E. (2005). Localized enlargement of the frontal cortex in early autism. Biol. Psychiatry 57, 126–133.

106. 106. Carper, R.A., Moses, P., Tigue, Z.D., and Courchesne, E. (2002). Cerebral lobes in autism: early hyperplasia and abnormal age effects. Neuroimage 16, 1038–1051.

107. Carver, L.J., and Dawson, G. (2002). Development and neural bases of face recognition in autism. Mol. Psychiatry 7 (Suppl 2), S18–S20. Casanova, M.F., Buxhoeveden, D.P., Switala, A.E., and Roy, E. (2002). Minicolumnar pathology in autism. Neurology 58, 428–432.

108. Casanova, M.F., van Kooten, I.A., Switala, A.E., van Engeland, H., Heinsen, H., Steinbusch, H.W., Hof, P.R., Trippe, J., Stone, J., and Schmitz, C. (2006). Minicolumnar abnormalities in autism. Acta Neuropathol. (Berl) 112, 287–303.

109. Castelli, F., Frith, C., Happe, F., and Frith, U. (2002). Autism, Asperger syndrome and brain mechanisms for the attribution of mental states to animated shapes. Brain 125, 1839–1849. Cheour, M., Martynova, O., Naatanen, R., Erkkola, R., Sillanpaa, M., Kero, P., Raz, A., Kaipio, M.L., Hiltunen, J., Aaltonen, O., et al. (2002). Speech sounds learned by sleeping newborns. Nature 415, 599–600.

110. Cherkassky, V.L., Kana, R.K., Keller, T.A., and Just, M.A. (2006). Functional connectivity in a baseline resting-state network in autism. Neuroreport 17, 1687–1690.

111. Chubykin, A., Liu, A., Comoletti, D., Tsigelny, I., Taylor, P., and Sü̈dhof, T. (2005). Dissection of synapse induction by neuroligins: effect of a neuroligin mutation associated with autism. J. Biol. Chem. 280, 22365–22374.

112. Chung, M.K., Dalton, K.M., Alexander, A.L., and Davidson, R.J. (2004). Less white matter concentration in autism: 2D voxel-based morphometry. Neuroimage 23, 242–251.

113. Dong, Guangheng, Elise E Devito, Xiaoxia Du, and Zhuoya Cui. "Impaired Inhibitory Control in 'Internet Addiction Disorder': A Functional Magnetic Resonance Imaging Study." *Psychiatry Research* 203, no. 2–3 (September 2012): 153–158. doi:10.1016/j.pscychresns.2012.02.001.

Dong, Guangheng, Yanbo Hu, and Xiao Lin. "Reward/Punishment Sensitivities Among Internet Addicts: Implications for Their Addictive Behaviors." *Progress in Neuro-Psychopharmacology & Biological Psychiatry* 46 (October 2013): 139–145. doi:10.1016/j.pnpbp.2013.07.007.

114. Han, Doug Hyun, Nicolas Bolo, Melissa A. Daniels, Lynn Arenella, In Kyoon Lyoo, and Perry F. Renshaw. "Brain Activity and Desire for Internet Video Game Play." *Comprehensive Psychiatry* 52, no. 1 (January 2011): 88–95. doi:10.1016/j.comppsych.2010.04.004.

115. Hong, Soon-Beom, Jae-Won Kim, Eun-Jung Choi, Ho-Hyun Kim, Jeong-Eun Suh, Chang-Dai Kim, Paul Klauser, et al. "Reduced Orbitofrontal Cortical Thickness in Male Adolescents with Internet Addiction." *Behavioral and Brain Functions* 9, no. 1 (2013): 11. doi:10.1186/1744-9081-9-11.

116. Hong, Soon-Beom, Andrew Zalesky, Luca Cocchi, Alex Fornito, Eun-Jung Choi, Ho-Hyun Kim, Jeong-Eun Suh, Chang-Dai Kim, Jae-Won Kim, and Soon-Hyung Yi. "Decreased Functional Brain Connectivity in Adolescents with Internet Addiction." Edited by Xi-Nian Zuo. *PLoS ONE* 8, no. 2 (February 25, 2013): e57831. doi:10.1371/journal.pone.0057831.

117. Hou, Haifeng, Shaowe Jia, Shu Hu, Rong Fan, Wen Sun, Taotao Sun, and Hong Zhang. "Reduced Striatal Dopamine Transporters in People with Internet Addiction Disorder." *Journal of Biomedicine & Biotechnology* 2012 (2012): 854524. doi:10.1155/2012/854524.

118. Kim, Sang Hee, Sang-Hyun Baik, Chang Soo Park, Su Jin Kim, Sung Won Choi, and Sang Eun Kim. "Reduced Striatal Dopamine D2 Receptors in People with Internet Addiction." *Neuroreport* 22, no. 8 (June 11, 2011): 407–411. doi:10.1097/WNR.0b013e328346e16e.

119. Ko, Chih-Hung, Gin-Chung Liu, Sigmund Hsiao, Ju-Yu Yen, Ming-Jen Yang, Wei-Chen Lin, Cheng-Fang Yen, and Cheng-Sheng Chen. "Brain Activities Associated with Gaming Urge of Online Gaming Addiction." *Journal of Psychiatric Research* 43, no. 7 (April 2009): 739–747. doi:10.1016/j.jpsychires.2008.09.012.

120. Kühn, S, A Romanowski, C Schilling, R Lorenz, C Mörsen, N Seiferth, T Banaschewski, et al. "The Neural Basis of Video Gaming." *Translational Psychiatry* 1 (2011): e53. doi:10.1038/tp.2011.53.

121. Lin, Fuchun, Yan Zhou, Yasong Du, Lindi Qin, Zhimin Zhao, Jianrong Xu, and Hao Lei. "Abnormal White Matter Integrity in Adolescents with Internet Addiction Disorder: A Tract-Based Spatial Statistics Study." *PloS One* 7, no. 1 (2012): e30253. doi:10.1371/journal.pone.0030253.

122. Rideout, Victoria J., Ulla G. Foehr, and Donald F. Roberts. "Generation M2: Media in the Lives of 8- to 18- Year Olds." *Kaiser Family Foundation Study* (2010). http://kff.org/other/poll-finding/report-generation-m2-media-in-the-lives/.

123. Weng, Chuan-Bo, Ruo-Bing Qian, Xian-Ming Fu, Bin Lin, Xiao-Peng Han, Chao-Shi Niu, and Ye-Han Wang. "Gray Matter and White Matter Abnormalities in Online Game Addiction." *European Journal of Radiology* 82, no. 8 (August 2013): 1308–1312. doi:10.1016/j.ejrad.2013.01.031.

124. Yuan, Kai, Ping Cheng, Tao Dong, Yanzhi Bi, Lihong Xing, Dahua Yu, Limei Zhao, et al. "Cortical Thickness Abnormalities in Late Adolescence with Online Gaming Addiction." Edited by Bogdan Draganski. *PLoS ONE* 8, no. 1 (January 9, 2013): e53055. doi:10.1371/journal.pone.0053055.

125. Yuan, Kai, Chenwang Jin, Ping Cheng, Xuejuan Yang, Tao Dong, Yanzhi Bi, Lihong Xing, et al. "Amplitude of Low Frequency Fluctuation Abnormalities in Adolescents with Online Gaming Addiction." Edited by Krish Sathian. *PLoS ONE* 8, no. 11 (November 4, 2013): e78708. doi:10.1371/journal.pone.0078708.

126. Yuan, Kai, Wei Qin, Guihong Wang, Fang Zeng, Liyan Zhao, Xuejuan Yang, Peng Liu, et al. "Microstructure Abnormalities in Adolescents with Internet Addiction Disorder." Edited by Shaolin Yang. *PLoS ONE* 6, no. 6 (June 3, 2011): e20708. doi:10.1371/journal.pone.0020708.

127. Zhou, Yan, Fu-Chun Lin, Ya-Song Du, Ling-di Qin, Zhi-Min Zhao, Jian-Rong Xu, and Hao Lei. "Gray Matter Abnormalities in Internet Addiction: A Voxel-Based Morphometry Study." *European Journal of Radiology* 79, no. 1 (July 2011): 92–95. doi:10.1016/j.ejrad.2009.10.025.

Figures and Diagrams

Figure 1:	A Happy family	Page 3
Figure 2:	Extended Happy Family	Page 7
Figure 3:	New Born Feet in Parent's Hands	Page 7
Figure 4:	Neurons and Neuroglial Cells	Page 14
Figure 5:	Left vs Right Brain assigned functions	Page 17
Figure 6:	Illustration of activity in and around brain	Page 19
Figure 7:	Dynamic Brain growth illustration like a cobweb	Page 23
Figure 8:	Normal sagital section of brain anatomy	Page 24
Figure 9:	Illustration of Brain Anatomy	Page 25
Figure 10:	Functional Areas of Brain	Page 26
Figure 11:	Illustration of Active brain waves	Page 30
Figure 12:	Biological Unit of the Society	Page 34
Figure 13:	Limbic System functional connections	Page 35
Figure 14:	Amygdala Functions	Page 36
Figure 15:	Sagital View functions of brain	Page 39
Figure 16:	Functional Brain Illustration	Page 40
Figure 17:	PET scan 0-12 months brain Activity and connections	Page 41
Figure 18, 19:	3 D illustration of Neuron Activity, and Neuroglial	Page 42
Figure 20:	Illustration of stress from Cortisol	Page 45
Figure 21:	Illustration of scattered phonemic presentation	Page 49
Figure 22:	Well presented phonemic theme	Page 50
Figure 23:	Head-Heart and Hand	Page 55
Figure 24:	Blocking Sound signals	Page 56
Figure 25,26:	Hearing and Seeing Words brain mapping illustration	Page 58
Figure 27:	Vibro -Tactile Stimulation	Page 59
Figure 28:	Gray Matter Attrition with Electronics	Page 62
Figure 29:	Illustration of tummy time positions	Page 72

Figure 30:	**Infant's Feet in the entrusted parents' hands**	**Page 74**
Figure 31:	**Repeat of Neuron and Synaptic junction**	**Page 75**
Figure 32:	**Overlap of Developmental disorders**	**Page 80**
Figure 33:	**Sensory perceptions and variables Illustration**	**Page 81**
Figure 34:	**Ascending Triangle from positive Environment**	**Page 83**
Figure 35:	**Descending Triangle from negative Environment**	**Page 84**
Figure 36:	**PET scan of 0-12 Neurodevelopment, cells-hardwiring**	**Page 102**
Figure 37:	**Illustration of physiological Immune Deficiency**	**Page 106**
Figure 38:	**Demonstration of Normal 4 year brain PET scan**	**Page 135**
Figure 39:	**Demonstration of Abused 4 year brain PET scan**	**Page 135**
Figure 40:	**Demonstration of Spect study of meditation effect**	**Page 146**

Index

A

abuse, 3, 7, 42, 79, 121, 137
  physical, 7, 149
Acad, 178
ACC (anterior cingulate cortex), 25
addiction, 26, 29, 55
ADHD (attention deficit hyperactivity disorder), 19, 24, 34, 49, 57–58, 61–62, 69, 72, 74, 76–78, 110, 112, 125–28, 131–32, 136–37, 144, 153, 155
ADHD and Autism treatment, 171
aggression, 7, 42–43
Alexander, 179
amygdala, 33, 35, 42, 45, 68, 89–90, 127
Anderson, 177–78
Atomic and Molecular Physics, 170
attachment, 68–69, 71, 79, 89, 109, 123, 128, 141
autism, 69, 77, 108
  clinicopathological study of, 177
  early, 178
autistic adolescents, retarded, 177
autistic children, 56, 76
autistic subjects, 177
autonomy, 102, 106, 109, 115–16, 127, 154
awh287, 173
axons, 12, 40, 59
Aylward, 177

B

behaviors, 12, 18–19, 38, 41–42, 46–47, 59, 61, 73, 77, 100, 106, 108, 122, 126–27, 137–38, 142–44, 150–52, 154–55, 165
  biosocial, 57, 76
  negative, 90, 95, 101, 104, 109
  newborn, 59, 62
  violent, 174, 176
belongingness, 68, 89
Best Practices to Breakthrough Impacts, 174
Biol, 177–79
birth order positions, 145–47

brain, 2–3, 6, 9–11, 13, 15–20, 22, 24–25, 28–29, 33, 35–36, 38–42, 44–46, 51–57, 59, 65–66, 68, 70–72, 74, 76–81, 84–86, 89, 92–93, 95, 100, 104, 106, 108, 111–12, 120, 125, 127–29, 132, 134, 136, 138, 140–44, 151, 154–55, 171, 173, 176–78
  activity, 44, 47, 140–41, 152
  anxious, 92
  cells, 41–42, 121–22
  developing, 28, 40, 42
  executive, 22, 37, 89, 110
  growth, 118–19
  human, 34–35
  plasticity, 19, 90, 126, 139
  reward system of, 11, 25, 134
  social, 172
  structure, 20, 24, 33, 66, 73, 106, 121–22
Brain, Mind, SAI Educare, 17, 19, 29, 128
brain development, 46
  early child, 20, 29, 74, 76, 126
brain mechanisms, 178
brain networks, 18, 29, 135, 154
  disorganization of, 29
breastfeeding, 59–60, 64–65, 80
Broca's area, 22, 37, 44
Buxhoeveden, 178
Buxhoeveden, Daniel P., 173

C

CA, 174, 176
Campbell, 178
care, newborn, 59, 71
Casanova, Manuel F., 173
case presentation, 57, 64, 77, 153, 155
CDC (Centers for Disease Control), 28–29
cephalocaudal development, 79
cerebellar cortices of autistic subjects, 177
cerebellum, 22, 24, 35, 37
Child & Adolescent Psychiatry Shanghai Mental Health Center, 170
Child Adolesc, 178

child development, 29, 47, 91, 107, 109
childhood hyperkinetic syndrome, 54, 88
childhood trauma, 176
Child Neuropsychology, 177
Child Trauma Academy, 13, 18
choice making, 13, 40, 95, 107
cingulate gyrus, 25, 55
classical music, 44, 65, 95, 120, 128, 161, 164, 166, 168
cognition, 26, 33, 44
cognitive associations, 13, 33, 35, 38, 43, 53, 74, 91–93, 106–7, 111, 141
cognitive development, 6, 15, 106, 109–10, 171
cognitive skills, 125
Cohen, 176
communities, 86, 98, 121–22, 136
computers, 126
contact, mother-infant skin-to-skin, 176
corpus callosum, 13, 81
correspondence, 173–74
cortisol, 10, 33, 41, 44, 56, 97, 125, 132
CPS (Child Protective Services), 61, 73, 136
curriculum, 16, 29–30, 47, 57, 61, 66, 73, 76–77, 130

D

Department of Child, 170
depression, 12, 26, 42–43, 54, 126
dialogue, 137, 142, 147, 150–52
Dimensional Brain-Behavior Relationships, 174
disorders, 8
  anxiety, 8, 12, 25, 45, 54, 68
  autism spectrum, 17, 19, 61, 72, 78, 110, 126, 130
  behavior, 8, 17, 74, 125, 137
  eating, 104–5, 118–19
  learning, 90, 106, 110, 121, 128, 136–37
disorganization, 38
DISTINCT White Matter Disruption and Dimensional Brain-Behavior Relationships, 172
DOI, 171–73
dopamine, 11, 23, 89–90

Dr. Money (psychiatrist), 17
drugs, 3, 23, 28, 55, 70, 89–90, 130, 136–37, 175
DSM-IV (Diagnostic and Statistical Manual of Mental Disorders, Fourth Edition), 8
dx.doi.org, 172–73

E

Early Brain development Research review, 171
Early Experience in Infant development, 175
Early Experience in Infant Development, 175
Early Interventions for Infants of Depressed Mothers, 173
Ebert, 178
ECBD (early child brain development), 3, 20, 29, 74, 76–78, 122, 126
educare, 15, 20, 30, 46, 136, 152
education, bilingual, 175
electronics, 10, 20, 23, 28, 55, 73, 78, 108, 110, 117, 128, 155
Elsevier, 177
emotions, 42–44, 54, 79, 87, 89
empathy, 108–9
experiences, 12–13, 15, 38–39, 41–42

F

family system, 146, 148–49
family unit, 9, 48, 98
feedback, 148–49
Field, 173, 177
Fischer, Kurt, 19, 30
fMRI studies, 66, 101, 110
Focus on Exceptional Children, 176
food introduction, 85
Frith, 178
frontal lobe, 95, 103, 110

G

genes, 10, 19, 73, 105, 117
genetics, 10
Germany, 172
gratification, 61, 63–64, 68–69, 79, 89, 140–41
gray and white matter, 28, 35, 66, 140
Growth and Development of Children, 2

guided imagery, 134, 139, 141–42, 144, 153, 161, 164–66, 168

H

hard wiring, 38, 46, 73, 85–86, 120, 139
Harvard University, 174
health, 10, 29, 31
hindbrain, 35, 52, 74, 89
hippocampus, 25–26, 89, 111, 141
home environment, 40, 57–58, 76, 107
human beings, 35, 138–39, 142, 156
human brain wiring, 172
hyperkinetic child syndrome, 61, 71, 110, 141, 153
hypothalamus, 24–25, 42, 45

I

Infant behavior and Development, 176
Infant Behavior Development, 175
Infant Mental Health, 176
infants, natural state of, 68, 123
Infants of Depressed Mothers, 173
insecurity, 82, 89, 93, 95
Institute of Music Psychology and Musician, 172
insula, 23–24, 45
Internet addiction, 55
Internet addicts, 55
Internet exposure, 55
interventions, 46, 63, 136, 152
   multisensory, 46–47, 150, 152
iPad, 11–12, 29, 56, 76, 78, 91, 94, 104–6, 110–11
iPhone, 94, 110–11, 119

J

Johnson & Johnson Institute, 17, 30, 65, 126

K

Kingery, 175

L

La Jolla, 174
language, 44–45, 54, 71, 83–84, 100, 105, 111, 113–14, 116, 120–21, 127
learning, emotional, 43, 89, 106, 122
left hemispheres, 44
life application, 46, 49, 127–28, 134, 154
limbic system, 23–25, 33–34, 42, 52–53, 70, 89–90
Local Brain Functional Activity, 174
locus, internal, 4, 46, 81–82, 103, 138
Longitudinal development of human brain wiring, 172
love, 1, 4, 69, 82, 98, 108–9, 122–23, 138–39, 145, 156–57, 161, 168
Lu, 174, 177

M

Mapping Early Brain Development, 174
Martha Ann Brain, 171
meditation, 132, 143
mesocorticolimbic system, 25
midbrain, 38, 62, 89, 103, 120, 141
Miller, 176–77
Minshew, 177
Mol, 177–78
motor function area, 22, 37
motor skills
   fine, 22, 37, 54, 82, 84, 87–88, 91, 98–99, 102, 111–12, 114, 116–17, 127
   gross, 15, 82, 84, 87, 90, 98–99, 101, 110, 112–13, 116–17, 127
multisensory integration, 16, 19, 30, 54, 57, 66, 74, 76, 78, 82, 87, 92, 95, 140, 153, 155
music, 44–45, 65–68, 80–82, 104, 106, 108, 118, 134
   emotion, 171
   physiological effects of, 45
Musician's medicine, 172
music listening, 45, 66, 68
   devotional, 44
music therapy, 65–67, 72, 80, 82, 87, 97, 103–4, 107–8, 110
myelination, 40, 59, 66, 81

N

NCS-A (National Comorbidity Survey Adolescent Supplement), 8
neocortex, 26, 34–35, 38, 42, 65, 73, 89–90, 138
Neurobiol, 177–78
neurobiology, 15, 17, 29, 35, 49, 57, 76, 78, 112
Neurobiology of a Developing Child from Birth and Emotional Development, 17
neurodevelopment, 19, 29, 35, 136
neuroendocrine responses, 42
neuroendocrine state, 42
neurogenesis, 38, 40, 46
  dynamic brain, 44
Neuroimage, 172, 174, 177–79
Neurology, 177–78
neurons, 16, 28, 35, 39, 69, 78, 120
NICU (neonatal intensive care unit) graduates, 29–30, 57, 76
nucleus accumbens, 23–24, 26, 45, 55, 68
nurture, 15–16, 47, 53, 76, 87, 89, 92, 121–22, 130, 136, 141

O

objectives, 140, 143, 145, 147, 150, 152
occipital lobes, 24
Orajel (topical anesthetics), 2, 97
orbitofrontal cortex, 45, 89
organization, 28, 40, 44, 54, 102
  neurodevelopmental, 9, 16, 137
orifices, 119–20

P

parent, role of, 59
parentese, 65, 69, 82, 84, 91
parenting skills, 16, 46, 122, 136, 141
  authoritative, 49, 78, 103, 111, 119, 122
parenting style
  authoritative, 97, 110, 149, 152
  need-based mixed, 149
  neglectful, 149
  permissive, 148–49
  rigid, 147–48
participation, social, 45, 61, 67
pathophysiology, 136
patients, 2–3, 76–78, 123, 125–26, 128, 130, 140, 178
peace, 4, 31, 68–69, 82, 97, 108, 138, 158, 166
perceptions, sensory, 13, 22, 37, 82, 93
Persistent Fear and Anxiety, 171
personality development, 39, 43
PET scans, 9, 18, 38, 44, 126, 140
Phonological Processing Skills of Children Adopted Internationally, 171
physiological immunodeficiency, 2, 97
prefrontal cortex, 55, 66, 108, 111, 138, 143
pregnancy, 20, 28, 35, 39, 118, 125
Psychiatry, 173, 177–78
psychopathologies, 3, 40, 73, 137, 141
  developmental, 176
psychosocial dwarfism, 3, 17, 125

R

Raine, Adrian, 101
redirection, 91, 95, 107, 110, 121, 123, 158
  positive, 95, 103, 158
reflective decisions, making, 97–98
relaxation, 65–66, 74, 80
reward system, 55, 103, 112, 116, 169

S

SAI Educare
  curriculum of, 57, 76, 78
  parenting course of, 49, 137
  parent self-audit in, 136
SAI Institute of Educare, 46–47, 49, 136, 152
Schneider, 177–78
screen time, 10–12, 29, 42–43, 53–54, 110–12, 119, 136, 141
sensory input, 12, 15–16, 38, 44, 47–48, 73, 79, 89, 95, 108, 111, 140
sensory integration, 51–54, 80, 88, 99
sensory nurture, 15, 20, 30, 60–61, 73, 77–78, 82–83
sensory withdrawal, 56, 70, 76–77, 140
separation anxiety, 2, 68, 85, 89, 92–93, 95, 100–101, 103, 107, 126

sleep, 59–60, 62–63, 71–72, 94–95
sleep training, 93, 100–101, 107, 111
   guidelines, 94
social learning theory, 42
society, 6, 15, 29–30, 117–18, 121
stranger anxiety, 2, 61, 68, 87, 91–92, 97, 99–101
stress, 12, 17–19, 26, 28, 122–25
stress hormones, 3, 10, 33, 132
striatum, 26, 55
   dorsal, 26
   ventral, 23, 26
synaptic connections, 11, 33, 110
synaptic junctions, 11, 39–40, 69

T

teaching techniques, 30, 47–49, 57, 62, 76, 78, 126–28, 132, 139–40
temporal lobes, 23–24, 26, 51, 65
Touch Research Institute, 44
touch therapy, 44, 53–54, 57, 61, 65–67, 69–70, 72, 77–78, 80–81, 87, 122, 126
training, sessions, 137, 139–40, 142
trauma, 3, 20, 38, 42, 51, 140
truth, 4, 18, 69, 138, 161
tummy times, 66–67, 70, 72, 80

V

van Engeland, 173, 178
violence, 3, 15, 42–43, 117–18
   cycle of, 8, 43, 136, 154–55
visual cortex, 22, 24, 37, 53

W

Wernicke's area, 22, 37, 44, 51
WHO (World Health Organization), 10, 16, 29, 31, 117, 155
Wuhan, 170
Wuhan Institute of Physics and Mathematics, 170

Y

yoga, 57, 76, 132, 143
young children, 178

Printed in the United States
By Bookmasters